Remembering Protest in Britain since 1500

Carl J. Griffin • Briony McDonagh
Editors

Remembering Protest in Britain since 1500

Memory, Materiality and the Landscape

Editors
Carl J. Griffin
University of Sussex
Brighton, UK

Briony McDonagh
University of Hull
Hull, UK

ISBN 978-3-319-74242-7   ISBN 978-3-319-74243-4 (eBook)
https://doi.org/10.1007/978-3-319-74243-4

Library of Congress Control Number: 2018937107

© The Editor(s) (if applicable) and The Author(s) 2018
This work is subject to copyright. All rights are solely and exclusively licensed by the Publisher, whether the whole or part of the material is concerned, specifically the rights of translation, reprinting, reuse of illustrations, recitation, broadcasting, reproduction on microfilms or in any other physical way, and transmission or information storage and retrieval, electronic adaptation, computer software, or by similar or dissimilar methodology now known or hereafter developed.
The use of general descriptive names, registered names, trademarks, service marks, etc. in this publication does not imply, even in the absence of a specific statement, that such names are exempt from the relevant protective laws and regulations and therefore free for general use.
The publisher, the authors, and the editors are safe to assume that the advice and information in this book are believed to be true and accurate at the date of publication. Neither the publisher nor the authors or the editors give a warranty, express or implied, with respect to the material contained herein or for any errors or omissions that may have been made. The publisher remains neutral with regard to jurisdictional claims in published maps and institutional affiliations.

Cover illustration: The Chartist Uprising Mosaic, Photograph reproduced by permission of Budd Mosaics. Original mosaic design by Kenneth Budd ARCA.

Printed on acid-free paper

This Palgrave Macmillan imprint is published by the registered company Springer International Publishing AG part of Springer Nature.
The registered company address is: Gewerbestrasse 11, 6330 Cham, Switzerland

To the memory of the wage labourer, the threshing machine breaker, the 'obsolete' commoner, the radical housewife, the 'utopian' Chartist, and 'stowte' John Bussey.

Contents

Remembering Protest   1
Carl J. Griffin and Briony McDonagh

Remembering Mousehold Heath   25
Nicola Whyte

Landscape, Memory and Protest in the Midlands Rising of 1607   53
Briony McDonagh and Joshua Rodda

Relating Early Modern Depositions   81
Heather Falvey

Remembering Protest in the Forest of Dean, c.1612–1834   107
Simon Sandall

Remembering Protest in the Late-Georgian Working-Class Home   135
Ruth Mather

Prosecution, Precedence and Official Memory: Judicial Responses and Perceptions of Swing in Norfolk   159
Rose Wallis

The Politics of 'Protest Heritage', 1790–1850 187
Steve Poole

Memory and the Work of Forgetting: Telling Protest in the
English Countryside 215
Carl J. Griffin

Afterword: Landscapes, Memories and Texts 237
Andy Wood

Index 245

Notes on Contributors

Heather Falvey is a Panel Tutor in Local and Social History for the Institute of Continuing Education at the University of Cambridge and for the Department of Continuing Education at the University of Oxford. She has published a number of chapters and articles on early modern custom and protest and is the Editorial Assistant for the *Economic History Review*.

Carl J. Griffin is Head of Department and Reader in Historical Geography at the University of Sussex. An historical geographer of rural England from the Restoration to the mid-nineteenth century, his work has embraced histories of popular protest, including the first recent revisionist study of the Swing riots, more-than-human histories, and histories of labour and welfare. He is author of *The Rural War: Captain Swing and the Politics of Protest* (2012) *and Protest, Politics and Work in Rural England, 1700–1850* (Palgrave, 2014). He is co-editor of *Rural History* and *Southern History*.

Ruth Mather is a Post-Doctoral Research Associate at the University of Exeter. Her research interests include the roles of class and gender in popular politics, the potential of material culture for historical study, and widening participation in historical research. She recently completed her PhD 'The home making of the English working class: radical politics and domestic life in late Georgian England, c. 1790–1820' at Queen Mary, University of London.

Briony McDonagh is a historical and cultural geographer at the University of Hull. She is the author of *Elite Women and the Agricultural Landscape, 1700–1830* (2017) and co-editor of *Hull: Culture, History, Place* (2017). She has published widely on the geographies of property, enclosure, protest and the law, on women's histories, and on the history of the British landscape. She is Chair of the Historical Geography Research Group of the Royal Geographical Society (with the Institute of British Geographers) and co-director of the University of Hull's *Gender, Place and Memory* research cluster.

Steve Poole is Professor of History and Heritage at the University of the West of England, where he also directs the Regional History Centre. He researches English history from below in the long eighteenth century, and also works with partners in the creative industries on public mobile/digital applications for the historic landscape. His recent publications include *John Thelwall: Radical Romantic and Acquitted Felon* (2009), 'Ghosts in the Garden: Locative Gameplay and Historical Interpretation from Below' (*International Journal of Heritage Studies*, 2017) and, with Nick Rogers, *Bristol From Below: Law, Authority and Protest in a Georgian City* (2017).

Joshua Rodda is research assistant on McDonagh's current British Academy-funded project, *Experiencing the Landscape*. He is an early career researcher and tutor working at the University of Nottingham and the University of Leicester, specialising in the religious, cultural and political history of England in the sixteenth and seventeenth centuries. His first book, *Public Religious Disputation in England, 1558–1626*, was published in 2014, and he is currently working on the fictional religious dialogue during and after the Reformation.

Simon Sandall is Senior Lecturer in Early Modern British History at the University of Winchester. His research interests are in the areas of custom, law and community, particularly how these relations underpinned popular politics and popular protest in Early Modern England. His initial work examined the nature of collective memory and its relation to the organisation of popular protest in the Forest of Dean between the sixteenth and nineteenth centuries and is currently examining the relation between shame and popular litigation during this period. He is the author of *Custom and Popular Memory in the Forest of Dean, c. 1550–1832* (2013).

Rose Wallis lectures in British social history at the University of the West of England and is Associate Director of the Regional History Centre

(UWE). Her research examines the relationship between magistrates and their communities, focusing on crime, criminal justice, protest and 'history from below' in eighteenth- and early nineteenth-century rural England. Her thesis, completed at UWE, is entitled 'The relationship between magistrates and their communities in the age of crisis: social protest c. 1790–1834'.

Nicola Whyte is a Senior Lecturer in History at the University of Exeter and author of *Inhabiting the Landscape: Place, Custom and Memory, 1500–1800* (2009). She has wide-ranging interests in the landscape and social history of the post-medieval and early modern periods. Her current research explores the meanings and experiences of landscape in everyday contexts. She is particularly interested in landscape and memory, attitudes towards the physical remains of the past, patterns of appropriation, reinterpretation and reuse.

Andy Wood is Professor of Social History at Durham University. He writes about the poorer and middling people of Tudor, Stuart and Georgian England, and has published on a wide range of issues, including popular politics, class relations, rebellion, the mid-Tudor crisis, the English Revolution, local communities, literacy, oral culture, memory and customary law. His most recent book *The Memory of the People: Custom and Popular Senses of the Past in Early Modern England* (2013) won the American Historical Association's 2014 Leo Gershoy Award. He is also the author of *The Politics of Social Conflict: The Peak Country, 1520–1770* (1999), *Riot, Rebellion and Popular Politics in Early Modern England* (2002) and *The 1549 Rebellions and the Making of Early Modern England* (2007).

List of Figures

Remembering Mousehold Heath

Fig. 1 Detail of a late sixteenth-century map of Mousehold Heath, with Norwich to the east. (NRO, MC3085: Reproduced with kind permission of Norfolk Museums Service (Norwich Castle Museum and Art Gallery))   31

Fig. 2 Detail of a copy of a map of Mousehold made in 1730, following a survey of the lands belonging to the Dean and Chapter in 1718. Stone Mines is shown top right, St James Hill, gravel pits, lime and chalk kilns are also depicted. (NRO, MC3085/4: Reproduced with kind permission of Norfolk Museums Service (Norwich Castle Museum and Art Gallery))   40

Landscape, Memory and Protest in the Midlands Rising of 1607

Fig. 1 1632 map of Papley (Northamptonshire) showing the enclosed and depopulated township. NRO, Map 2221. (Reproduced with permission)   60

Relating Early Modern Depositions

Fig. 1 The first page of the examination of Robert Barker of Wilderley in the parish of Duffield, husbandman yeoman, aged about 27 26. (Source: TNA DL4/108/36, p. 1 (Photographed by TNA) (Duchy of Lancaster copyright material in The National Archives is reproduced by permission of the Chancellor and Council of the Duchy of Lancaster))   97

Remembering Protest in the Late-Georgian Working-Class Home

Fig. 1   Peterloo Plaque, c.1819. (Printed, painted, and glazed
         earthenware. British Museum, London)   145
Fig. 2   Peterloo jug, c.1819. (Printed earthenware and lustre.
         Touchstones, Rochdale)   146

Remembering Protest

Carl J. Griffin and Briony McDonagh

This book is about protest and the multiple and contested ways it is remembered, about the work protest memories do and the uses of the past in the (historical) present. While several chapters speak to the present *en passant*, it is not a study of the way protests past are mobilised today – that worthy subject awaits its author – but rather a broader and temporally deeper analysis of the rememberings and tellings of protest in Britain in the period between roughly 1500 and 1850. Drawing on work in social and cultural history, cultural and historical geography, psychology, anthropology, critical heritage studies and memory studies, this collection of essays seeks for the first time to consider systemically the ways in which protest is remembered, not least by early modern and modern protestors themselves. This is not to say that this the first study of protest memory: recent studies by Steve Hindle and Andy Wood, along with the 'Tales of the Revolt' project led by Judith Pollman at Leiden examining memories of the Dutch Revolt, take precedence.[1] Paul Roberts' study of the prominent Chartist William Aitken also shows the power of autobiography as a powerful tool in how protest memories were produced.[2] Inspired by Andy Wood's pioneering

C. J. Griffin (✉)
University of Sussex, Brighton, UK

B. McDonagh
University of Hull, Hull, UK

The Memory of the People, the purpose of this book is to consider the dynamic and lived nature of the past protests, in communities and at large.[3] In so doing, it emphasises the contested and shifting nature of the meanings of past episodes of conflict, revealing how the past itself was (and remains) an important source of conflict and opposition. The book is thus novel in that it draws together the early modern and the modern, in that it considers the legacy of both the dramatic and the (relatively) mundane, and that it offers the first showcase of the variety of approaches that comprises the vibrant and intellectually fecund 'new protest history'.[4]

Remembering Protest is also book about the spaces, sites and things through which memory is assembled, mobilised and contested. While recognising the often-complex, networked and more-than-local nature of past communities, the analysis is therefore also foregrounded by the understanding that the cultures and spaces of everyday life – the taskscapes, to borrow an anthropological concept – were the terrains in which these struggles over meaning occurred. Here we draw on the work of anthropologists and cultural geographers, thinking about landscape as 'always in the making', a 'simultaneity of stories-so-far', stories which are political in being always unfinished, and in which we argue protest memories form a crucial component.[5] Thus, the book explores three key ideas: the importance and politics of memory; the way in which 'things' are and become the focus for telling and commemorating past protests; and landscape as a repository and canvas for remembering protest.

In what follows we conceive of protest as a range of acts and intentions that span from mass movements to those subtle and sometimes unseen acts of everyday resistance that comprise James Scott's 'hidden transcript'.[6] In mapping out our ambitions for the book in this introductory chapter, we wish to do three things. Firstly, we offer an overview of the recent turn to protest history amongst historians and geographers, as well as noting the importance of protest memories in the here-and-now. Next we explore in turn each of the three themes identified above – the politics of memory, material things, and landscape – and, in doing so, offer an introduction to the broader concepts that underpin the chapters, something each individual author cannot possibly do. We thus also hope to stimulate future studies by highlighting the conceptual richness of the approach. Finally, we briefly introduce the chapters that follow, drawing out key themes, challenges and approaches.

Protest History

Before the advent of protest history there was nothing, just condescension. As E. P. Thompson so famously put it in the preface to his landmark 1963 *The Making of the English Working Class*, his study was an attempt at 'rescue', not just of the everyday lives of 'poor stockingers... [and] 'obsolete' hand-loom weavers' but critically also of the 'Luddite cropper... [and] 'the "utopian" artisan'. As Thompson noted, only such peoples – such historical *subjects* – who were successful (in that their 'aspirations anticipated subsequent evolution') had been remembered: all other peoples ('the losers') and their causes forgotten.[7] Even success measured on such terms was insufficient to pique the interest of generations of political historians in protest histories. As Sir Lewis Namier, that great snob of English history, once derisively proclaimed to a prospective researcher of the *sans-culottes*: 'Why are you interested in those bandits?'. Indeed, to Namier revolution, whether successful or nor, was necessarily always 'retrograde'.[8]

Protests were to be forgotten. When English historians made reference to popular rebellion they invariably did so in the context of other issues and as uninteresting ephemera, footnotes (often literally) to the real stuff of economics and elite politics. Of food rioting – an expression of popular protest that tied together the early modern and modern periods – Donald Barnes claimed in 1930 that they were 'more or less alike'. '[N]othing is gained', Barnes continued, 'by giving a detailed account of each one.'[9] Thomas Ashton and Julia Sykes made a similar assertion. While 'rebellions of the belly' were endemic in the second half of the eighteenth century, the effort involved in their study was 'disproportionate to the value of any generalisation that would be likely to emerge'.[10] A partial rescue was affected by historians like Barbara and John Hammond and Frank Ongley Darvall. But in neither the Hammonds' *The Village Labourer* (1911), *The Town Labourer* (1917) or *The Skilled Labourer* (1919) nor Darvall's slightly later *Popular Disturbances and Public Order in Regency England* (1934) do we get any sense that the protests of the poor could be anything other than reactive or, at best, proto-, a form of politics in the becoming.[11] One can even see Namierian condescension internalised in the earliest work of that other pioneering rescuer of poor politicians, Eric Hobsbawm: his suggestive *Primitive Rebels* still locked in the teleological language of emergence, his subjects still pre-political.[12]

All subsequent studies, both by Thompson and Hobsbawm as well as by George Rudé and Gywn Williams and the generation of early modern and modern historians and historical geographers that followed, have been exercises in rescuing, in remembering protest. Such studies have allowed the voices (and practices) of discontent to be heard and foregrounded in historical scholarship, accepting that from a dramatic food or enclosure riot, through incendiarism and the sending of threatening letters, to the often-subtle acts of everyday defiance of authority such as wood-stealing and even foot-dragging, all exist on the same spectrum as acts of resistance. Such practices are all ways of people rejecting and protesting their lot. Protest, so we now understand it, is not simply synonymous with disturbance or riot. Rather – and this definition holds for this book – it is an expression of dissent registered against social 'betters', whether exploitative employers, supercilious clergy, hard-nosed parish officers, enclosing landowners, or aloof politicians.

Without doubt Charlesworth, Clark, Hay, Linebaugh, Manning, Neeson, Randall, Reed, Rule, Sharp, Slack, Stevenson, Underdown, Walter, Wells, Wrightson, amongst others, drawing on the seminal works of Rudé, Hobsbawm and Thompson, firmly established protest history on the scholarly map.[13] But if the period from the mid-1970s through to c.1990 represented the blossoming of the field, soon the energy and intellectual dynamism dissipated as many protest historians assumed senior management roles in the academy or the emphases of their research shifted. None of this is to say the field was absolutely moribund by the start of the new millennium, rather that the rate of production slowed and much of that which was published represented the culmination of earlier work, for instance, Randall and Charlesworth's 2000 edited collection on the moral economy related to a conference held in the early 1990s in honour of attendee Thompson.[14]

Since the early 2000s, slowly at first and emphatically since the turn of the current decade, protest history has undergone a creative and critical renewal. First evident in studies of early modern England and subsequently extending to work on modern England and (to a lesser extent) Wales and Scotland, this reinvigoration has seen both an extension of the intellectual envelope to embrace new concerns as well as revisionist studies of earlier landmark publications and their legacy. This renewal and remaking is perhaps best attested by a slew of monographs and other significant publications in the past ten years by both a new generation of scholars – with several doctoral theses awaiting publication – as well as new studies by already established historians.[15]

While this is not the place to offer a detailed description of the trends and directions of what has been labelled the 'new protest history', some points are worth pulling out. Recent work has drawn attention to the importance of more-than-human and environmental drivers of protest, such work also thus emphasising the importance of considering material worlds as much as discursive and textual worlds in our analyses. It has also been alert to the gendered nature of protest as well as the role of gender in protest, thereby drawing our attention to the importance of intersections of difference and power. Micro-historical analyses have likewise forced us to think carefully about the spaces of everyday life and the symbolic importance of place and landscape, important not just as being the contextual backdrop against which protest is played out but also as something that co-constitutes – and in part is also constituted by – protests.[16]

Another emergent theme relates to the importance of memory. If we have long understood the importance of custom to the study of popular protest – Thompson and his acolytes recognising that appeals to past practices served to popularly and sometimes legally legitimise all aspects of popular culture and social relations – the study of memory and popular protest has remained obscure. But this has started to change. We are beginning to understand the importance of both how past protests have been and continue to be commemorated – take, for example, Claire Griffiths' work on the ways in which the TUC commandeered the memory of Tolpuddle in and since the 1930s – and the way in which the memory of past protests is critical in justifying and vivifying future protests. Much innovation here has come from early modern historians. In the work of Andy Wood and Nicola Whyte we see the complex ways in which memory was utterly central to the forms and experiences of everyday life in plebeian households. This is not just about custom, but also about how everyday life represented a deep and intimate connection between landscape, place, identity and, critically, the past. Memory was not only in the mind and grooved into the body, but also written and read in the matter of place. If much of this was about how the collective, shared memory of the past was used to inform everyday life in the present, it is also about past (and thus future) episodes of social conflict, past successes and failures defining moments in the memory.

Similarly, early modern scholars have begun to explore the ways in which past protests were subsequently (re-)imagined and the work their imagining did. Thus, in Steve Hindle's study of representations of the Midland Rising of 1607 and in the final chapter of Wood's *The 1549*

Rebellions and the Making of Early Modern England examining 'later' representations of the 'commotion time', we see both the importance of afterlives of dramatic episodes of social conflict and the rich possibilities for extending such studies to other times and places.[17] Indeed, hitherto this approach has neither been extended to studies of modern Britain nor more broadly to the *uses* of past protest. One could also argue though that whereas emergent work on early modern England has developed in a decidedly post-Thompsonian mode, work on relatively more recent protests has drawn strongly from other conceptual influences. For instance, in Iain Robertson's suggestive *Heritage from Below* we see the influence of Hobsbawm and Thompson fused with work by cultural geographers and from the critical heritage studies movement in writing defiantly post-structuralist modest stories about the subtle and oft-hidden ways in which past protests are told and retold towards new ends. To come full circle, one could even read this introduction as part of a further attempt to explore how scholarly analyses of protests past are part of the same process of reinscribing and taking ownership of past protests to serve particular progressive ends in the present (and here one might remember the Hammonds' attempts to historically situate and intellectually underpin their prized Fabianism by yoking the archive of early nineteenth-century protests to their cause).

Protest Memories in the Here-and-Now

This book does not just mark the rebirth of protest history. It also coincides with a notable upsurge in public interest in the commemoration of past protests, this attested by a plethora of new (and campaigns for new) public memorials. This desire to rematerialise past protests is examined in detail in the chapter by Steve Poole in this book, but it is worth making a few points here. This trend takes many forms. Arguably the most high-profile memorialisation of past protest are those looking towards the bicentenary of the massacre at Peterloo, this involving high profile public meetings/performances, the campaign for a 'permanent' memorial to the slain by Turner Prize-winning artist Jeremy Deller, as well as a film now in production by the doyen of radical-left cinema Mike Leigh. At the most recent 'anniversary memorial', attended by several hundred people, actor Christopher Eccleston, in simulation of Charles Ethelston the magistrate who presided over the massacre, hammily read out the Riot Act.[18] At the other end of the spectrum are, as examined by Robertson, those modest, unofficial and unheralded community memorials marking the 'later' clearances in the Scottish Highlands. Further, in a study of the Hebrides, Robertson also suggests that we should read the decayed 'blackhouse' as a memorial in itself, an assemblage of the material and memory, or what Robertson calls a 'hardscrabble heritage'.[19] There is also a parallel, quite different but no less discernible trend in past protests becoming the subject of popular 'nostalgia', social conflict rewritten as what elsewhere one of us has called 'pleasant histories', this a new ironic form of condescension.[20] It is also important to note that protest memorials can themselves be generative of protests anew, both in the form of conflicts over new memorials (as in the case of Peterloo) but also over the defacing and destruction of earlier protest memorials (as per the demolition of the Newport Chartist memorial – which adorns the cover of this book – in October 2013).[21] Or, as Christina Jerne has recently put it in the context of 'mass commemorations' of mafia victims that took place in Bologna, commemorations can be 'catalysts' in forging new social movements, just as can extant monuments dedicated to historical figures whose worldview many now find rightly abhorrent (as per the recent Rhodes Must Fall campaign, or the ongoing controversy over Confederate memorials in the United States).[22]

There is also a growing sense that while removed from the cultural and material contexts of the past, protest movements and groups in the early twenty-first century are once again drawing upon past protests to help both inform and justify their actions in the present. For instance, elsewhere the editors of this book have explored the ways in which the recent Occupy movement has directly drawn upon, as Occupy activists have seen it, their protest antecedents. One Occupy group coalesced in the early summer of 2012 at Runnymede, Surrey, on a piece of waste woodland. The site in itself was not materially significant, forming a small and all but forgotten part of the Runnymede Campus of Brunel University closed in 2007 and sold to a developer for £46.5 million. However, the symbolism and location of the site was important, being a slog of a cricket ball away from the Magna Carta memorial, itself located on National Trust land. Moreover, the group decided to call themselves Diggers 2012, a deliberate and careful allusion to the squatter communities established at nearby Walton and Cobham in the late 1640s, and to issue a manifesto – titled *Declaration from the Dispossessed* – consciously modelled on Gerrard Winstanley's 1649 *Declaration from the Poor*. The Runnymede camp was envisioned by those living there as just such a radical community, a challenge to a 'system in crisis', and in justifying their occupation and fighting the subsequent eviction proceedings, the group explicitly and knowingly remobilised earlier protest episodes. Thus protest past is employed in protests present in the effort to remake the social, economic and political relations of the future. Indeed, as the chapters of the book bear out, remembering protest has always been a political act writ through with the concerns of the present and with a desire to shape the future. Such understandings of the past in the present therefore matter now more than ever, for how we remember past struggles – and the cultural and political erasure of past struggles – is a battleground in how we resist new forms of 'enclosure' and oppression today.[23]

Memory Politics

There can be little doubt that memory has become one of the defining intellectual ideas, even idioms, of the academy in recent decades. So much so that it is its own field of study ('memory studies') with its own well-regarded and lively journal *Memory Studies*, first published in 2008. While no discipline in the humanities and social sciences can be said to have *not* gone through a 'memory turn', the relationship between history and memory is an especially awkward one. And there is an irony here, for whilst the turn to memory in work by sociologists has been labelled an 'historical turn', memory has long been held as history's other.[24] If history represents the pursuit of knowing the past, memory has a more quicksilver quality, elusive yet everywhere, often counter- and contradictory. As Pierre Nora asserted, until recently it could usefully be stated that history, as an intellectual practice, represented a 'colonisation of memory', an attempt to concretise, to secure the past, a 'critical discourse' 'antithetical to spontaneous memory'. In this way, 'modern memory', our shared memory of the past, had been seized by history, had been made reliant on the material, the visible. Our memory had become archival.[25] Arguably, the highpoint – or perhaps the nadir – came in the publication of Hobsbawm and Ranger's *The Invention of Tradition*, their influential edited collection of essays 'debunking' the way in which claims to tradition rested on myths and legends, much of what passed for old instead a product of modernity, plastic.[26] If this act of purification might still hold in the telling of national histories – the 'official' story of the nation, as so ably detailed and deconstructed by Peter Mandler in his *History and National Life* – and in much community history – for example, in the original intention of the *Victoria County History* to write an encyclopaedic history of each English county – the idea that the work of history is to write the past has been unpicked, undone.[27]

This is also true of our understanding of memory. First, it is important to note that Raphael Samuel and Paul Thompson's edited collection *The Myths We Live By*, drawing on work in cultural studies and folklore, and inspired by the possibilities of oral history, represented a fecund showcase of the ways in which myths are central to much history. In their wide-ranging introduction, Samuel and Thompson argued not only that myth is a 'fundamental component of human thought', but also that historians need to take myth seriously as central to the ways in which individual, collective and national stories are framed. In this, so they assert, myth does not relate to a 'false past', rather that myths reflect 'displacements, omissions, and reinterpretations… shaped accounts in which some incidents [are] dramatized, others contextualized, yet others passed over in silence, through a process of narrative shaping' drawing in reality, subjectivity, imagination, myth, the conscious and unconscious.[28] This also applies to understandings of memory. As our writings of the past have shifted from the substantial, the solid, the durable, so has our conception of memory. Rather than being static and fixed, or, in contradistinction, spontaneous, critical work in the humanities and social psychology has led to an understanding that memory is both mutable and changeable, a mechanism, a device to help us make sense of ourselves in time. If, as Brian Conway has noted, it is 'difficult to delineate the precise relationship between these phenomena – individual and collective memories, the past and the present, and what element of memory is internal and what is external – it is because the distinctions are conceptual rather than lived.[29] Thus, as the psychologist Jens Brockmeier asserted, the dualisms that once informed our conceptions of memory are collapsing, collective-individual memory, intentional-unintentional, and, crucially, memory-forgetting giving way to a realisation that memory plays are more complex and contingent on context. To comprehend truly the intricacies of memory, so Brockmeier claims, we first need to understand the specificities of the local context, for it is in the realm of everyday public life that memory is lived and ultimately contested.[30]

Recent work has therefore nuanced – and sometimes directly challenged – sociologist Maurice Halbwachs' seminal 1925 work *Les Cadres Sociaux de la Mémoire*, not least in the turn to the local and vernacular within memory studies.[31] This is accompanied by the recognition that 'memory politics' is about much more than the ways memory is employed by agents acting in the name of national – and nationalist – concerns.

We would argue that such a reading of memory has long been implicit within the work of social historians utilising critical approaches to power, agency and resistance in interrogating the 'politics of the parish' and – as we note above – has recently come to the fore more explicitly in the work of Whyte, Wood, Hindle and others.[32] We note too the related turn to materiality both within memory studies and indeed across the humanities more generally. In what follows, our contributors are all interested in the spaces, things and landscapes through which memory is constituted and protest memorialised, mobilised – or indeed forgotten. Or, to put it another way, they are concerned with the assemblages of people and matter – the taskscapes – through which memory is made.

Memory, Matter, Materiality

Arguably it is in work on memorialisation – memory made matter – that this conceptual coming together is most evident, and where the process of putting the past to work in highly selective ways is most obvious. Much of this work has focused either on memory made matter, the casting into stone as Nuala Johnson puts it,[33] in the production of memorials, and in official celebrations, for instance the TUC's attempts in the 1930s – and beyond – to revive the 'memory' of Tolpuddle.[34] While these two processes adopt, both literally and metaphorically, very different forms, both involve and invoke placed struggles that as well as valorising particular sites in memory (former residences, battlefields and places of struggle, as well as symbolic sites) also attempt to concretise particular memories in the more-than-local consciousness. This is what happened, this is what matters, this is who matters. If such attempts to colonialise individual memory are necessarily always political in that they privilege one memory over others, so too are the affective 'atmospheres' that memorials and the ritualistic performance of commemorative events create. As Shanti Sumartojo has recently suggested in the context of the experience of marking Anzac Day (25 April) in Australia, through repetition of certain performances and the telling of certain narratives, individuals are bound and affectively through the feelings that commemorative events engender, to a shared memory. The collision, and management of, emotion, repetition, spectacle and the act of sharing, subtly act to enforce the official narrative as a known, felt truth.[35] Or, as Duncan Bell has put it, memory is employed 'in an often-bewildering variety of ways' that acts to obscure 'vectors of power'.[36] In this, one is reminded of Gramsci's concept of cultural hegemony, that through elite power and force and through repetition, those in a position of subjugation can accept elite views of being in the world as representing the natural state of things. None of this is to say that such colonial(ising) practices are inevitable and irresistible, for, as Yvonne Whelan has shown in relation to British monuments in colonial and postcolonial Ireland, they acted, and continue to act, as foci for opposition and resistance.[37] In a different context, Robertson has also shown that in opposition to 'official' memorials (and memorialising practices), communities have and continue to create their own countermemorials, often marking the violences enacted by elites on the poor in what Robertson describes as memorialisation from below.[38]

Beyond memorials, memory is invested in other more everyday and mundane things too. While it might be overstating the case to claim that all museums are now critical spaces in which once-dominant and hegemonic narratives are invariably challenged, it is increasingly common for regional and national museums to at least address the place of past protests through displaying protest artefacts.[39] As the following chapters by Poole and Mather attest, not only did protests give certain objects a particular charge – the humerus bone from an adult male 'rioter' who perished in the flames when the Bristol Custom House was set on fire during the Reform Riots in 1831 and now on display in the M Shed museum in that city being a particular macabre example[40] – but they also generated a veritable industry in protest mementoes. From commemorative jugs and trophies awarded for the 'successful' repression of riots to the manufacturing of cheap, popular domestic items through which working women and men could remember those slain in such massacres as Peterloo or honour the impact of activists (such as the commemorative mug produced on the death of Chartist leader Ernest Jones in 1869) protests produce things.[41] While such acts of inclusion in museums can act as another layer of condescension by sanitising objects through decontextualising them, it is important to note their inclusion is at once an acknowledgement of collective memories in place as held in objects and, for more recent objects, a vital trigger to new memory work in the community.

It is also important to note that, as the work of Wood and Whyte has shown, the matter of dwelt space – whether a building, field, common, or tree – was also vitally important as a repository of community memory.[42] In relation to how protests were lodged in the memory of the community, certain things and spaces could assume particular importance. The point is an obvious, but important one: sites of riots, new and repaired buildings on the site of incendiary fires, the site of bodily attacks, to give a small range of examples, all endured and persisted as material markers of past protests. The erection of gibbets played on this dynamic. As Sarah Tarlow and Zoe Dyndor have suggested, the gibbet was a symbolically *placed* reminder of the power of the state to suppress protest, the material presence of the gibbet a way in which communities were not allowed to forget.[43]

LANDSCAPES, TASKSCAPES, MEMORYSCAPES

We are also now beginning to better understand that memory has its own histories and geographies. As Wood has recently noted in his *The Memory of the People*, early modern people took great care in remembering the things that mattered to them, both through cultures of collective recall but also through material mnemonics in the landscape. There was, Wood notes, an 'intimate connection' in the making and maintaining of memory between landscape, place and identity. Memory itself might not be a thing, but it was manifest in the material, the environment the constant reminder of the past.[44] To John Clare, variably described as the nature poet or the 'Northamptonshire Peasant Poet', memory was not only jolted by the material but actually writ in material entanglements. Reflecting on his earlier life, although then still only 31, Clare mused:

> I was never easy but when I was in the fields passing my sabbaths and leisure with the shepherds and herdboys as fancys prompted sometimes playing at marbles on the smooth-beaten sheeptracks or leapfrog among the thymy molehills sometimes running among the corn to get the red & blue flowers for cockades to play at soldiers or running into the woods to hunt strawberries or stealing peas in churchtime when the owners were safe to boil at the gypseys fire who went half-shares at our stolen luxury we heard the bells chime but the field was our church.

If the only thing of protest about this is the very fact that a cash-strapped and increasingly disillusioned Clare wrote it, everything about it speaks to the importance of things in place as stores of memory.[45] Of course, Clare's writings were as much an attempt to make sense of himself in place as it was an attempt to make sense of the places he inhabited (and made). To go beyond the personal and elevate the material to meaningfully collective mnemonics, it required key members of the community to interpret and act as custodians. Holding popular memories required work and policing. As Whyte has suggested, it was often women who acted as the 'custodians' of memory, those charged in the community with the propagation and promulgation of the significant events of the community, thereby policing what mattered and what did not.[46]

In this recent work we see an emphasis on the importance of memory as being the wellspring of custom, thus the work of memory mattered because it helped to establish claims to individual and collective rights. Memory was put to work to do good work and sustain the community. This worked in two ways. First, custom was shaped and inscribed through oral transmission (in the spaces of the household and community), textually (through reference to the documents of the community, for instance baptismal registers, and documents in the hands of individuals, such as deeds and settlement certificates), and through material practices (markers and monuments in the landscape). As Wood notes, '[e]lite contemporaries were well aware of how deeply custom was grafted onto the environment: as Edward Coke put it in 1641, "Custom lies upon the land"'. In this way, 'custom *made* the past usable'.[47] These 'technologies' of memory, if not immutable in how they are mobilised and performed, serve to 'give a future to the past' and act as solid, shared referents to an accepted version of the past.[48]

Second, through being repeated, shared and performed, such 'devices' acted as mnemonics, aids to remembering that were important in making claims in the future. In this way custom was necessarily curated, some points to the past carefully selected and others excluded. Remembering – selectively, politically, unevenly but always with purpose – was that which underpinned community cohesion.[49] It was that which was called upon to make a judgement, a value judgment to evoke E. P. Thompson's seminal 'moral economy' thesis, when the agrarian equipoise was threatened. And in the face of threats to their way of being, commoners appealed to local custom not as a 'vague body of tradition', but rather as a regulator of community tension given legitimacy as 'a rigorous, detailed, and precise corpus of local law'.[50] Time after time when the validity of rights was called into question, the legal case for the defence relied on the testimony of the oldest members of the community, their memory of the practice of rights called upon – and called into question – in court.[51] Custom was never fact, rather as Thompson suggested, it was ambiance, a Bourdieuian *habitus* in which everyone strove to maximise their advantage.[52] In this context, memory was necessarily constantly called into question, and no doubt highly selective, embellished, with past conflicts variably mobilised or ignored depending on their success.

Likewise, in narrating our own lives, we invariably hide as much as we reveal, embroider as well as underplay, fictionalise and forget. As Hall in his aforementioned rereading of Ashton-under-Lyme Chartist William Aitken's autobiography tells us, the writing of autobiography – a still emergent form in the 1860s – 'was never a simple case of retrieving timeless, unchanging memories… and fitting them into a narrative form. Memory involves forgetting as well as remembering; with the passage of time, details of long ago conversations and events fade and change'.[53] The protest archive, we do well to remember, is already a partially remembered and staged past. All documents, whatever their genesis, are like autobiographies: this is what is important, this is what you need to know.

The Book

Taken together, the chapters in the volume span analyses of major incidents of riot and rebellion to less notorious and more localised episodes of unrest. Either way, as well as adding to the historiography of the protests studied, the conceptual implications of each chapter, and hence the book, transcends the precise geographical foci and speak to universal themes in how we remember protest. The chapters are arranged in a broadly chronological fashion moving from Nicola Whyte's discussion of the camps on Mousehold Heath in 1549 to Rose Wallis and Carl Griffin's respective discussions of the Swing riots of 1830 and 1831, though in examining how protest is remembered each author necessarily shuttles back and forth in time, sometimes over several centuries. In bringing together studies of the early modern and modern periods we deliberately intend to challenge neat periodisations. For while we agree with Judith Pollman and Erika Keijpers' assertion that 'on a local level early modern memories could be as ubiquitous and pervasive as they are at any time in the twenty-first century', their claim that in a 'political, legal and moral sense' the past was more important in early modern Europe because as a source of authority it had few competitors we find problematic.[54] We appreciate the *apparent* irony between on the one hand acknowledging the often non-linear nature of memory and relatedly the potential for non-teleological tellings of protest memories, and, on the other hand, the more-or-less chronological ordering of the book. Our justification? In bringing together scholars of the early modern and modern periods, our aim is to critically consider the differences and similarities in the processes and practices of remembering protest between the two periods. And besides, memory might challenge the neat ordering of lived time, but it would be perverse to deny that, say, Swing activists' protests were in part informed and shaped by the knowledge – by the memory – of past protests.

While undoubtedly the textualising tendencies of modernity helped to provide alternative ways of remembering the past – not least in the written record of communities but also in legal codification and practices – memory mattered precisely because it offered a way in which plebeians could challenge patrician tellings of the past. Indeed, whatever the challenges of commercialising imperatives, to many communities custom remained the defining cultural and social code throughout the eighteenth and well into the nineteenth century. As Thompson noted in *Customs in Common*:

> If the memories of the old, perambulation and exhortation lay towards the centre of custom's interface between law and praxis, custom passes at the other extreme into areas altogether indistinct – into unwritten beliefs, sociological norms, and usages asserted in practice but never enrolled in any bylaw. This area is the most difficult to recover, precisely because it belongs only to practice and to oral tradition. It may be the area most significant for the livelihood of the poor and the marginal people in the village community.

Documents often represented partisan accounts and understandings, 'the outcome of bargaining and compromise between several propertied parties', the poor with 'no voice on the homage'.[55] None of this is to deny differences in emphasis or that change occurred, rather that memory remained for the poorest members of society a vital way in which they could counter the claims of elites. Besides, while Wood notes that '[m]uch of early modern popular memory remains an undiscovered country', the same can also be said for many of the working communities of modern Britain.[56] Here too we see significant commonalities in the ways rural and urban communities assembled and mobilised protest memories, not least in their reliance on the material world as an important repository for remembering protest. Of course, as Falvey's essay so powerfully demonstrates, the archive is not only necessarily incomplete and partial, but we need to be careful in using documents whose very creation was to serve hegemonic ends. Legal depositions, as Falvey notes, were always taken, transcribed and archived in the context of elites attempting to enforce, to perform, their power. We need, as such, to be mindful of these contexts, to read the archive of protest memory at once with a charry eye and simultaneously against the grain. This matters for even our reimaginings of the transcripts of the poor, of the quotidian and the customary, are often reliant on reading the scripts of elites.

Thus, the contributors to the volume collectively detail memory's rich material presence within the early modern and modern landscape. While the plebeian parks advocated by the radicals of early nineteenth-century London were never laid out (on which, see Steve Poole's chapter), radicalism, dissent and protest were remembered, mobilised and practiced via a range of sites, spaces and things. This included memorials, monuments, graves and plaques, but also boundary features, trees, landmarks and even the land itself, especially where the geographies of property were disrupted by hedge-breaking or riotous ploughing (as detailed in the chapters by Whyte and by Briony McDonagh and Joshua Rodda). These material markers functioned alongside practices of textual inscription, as protest memories were recorded in court papers, maps and place-names. While as Wallis documents, the prosecutions of Swing rioters in Norfolk and other counties functioned on one level to create the official narrative of unrest – as did the capital punishments that were meted out, especially where the executions took place in public – court records and official papers also inadvertently recorded more plebian memories of protest (on which, see Heather Falvey and Simon Sandall's contributions). As Ruth Mather relates, domestic space might also be an important repository for radical memory, as in her example of the Peterloo relics or other cheap commemorative objects displayed in the homes of working-class families. Thus, memory was made tangible and usable through material objects and spaces, including via temporary occupations of space for marches, camps or anniversary dinners which existed alongside more official performances of civic pride and memory.

If much of this book is concerned with the work that individuals and communities did to remember protests, it is also, both conceptually and archivally, important to understand memory's antonym, forgetting. In his chapter, Griffin starts from the theoretical standpoint that in deciding what was important to remember communities necessarily also needed to conceive what was not important, what was not useful or necessary for the future. Through the lens of a range of rural protests from the early eighteenth-century 'Blacks' to the Swing quasi-insurrection, he shows that in order to forge a future and rebuild communities after often-painful state-sponsored repressions, communities invested in the making of decidedly partial narratives that became the accepted collective memory.

The authors in this volume are thus careful not to set up false binaries: official vs alternative narratives of protests past; real vs false memories – although the dominant approach is the writing of protest histories from below. Rather, they point to the multiplicity of memories and the complex negotiations over meaning that took place. As Poole notes, the protagonists of his chapter 'all shared… a broad understanding of the importance of memory as an ideological field of conflict'. Much the same was true of many of the individuals and communities documented elsewhere in the volume, yet it is the voices of those farthest down the social scale that are often the hardest to hear. Remembering protest was also a gendered act, and while women's protest acts and memories receive consideration in the contributions of Mather, McDonagh and Rodda, and Falvey, more might be done by protest historians to explore the gendered, racialised and intersectional aspects of remembering, as well as the classed. In putting together this book, we thus hope to stimulate ongoing conversations and future research directions as much as chart (read: *remember*) protest histories past.

Acknowledgements The editors of *Remembering Protest* organised with Dr Katrina Navickas and Dr Iain Robertson a series of three well-attended and very successful conferences held at the University of Hertfordshire (2011), the University of the West of England (2012) and the University of Gloucestershire (2013). While the chapters in this book do not come directly out of the conferences, it was at the final conference in Cheltenham that the idea for this book was hatched. We would therefore like to pay thanks to all those protest historians – a heady mix of the salaried academic, the student, those involved in heritage industries and trade unions, and that bastion of British social history, the enthusiastic amateur historian – who made the conferences such an intellectually fecund space. Katrina and Iain deserve our particular thanks for their inspiration and dedication to researching critical protest histories. Iain was also involved in the early stages of this publication project and we hope the finished book meets with his approval.

Notes

1. Steve Hindle, 'Imagining insurrection in seventeenth-century England: representations of the Midland Rising of 1607', *History Workshop Journal* 66 (2008), 21–61; Andy Wood, *The 1549 Rebellions and the Making of Early Modern England* (Cambridge University Press: 2007). On 'The Tales of the Revolt' project see https://vre.leidenuniv.nl/vre/tales/emm/Pages/Home.aspx, accessed 25 August 2017.
2. Robert Hall, 'Chartism remembered: William Aitken, liberalism, and the politics of memory', *Journal of British Studies* 38 (1999), 445–70.
3. Andy Wood, *The Memory of the People: Custom and Popular Senses of the Past in Early Modern England* (Cambridge University Press: 2013).

4. See note 15.
5. Barbara Bender, 'Introduction: Contested Landscapes', in Barbara Bender and Margot Winer (eds), *Contested Landscapes: Movement, Exile and Place* (Berg: 2001), 1–18, 3; Doreen Massey, 'Landscape/space/politics: an essay', 8 and 22, Massey's essay was produced as part of the AHRC-funded project 'The future of landscape and the moving image' and appeared on the project website http://thefutureoflandscape.wordpress.com. See also Briony McDonagh and Stephen Daniels, 'Enclosure stories: narratives from Northamptonshire', *Cultural Geographies* 19 (2012), 107–21.
6. James C. Scott, *Domination and the Arts of Resistance: Hidden Transcripts* (Yale University Press: 1990).
7. Edward P. Thompson, *The Making of the English Working Class* (Penguin: 1968/1963), 13.
8. John C. Cairns, 'Sir Lewis Namier and the history of Europe', *Historical Reflections/Réflexions Historiques* 1 (1974), 22.
9. Donald Grove Barnes, *A History of the English Corn Laws, 1660–1846* (Routledge: 1930), xiv–xv.
10. Thomas S. Ashton and Joseph Sykes, *The Coal Industry of the Eighteenth Century* (Manchester University Press: 1929), 126, 131.
11. John Hammond and Barbara Hammond, *The Village Labourer, 1760–1832: A Study in the Government of England Before the Reform Bill* (Longmans: 1911); Idem., *The Town Labourer, 1760–1832: The New Civilization* (Longmans: 1917); Idem., *The Skilled Labourer* (Longmans: 1919); Frank Darvall, *Popular Disturbances and Public Order in Regency England: Being an Account of the Luddite and Other Disorders in England During The Years 1811–1817 and of the Attitude and Activity of the Authorities* (Oxford University Press: 1934).
12. Eric Hobsbawm, *Primitive Rebels: Studies in Archaic Forms of Social Movements in the 19th and 20th Centuries* (Manchester University Press: 1959).
13. The following references are indicative of the approach of each individual and the oeuvre rather than an exhaustive bibliography: Andrew Charlesworth, *An Atlas of Rural Protest 1548–1900* (Croom Helm: 1983); Anna Clark, *The Struggle for the Breeches: Gender and the Making of the British Working Class* (University of California Press: 1995); Peter Linebaugh, Douglas Hay, John Rule, Edward P. Thompson and Cal Winstow, *Albion's Fatal Tree: Crime and Society in Eighteenth-Century England* (Allen Lane: 1975); Roger Manning, *Village Revolts: Social Protest and Popular Disturbances in England, 1509–1640* (Oxford University Press: 1988); Jeanette Neeson, *Commoners: Common Right, Enclosure and Social Change in England, 1700–1820* (Cambridge University Press: 1993); Adrian Randall, *Before the Luddites: Custom, Community and Machinery in the English Woollen*

Industry, 1776–1809 (Cambridge University Press: 1991); Mick Reed and Roger Wells (eds), *Class, Conflict and Protest in the English Countryside, 1700–1880* (Alan Sutton: 1990); John Rule, *The Experience of Labour in Eighteenth-Century Industry* (Croom Helm: 1981); Buchanan Sharp, *In Contempt of All Authority: Rural Artisans and Riot in the West of England, 1586–1660* (University of California Press: 1980); Paul Slack (ed.), *Rebellion, Popular Protest and the Social Order in Early Modern England* (Cambridge University Press: 1984); John Stevenson, *Popular Disturbances in England 1700–1832* (Routledge: 1992); David Underdown, *Revel, Riot, and Rebellion: Popular Politics and Culture in England 1603–1660* (Houghton Mifflin Harcourt: 1987); John Walter, *Understanding Popular Violence in the English Revolution: The Colchester Plunderers* (Cambridge University Press: 1999); Roger Wells, *Insurrection: The British Experience, 1795–1803* (Alan Sutton: 1983); Keith Wrightson, *English Society 1580–1680* (Routledge: 1982). Eric Hobsbawm and George Rudé, *Captain Swing* (Lawrence and Wishart: 1969); George Rudé, *The Crowd in History: A Study of Popular Disturbances in France and England* (Wiley: 1964); Edward P. Thompson, 'The moral economy of the English crowd in the eighteenth century', *Past and Present* 50 (1971), 76–136; *Idem.*, *Whigs and Hunters: The Origin of the Black Act* (Allen Lane: 1975).
14. Andrew Charlesworth and Adrian Randall (eds) *Moral Economy and Popular Protest: Crowds, Conflict and Authority* (Macmillan: 2000).
15. Malcolm Chase, *Chartism: A New History* (Manchester University Press: 2007); *Idem.*, *1820: Disorder and Stability in the United Kingdom* (Manchester University Press: 2013); Carl Griffin, *The Rural War: Captain Swing and the Politics of Protest* (Manchester University Press: 2012); *Idem.*, *Protest, Politics and Work in Rural England, 1700–1850* (Palgrave: 2014); Paul Griffin, 'The spatial politics of Red Clydeside: historical labour geographies and radical connections' (unpublished PhD thesis, University of Glasgow, 2015); Ruth Mather, 'The home-making of the English working class: radical politics and domestic life in late-Georgian England' (unpublished PhD thesis, Queen Mary, University of London, 2017); Briony McDonagh, 'Subverting the Ground: private property and public protest in the sixteenth-century Yorkshire Wolds', *Agricultural History Review* 57.2 (2009), 191–206; *Idem.*, 'Making and breaking property: negotiating enclosure and common rights in sixteenth-century England', *History Workshop Journal* 76 (2013), 32–56; Katrina Navickas, *Loyalism and Radicalism in Lancashire, 1798–1815* (Oxford University Press: 2009); *Idem.*, *Protest and the Politics of Space and Place, 1789–1848* (Manchester University Press: 2015); Iain Robertson, *Landscapes of Protest in the Scottish Highlands After 1914: The Later Highland Land Wars* (Ashgate: 2013); Simon Sandall, *Custom and Popular Memory in the Forest of Dean, c.1550–1832* (Scholars' Press: 2013); Wood, *The 1549*

Rebellions; *Idem.*, *The Memory of the People*; Rose Wallis, 'The relationship between magistrates and their communities in the age of crisis: social protest c. 1790–1834' (unpublished PhD thesis, University of the West of England, 2006); Nicola Whyte, *Inhabiting the Landscape: Place, Custom and Memory, 1500–1800* (Windgather Press: 2009).

16. For useful overviews of new protest history, see Katrina Navickas, 'What happened to class? New histories of labour and collective action in Britain', *Social History*, 36.2 (2011), 192–204; Griffin, *Protest, Politics and Work*.
17. Hindle, 'Imagining insurrection'; Wood, *The 1549 Rebellions*. On transhistorical approaches to the commons, see Briony McDonagh and Carl Griffin, 'Occupy! Historical geographies of property, protest and the commons, 1500–1850', *Journal of Historical Geography* 53 (2016), 1–10.
18. On the memorialisation of Peterloo, see: https://www.theguardian.com/uk-news/2017/aug/19/manchester-event-marks-peterloo-massacre-anniversary, http://www.manchestereveningnews.co.uk/news/greater-manchester-news/peterloo-massacre-event-albert-square-13503827 and, http://www.peterloomassacre.org, all accessed 23 August 2017.
19. Iain Robertson, 'Memory, heritage and the micropolitics of memorialisation: commemorating the heroes of the land struggle', in E. Cameron (ed.), *Recovering From the Clearances* (Kershader, Isle of Lewis: The Islands Book Trust, 2013); *Idem.*, 'Hardscrabble heritage: The ruined blackhouse and crofting landscape as heritage from below', *Landscape Research* 40 (2015), 993–1009.
20. Carl Griffin, 'As lated tongues bespoke: popular protest in south-east England, 1790–1840', (unpublished PhD thesis, University of Bristol, 2002), 1–2. This is especially noticeable in the case of rural protests. For instance, see: http://www.bordonpost.co.uk/article.cfm?id=112705&headline=NOSTALGIA:%20Workhouses%20were%20unusual%20target%20of%20'Swing'%20rioters&sectionIs=news&searchyear=2017, accessed 23 August 2017.
21. http://www.walesonline.co.uk/news/local-news/chartist-mural-demolished-protesters-vent-6134407, accessed 23 August 2017.
22. Christina Jerre, 'Event-making the past: commemorations as social movement catalysts', *Memory Studies*, in press (2017), doi https://doi.org/10.1177/1750698017709871.
23. On this point, see McDonagh and Griffin, 'Occupy!', 9.
24. Daniel Levy, 'The future of the past: historiographical disputes and competing memories in Germany and Israel', *History and Theory* 38 (1999), 51–66.
25. Pierre Nora, 'Between memory and history: les lieux de memoire' in Jacques Revel and Lynn Hunt (eds), *Histories: French Constructions of the Past* (The New Press: 1995), 633, 636.

26. Terence Ranger and Eric Hobsbawm (eds), *The Invention of Tradition* (Cambridge University Press: 1983), see esp. Hobsbawm's introduction, 1–14.
27. Peter Mandler, *History and National Life* (Profile Books: 2002); John V. Beckett, Matthew Bristow and Elizabeth Williamson, *The Victoria County History 1899–2012: a Diamond Jubilee celebration*, 2nd edition (University of London, Institute of Historical Research: 2013). On the challenge to the idea of writing *the* past see: Keith Jenkins, *Rethinking History* (Routledge: 1992) and Michael S. Roth, *The Ironist's Cage: Memory, Trauma, and the Construction of History* (Columbia University Press: 1995).
28. Raphael Samuel and Paul Thompson, 'Introduction', in *Idem.* (eds), *The Myths We Live By* (Routledge: 1990), 4–5.
29. Brian Conway, 'Active remembering, selective forgetting, and collective identity: the case of Bloody Sunday', *Identity* 3 (2003), 309.
30. J. Brockmeier, 'Introduction: searching for cultural memory', *Culture and Psychology* 8 (2002), 5–14, 9–10.
31. Maurice Halbwachs, *Les Cadres Sociaux de la Mémoire* (Librarie Félix Alcan: 1925); *Idem.*, *On Collective Memory*, translated by Lewis A. Coser (Chicago, Chicago University Press: 1992). For the long and complex history of memory studies and the wider context for Halbwachs' writings see: Jeffrey K. Olick, Vered Vinitzky-Seroussi and Daniel Levy, 'Introduction' in *Idem.*, *The Collective Memory Reader* (Oxford University Press: 2011), 3–62. On local, vernacular and counter-memory, see for example George Lipsitz, *Time Passages: Collective Memory and American Popular Culture* (University of Minnesota Press: 1990); on counter memory and the local: Guy Beiner, *Remembering the Year of the French: Irish Folk History and Social Memory* (University of Wisconsin Press: 2007).
32. On the politics of the parish, see Keith Wrightson, 'The politics of the parish in early modern England', in Paul Griffiths, Adam Fox and Steve Hindle (eds), *The Experience of Authority in Early Modern England* (Macmillan: 1996), 10–46.
33. Nuala Johnson, 'Cast in stone: monuments, geography, and nationalism', *Environment and Planning D: Society and Space* 13 (1995), 51–65.
34. Clare Griffiths, 'Remembering Tolpuddle: rural history and commemoration in the inter-war labour movement', *History Workshop Journal* 44 (1997), 144–69.
35. Shanti Sumartojo, 'Commemorative atmospheres: memorial sites, collective events and the experience of national identity', *Transactions of the Institute of British Geographers* 41 (2016), 541–53.
36. Duncan Bell, 'Agonistic democracy and the politics of memory', *Constellations* 15 (2008), 148–166, 149.

37. Yvonne Whelan, 'The construction and destruction of a colonial landscape: monuments to British monarchs in Dublin before and after independence', *Journal of Historical Geography* 28 (2002), 508–33.
38. Robertson, 'Memory, heritage and the micropolitics of memorialisation'.
39. For a fascinating study of the politics of politics in museums, see Tom Carter and Iain Robertson, '"Distilling more than 2000 years of history into 161,000 square feet of display space": limiting Britishness and the failure to create a museum of British history', *Rural History* 27, (2016), 213–37.
40. On the 'Arm Bone' see: http://museums.bristol.gov.uk/details.php?irn=152065, accessed 3 October 2017.
41. https://www.wcml.org.uk/our-collections/object-of-the-month/ernest-jones-commemorative-jug/, accessed 3 October 2017.
42. Whyte, *Inhabiting the Landscape*; Wood, *The Memory of the People*.
43. Sarah Tarlow and Zoe Dyndor, 'The landscape of the gibbet,' *Landscape History* 36 (2015), 71–88.
44. Wood, *The Memory of the People*, esp. ch. 4.
45. John Clare, *Selected Poetry and Prose: John Clare;* edited by Merryn and Raymond Williams (Methuen: 1986), 90.
46. Nicola Whyte, 'Custodians of memory: women and custom in rural England c.1550–1700', *Cultural and Social History* 2 (2011), 153–73.
47. Wood, *The Memory of the People*, 259, 14, emphasis added.
48. On this concept see: W. Kansteiner, 'Finding meaning in memory: a methodological critique of collective memory studies', *History and Theory* 41 (2002), 179–197.
49. Robertson, *Landscapes of Protest*, esp. ch. 6. Mnemonics could take other non-material forms too, especially song: Heather Falvey, 'The articulation, transmission and preservation of custom in the forest community of Duffield (Derbyshire)', in Richard Hoyle (ed.), *Custom, Improvement and the Landscape in Early Modern Britain* (Ashgate: 2011), 83–4.
50. Thompson, 'Moral economy', *passim*; Alan Everitt, 'Farm labourers', in Joan Thirsk (ed.), *The Agrarian History of England and Wales, Volume IV: 1500–1640* (Cambridge University Press: 1967), 459.
51. As Brian Short notes, the version of events detailed might have been distorted by 'cued recall', the cues to aid recall acting to frame the past in partial ways: 'Environmental politics, custom and personal testimony: memory and lifespace on the late Victorian Ashdown Forest, Sussex', *Journal of Historical Geography* 30 (2004), 470–495, 488.
52. Edward P. Thompson, *Customs in Common: Studies in Traditional Popular Culture* (New Press, 1994), 102.
53. Hall, 'Chartism remembered', 449.

54. Erika Kuijpers and Judith Pollmann, 'Introduction', in Erika Kuijpers, Judith Pollmann, Johannes Muller and Jasper van der Steen (eds), *Memory Before Modernity: Practices of Memory in Early Modern Europe* (Brill: 2016), 11, 21. On the distinctions some earlier scholars have drawn between pre-modern (cyclical) and modern (linear) temporalities, see Mircea Eliade, *The Myth of Eternal Return: Cosmos and History* (Princeton University Press: 1971). Jacques Le Goff, *Time, Work, and Culture in the Middle Ages* (University of Chicago Press: 1982).
55. Thompson, *Customs in Common*, 100–1.
56. Wood, *The Memory of the People*, 30.

Remembering Mousehold Heath

Nicola Whyte

Processes of memorialisation and memory work have long been a focus of academic debate across disciplines. A growing body of literature is now concerned with acts of commemoration and memorialisation not as a means of preserving some authentic version of history, as valued by the nation-state, but rather as a social process that realises the operations of memory as a blend of official, yet also deeply personal engagements with the past. Halbwachs noted long ago how official narratives of the past can provide a framework through which people find a language to express their memories and personal experiences. Halbwachs was concerned with how autobiographical memory dialectically relates to the collective memory of a social group and to the broader historical memory of society.[1] As later work has shown, to subsume all memories and experiences into a shared narrative overlooks the possibility of alternative memories, and conflictual meanings of the past. Formal narratives are continuously interrogated and disrupted by individuals in their day-to-day practices and, as Frentress and Wickham note, opposition movements that employ prescribed historical narratives commemorate the past with different emphases and political valencies.[2] Historical memory can therefore provide a prompt for alternative, less consensual sometimes conflictual responses

N. Whyte (✉)
University of Exeter, Penryn Campus, UK

and meanings, and can act as a conduit for the expression of alternative values and associations. In his writing on the production of space Lefebvre suggests the creation of 'counter-space', formed in opposition to hegemonic spaces. This he argues is central to the functioning of the political economy and realisation of the potential for revolutionary change by overthrowing the prescribed socio-political order.[3]

Writers interested in the conditions of modernity have argued that the present concern to create sites of memory has had the adverse effect, rupturing people and society from the very past they wish to remember. They argue that there is an unprecedented urgency within modern societies to memorialise the past because it has already diminished from memory, slipped away from the grasp of the living.[4] As other scholars have argued, we must be careful not to valorise the original intentions and purpose of monuments and landscapes, and thus ignore the ongoing and even spontaneous processes of re-interpretation and renewal.[5] Memory has not atrophied, but rather the relationship between society and its past always takes on new forms, being wrought in the dialogical space between official and unofficial perspectives. Meanings do not merely shift with the passage of time, they are renewed through the evocation of various, multiple and unpredictable pasts. For Jay Winter, 'historical remembrance' best encapsulates this blend of practices, 'not just history, not just memory but a story that partakes of them both'.[6] Explorations of the processes that produce and reproduce historical remembrance, leads inevitably to an unsettling of prescribed historical narratives, as people interpret and employ the past for diverse ends, both as a social resource and means to articulate their own life-histories. As many writers have shown, it is important to release memory from official narrations of history, which bring closure to meaning when we might leave space for multiplicity and plurality.[7]

Radstone and Schwarz argue that we are living in an age of an unprecedented politicisation of memory.[8] But whether it is right to draw such a clear distinction between a past characterised by any less, or even unpoliticised memory practices, needs to be brought into question. Important work has investigated the relationship between history and collective memory and how meaning was mediated and contested through ritual performance, and ceremony, and how monuments and memorials functioned as sites of memory in the past.[9] Building on this work, we are interested here in articulations of landscape and place that draw upon a deep connection with the past and how in turn the landscape is constitutive of memory practices over long periods of time. Halbwachs was concerned with the spatial contexts within which historical memories take form, emphasising how through processes of inscription the past is etched upon the landscape, with the landscape in turn providing a repository of reference points for later inhabitants.[10] While we might take issue with the notion that the landscape is merely a static repository of memories, it is in the ways people encounter, draw meaning and make attachments to landscapes and places that need to be situated at the forefront of our investigation into the ways social conflicts and protests were remembered, remade and perhaps forgotten over time.

Historians, especially those interested in the pre-modern epoch, have often neglected to take on board the centrality of landscape and materiality as constitutive elements in memory work. The debate has tended to focus instead on the relative authority of oral and written methods of recording and remembering the past.[11] Engagement with recent research on landscape not only allows for greater plurality and multiplicity in the ways monuments, places and landscapes were interpreted, it also troubles their schematic classification into chronological sequences. Rather than attempting to fix monuments, material traces and landscapes in time and place, greater attention is now paid to making sense of the fluid, non-consensual processes of memory making and re-making that are prompted by encounters with landscapes and places formed of diverse and often conflicting ideas about the past.[12] This splintering of meaning points to the fragility of memory, yet it also suggests temporal dynamism, and the notion that relationships are continually in the process of being formed and reformed across time and space.[13] Chronological sequences and typologies tend to conceal connections that might be made through everyday practices of inhabitation and dwelling.[14] It is precisely in the malleable nature of memory practices and the unstable materiality of landscapes that renders the past a continuously powerful resource in the present.

The remainder of this chapter will explore the memories and meanings attached to a particular landscape, that of Mousehold Heath which lies on the eastern fringes of the city of Norwich and is often remembered as the place where Robert Kett and his followers made camp in 1549. The economic, social and political contexts of the 1549 rebellions have been extensively researched, and it is not my purpose to rehearse these debates.[15] Rather, I am interested in developing a different line of enquiry by considering instead the relationship between landscape and memory in the decades and centuries following the rebel camp. We will examine how Mousehold Heath has been constituted and reconstituted as a place for political protest and resistance from the sixteenth century to the present day. Tensions relating to access and land use rights emerge as a central theme in the following discussion. But more generally and importantly Mousehold was claimed by various groups as a place to meet, to work, to make camp, and to articulate social and political messages. Our purpose here is to understand the 1549 rebellion as one constituent in an assemblage of popular protests which drew upon the deep, spatio-temporal connectivity linking memory and materiality in a particular landscape.

Remembering the Commotion Time

Since the mid-twentieth century, Norwich and Mousehold Heath have been written into a conventional historical narrative about the coming of the age of democracy and the freedom and liberty of the people, traced back to the events of 1549. In 1949, Alderman Fred Herderson celebrated Robert Kett by commissioning a stone plaque to be set upon the Castle walls: 'in reparation and honour to a notable and courageous leader in the long struggle of the common people of England to escape from a servile life into the freedom of just conditions'. A number of plaques, tagging the sites of encounters between the gentry and rebels, have since been inserted into walls and pavements about the city, and further afield. Standing by the old road from Wymondham to Norwich, Kett's Oak in Hethersett can be seen today 'preserved' perhaps rather ironically behind a circular enclosure of iron railings. In Wymondham, eight miles south of Norwich and the place of Kett's birth, a local school carries his name, and a recent plaque echoes the sentiment of that made in 1949, but now Kett is claimed as a hero for Norfolk:

> Seeking a fairer society in Norfolk Robert Kett supported by his brother William led a rebellion of more than 15 000 people in 1549. The rising was crushed and over 3000 died. On 7th December 1549 Robert was hanged for treason at Norwich Castle and William from Wymondham Abbey's west tower. This plaque was erected in 1999 to remember the man and his struggle for a more just society in Norfolk.

There are doubtless many more local place-names claiming some connection with Kett, but it is the slab of concrete laid in the turf of Mousehold Heath that draws our attention. Etched with the words '1549 Remember Robert Kett. The land is ours', the memorial encapsulates the timeless struggle of the commons against their landed oppressors.[16] Processes of inscription, which may appear passive, with all too familiar memorials being overlooked and forgotten in the familiar contexts of day-to-day-life, are revived through practices of incorporation, rituals and performances.[17] This action of historical remembrance has been embodied in recent political gatherings and processions which claim Kett as the heroic yet ordinary commoner taking on the establishment. In December 2011, the Green Party made an explicit connection between current political events and those of the sixteenth century in the route chosen for an Occupy march through the city: 'on Wednesday 7th December at 5pm… the Robert Kett Memorial March… will leave the Occupy Norwich camp at the Haymarket at 5.30, and proceed to the Gate House of Norwich Castle, where Kett was hanged on 7th December 1549. His crime was leading a rebellion against poverty, injustice and the privatisation of the common land'.[18]

Since the middle of last century, the representation of Kett as defender of common rights, liberty and freedom has been at the foreground of historical representation. But until the nineteenth century, antiquarian writers sought to denigrate Kett as a villain and traitor, the usurper of the natural social order.[19] Since Alexander Neville wrote his memoirs of the rebellion, first published in Latin and later translated by Richard Woods in 1615, other writers, notably Holinshed in the 1570s and 1580s and Blomefield writing in the mid-eighteenth century, reinforced a negative view of Kett as the transgressor.[20] In the immediate aftermath of the rebellion, as Blomefield records, the authorities sought to take control of public memory, by amercing people in the courts for seditious words evoking the memory of Kett and the rebel camp. The city authorities attempted to reinforce this sentiment by instituting an annual church festival in celebration of the suppression of the rising and execution of Kett, whose decomposing body could still be seen for a time hanging in chains from the castle gates.[21] Of course, we must not assume that while on the face of it parishioners appeared to take part in such commemorations, they necessarily agreed with the message.[22] As Andy Wood has shown, the oral testimonies recorded during litigation proceedings concerning cases of sedition and land use rights demonstrate how remembrance of the commotion time was used in a highly politicised language of social conflict in the decades following.[23] But by the turn of the seventeenth century, with the exception of elite accounts of the rebellion, the visibility of the 'commotion time' diminishes in the documentary record. Wood argues that for people who had lived through the violence, disorder and tragedy of the fighting that consumed Norwich in 1549, many were engaged in an active process of forgetting: 'memories of the commotion time were drowned under the steady wash of collective amnesia'.[24] While some welcomed a collective forgetting, as Wood suggests the memory of the commotion endured in popular memory for up to three generations before the events of 1549 lost their authority and relevance to the living.[25]

The lack of documentary material explicitly evoking Kett or the commotion time presents an obvious challenge for our exploration of the ways people remembered popular protest across the period. But perhaps, as Jay Winter argues, we should be careful not to assume that 'silence is the space of forgetting', and speech is where remembrance happens.[26] One way of developing our interpretation of historical remembrance in the case of Kett and more broadly, is to shift the focus of enquiry to understanding people's long-term engagements with landscape and materiality in the work of memory as practice. The re-appropriation of Mousehold as a site of political protest has been noted, but little attention has been paid to investigating what this longevity meant in practice, nor its later manifestations.[27] This association goes back to 1381, and as we have seen is evident in 1549, and extends into the nineteenth century. In the more recent past, Mousehold Heath was associated as a place to hold public meetings, where various dissenting groups met, and where local workers gathered to show their grievances against plans for the enclosure of the heath. As recently as 2012, an Occupy camp was made on the heath to raise issues of homelessness in Norwich.

We shall come to consider these later conflicts and uses of the heath, but we first turn to a series of maps of Mousehold Heath dating to the late sixteenth century, which were commissioned in the 1580s in part at least to accompany court proceedings concerning the rights of neighbouring manors over the heath grounds.[28] In the sixteenth century, local inhabitants from 11 villages and parishes bordering the heath, claimed a range of use rights including grazing for livestock, the right to dig for sand, lime and clay, to make bricks and to gather furze and flags for fuel. Adding to the jurisdictional complexity of the landscape, neighbouring lords claimed warrening and foldcourse (sheep grazing) rights over portions of the heath. By this time, some enclosure had already been carried out, and some parcels of heath operated as doles, which entitled landholders to harvest flags and hay for example, but with the provision that once the crop was taken grazing rights would be reinstated over the land (Fig. 1). The map, while revealing an ostensibly elite ordering of the world,

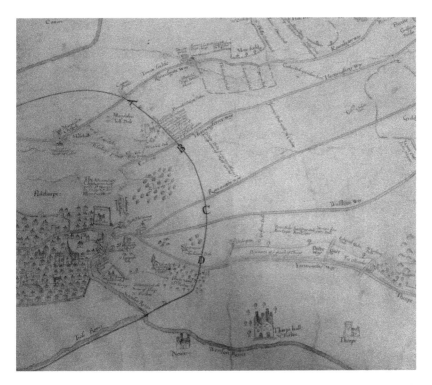

Fig. 1 Detail of a late sixteenth-century map of Mousehold Heath, with Norwich to the east. (NRO, MC3085: Reproduced with kind permission of Norfolk Museums Service (Norwich Castle Museum and Art Gallery))

provides an important insight into the re-workings of time in place, and how landmarks and places surviving from multiple pasts were drawn into social and political narratives about the present.[29]

At first glance, the map might be interpreted in the context of the economic interests of local manorial lords, Miles Corbet and Edward Paston, who were engaged in legal proceedings against the tenants and commoners grazing rights to the heath. Yet the contents of the map would suggest that they were interested in depicting more than farming matters. The city of Norwich, with its castle and cathedral, is shown, suggesting the importance of the proximity of the heath to the city. Mousehold itself is delineated in the drawing and labelling of a number of old sites and landmarks, route-ways and natural features. The map includes 'the Lollards Pytt where the martyrs dyed'; St William in the Wood 'whence it is saide that in tymes past an infant named Willm was buried whom the Jewes had murdered in the city of Norwich'; the Oak of Reformation 'so called by Kett the rebel', alongside a number of other buildings and structures apparently associated with monastic ownership and the Catholic past: St Leonard's Hill, St Michael's Chapel, and St James' Hill. Norwich cathedral and castle are shown environed by the city walls and river to the east where Bishops Bridge provides entry into the city from Mousehold. Other landmarks include the Hospital, Magdalen Gate and Magdalen Hill. On a map detailing the jurisdiction of manorial customs and land use rights their functions and meanings are not immediately obvious to us today.

Following the recent work on the adaptation, appropriation and reinvention of the relics of the past surviving in the landscape, the Mousehold map conveys a set of political messages about the past.[30] When read in conjunction with contemporary accounts of Kett's rebellion, it appears to chart, in part at least, the topography of the commotion time, which would have been well known, of course, to local gentry at the time. Both the Paston and the Corbet families were heavily involved in the fighting and eventual overthrow of the rebellion. Many of the landmarks depicted were places where the events of the rebellion unfolded, including: St Leonard's Hill, where the rebels made camp; Mount Surrey, the former site of St Leonard's Priory, appropriated by Kett as the centre of operations; Magdalen Hill, the scene of fighting; Bishops Gate, the scene of fighting and 'willful destruction'; and, of course, the 'Oak of Reformation', where Kett held his judicial court. It is plausible that this was an established landmark used before the Edwardian reformation, as the meeting place of the mayor, alderman and inhabitants of Norwich, who apparently made a yearly procession to an oak in the wood to hear sermons. The rebels were remembered for felling trees in the wood, but Thomas Paston stood accused of encroaching on commoners' grazing rights by enclosing the wood and by stopping up the right of way 'under Leonard's wall', which also severed the connection between the city and Mousehold Heath, and interrupted the procession to the old oak.[31] Considered in this light the two historical events, the dissolution and rebellion, were apparently conflated in order to endorse the dominant narrative of Kett the destroyer – destroyer of the material and social fabric of the city of Norwich and its environs. This conflation and re-working of historical narratives has been noted in other contexts, and is further suggested in the renaming of St Michael's Chapel as Kett's Castle by the nineteenth century.[32] When examined in the context of the dispute over Mousehold

Heath, the map may have been intended to be read not merely as a record of the victory over the rebels, but a celebration of the conquest over the defenders of common rights. In mapping the physical relics of the past alongside the disputed stretch of heathland a highly symbolic story emerges, one that visually portrays manorial ascendency over land and local society.

Early cartographic material can be interpreted as embedding temporal as well as spatial narratives about landscape and place. Crumbling ruins continued to serve important and diverse functions as tangible markers of time in place, and were integral in the attempts to claim authority over Mousehold Heath in the late sixteenth century. These were not newly designed monuments erected for the purposes of capturing and instilling memory, as the writers of modernity have insisted, but they were claimed as sites of memory nonetheless precisely because of their origins in the past. Read in this light, the map suggests an interest in the significance of Mousehold in a long history of social conflict and elite victories over religious and political disorder. It also demonstrates the layering of meaning in the landscape, whereby the potency of the Reformation past was mobilised to serve the more secular interests of the present. Victory over the commons was fleeting, and certainly could not easily continue in a landscape created by the continuous reproduction of customs and practices, which were essential to the rhythms of everyday life, and forging attachments though landscape and memory. The 1589 map of Mousehold was thus as much a political account of the past and idealised projection of the future, as it was an economic portrayal of land and resources, indeed for contemporaries the two could not be easily separated. It clearly signifies a particular way of seeing, a lord's view of the world, one that chronicles past events and actions attaching them to physical places, and embedding a hierarchical understanding of social relations in the landscape. Kett's rebellion had been quashed, as had Catholicism and the Jews (forcibly expelled from the city in the twelfth century), allowing the perceived natural order to prevail.[33] On the surface, this is an explicitly top-down view of the landscape, but as we shall see it is one that becomes meaningful in the way the sites and landmarks worked in dialogical relationship with non-elite understandings based on oral memory and everyday practice. Kett's camp was one of an assemblage of historical events traced in the relics of the past surviving on Mousehold Heath.

COUNTER-SPACE

Deposition evidence, gathered in 1589, offers valuable evidence of the ways local people interpreted and understood Mousehold as counter-space to that envisaged by manorial elites. The notion of counter-space should not imply a separate, discrete entity and container of action, but rather a layer of meaning in the landscape, existing alongside and in tension with elite ideas of spatial ordering. This folding together of different conceptualisations of landscape is important for understanding the multiple ways in which old landmarks and features were valued and afforded meaning. Local inhabitants gave account of the spatial parameters of customary rights to the heath, based upon knowledge borne of memory and practice. They claimed a substantial tract of the heath as Free Mousehold, allegedly an area operating outside manorial jurisdiction and control. Sixty-year-old labourer Richard Gilleford, for example, knew the heath called Free Mousehold 'right unto the cyttie of Norwich'. Just as the attempts to ascertain the bounds separating manors were open to question and often highly charged accusations of fraudulent goings-on, the attempts to mark and claim Free Mousehold by tenants and commoners were similarly contentious and ambiguous. The issue, which should not be construed as a problem, is that when we move from considering the projections of social and material order made by elite landowners, which offer a simplified view of landscape as portrayed in a map for example, and turn instead to the memories, practices and imaginations of local people we find complex, contingent and often-contradictory processes of landscape making.

The occupation of Mousehold in 1549 had been short-lived, and yet caused lasting disruption to the commoning community.[34] When the commotion time was evoked in local memory, it was used to signal a rupture in everyday life, when the activities of manorial lords and their bailiffs momentarily relinquished their grip, only to be reinstated with considerable force in the decades following. Local inhabitants dated their troubles to the coming of Corbet and Paston forty years previously, in 1549. William Garred, a sixty-year-old lime burner of the City of Norwich, argued that the Queen was lord of Mousehold and not Corbet and Paston, who had nevertheless claimed to be lords for the last forty years.[35] We can understand this in the context of Andy Wood's work on the ways communities called upon a higher authority, such as the monarch, to return good order by calling to account transgressors of prescribed custom and practice.[36] This conceptualisation of the organisation of landscape on the ground worked in tension with elite projections of the prescribed order. Sixty-three-year-old husbandman William Cubitt, told the court he had been born in Woodbastwick and that when he was a boy had seen the bailiff of the hundred drive cattle across Mousehold, suggesting freedom of movement over the heath. He accused Miles Corbet of digging false boundary marks and extending the perambulation of Woodbastwick further into the heath than he was entitled to do, and by such actions how Corbet sought to regulate and curtail access to the heath. Cubitt went on to describe how everyday practices of farming and experiences of the landscape had altered since the commotion of 1549, especially tenants' rights to keep sheep. He explained how the inhabitants of Woodbastwick used to keep 'till of late tyme since the comoccon' 'cullets' of sheep upon Mousehold. In recent years, however, the tenants of the manor were forced to leave their keeping of the cullet flock, because Corbet's shepherd allegedly chased their sheep from Mousehold, so they could not keep them 'quietlie as of ancient tyme they had done'.[37] Tightening regulation, by chasing away livestock and intimidating commoners, together with the appropriation, destruction and imitation of boundary marks, was key to achieving encroachment on the ground. It is by examining contemporary concepts of custom and right that we can shed additional light on the ways people negotiated the terms of their day-to-day existence, and how the past was a valuable resource in giving substance and legitimacy in the struggle for self-sufficiency among households.[38]

   The court evidence reveals tensions between middling tenants and commoners against manorial lords who they accused of trespassing on scarce resources not by enclosing but by actively seeking to disrupt everyday life. In view of the denigration of Kett as a traitor by contemporary elites, it is perhaps understandable that tenants and commoners, including husbandman, yeoman, labourers, fishermen and brickmakers, were reticent about evoking the memory of the rebel camp other than to indicate the disruption of the 'commotion' to everyday life. This disturbance was acutely felt in the entrenchment of unjust manorial policy, which threatened the economic and social subsistence of their and their neighbours' households. For local tenants and commoners, the principles of custom and right laid the foundations for an orderly society, based upon quietness and neighbourliness.[39] Manorial lords were accused of undermining and de-stabilising the social order, and impoverishing middling households by disrupting their means to dwell.[40] The commotion thus punctuated present time, giving the narrative of disenfranchisement and depletion important context. This tension is relayed in the deposition of eighty-four-year-old John Monforth, who explained that before John Corbet was lord of the manors of Woodbastwick and Laviles the manorial flock usually fed upon the demesne and other unenclosed lands, but since the enclosure of a great part of these grounds the manorial flock was kept on Mousehold 'and not so usuallie kept uppon the said demeasne & sev[er]all grounds as hath in annctient tyme bene used & accustomed'. He went on to describe how before Corbet and his father became owners of the manor, the inhabitants of Woodbastwick kept 'cullets' of sheep together with the manorial flock upon the parcel of heath. However, in recent years they could not keep as many sheep on the heath because the ground was so 'overlaide w[i]th the lordes flock of [Wood]Bastwick'.[41]

For everyone involved in contesting the right to be in the landscape, their various overlapping, personal and collective stories instilled value and potency to the concept of Free Mousehold, not as a fixed and bounded entity, but as a landscape created through individual, household and collective processes of memory making through everyday practice. Recent theories of inhabitation and dwelling, are useful to work with here for foregrounding lived experience, movement, memory and practice in knowledge making and identity formation. The emphasis on movement and wayfinding, and temporality in the work of Tim Ingold and others, invites historians to rethink conventional ideas of the landscape as a physical terrain to be categorised according to its constituent elements.[42] Rather, this work turns our attention to the experience of landscape as one of interconnected processes and possibilities. In contrast to recent writing among cultural geographers, in particular, which has privileged the experience of the individual, in our period of focus landscapes were not simply borne of personal experience but were created in company with others. Of course, deponents related their own subjective memories and experiences of working the land, meeting and socialising with neighbours, and moving from one place to another, yet still the shared experience of being in the landscape and reaching a common understanding was vital in the social process of landscape.

These approaches are important for our understanding of the continuing relevance of meanings associated with particular landscapes, where apparently diverse and unconnected landmarks, monuments, ruins, natural features and places of everyday work, were held together in relational tension with one another. Among those asked to give evidence, Edmund Cosen, a sixty-year-old fisherman who had known Mousehold lying in

Thorpe for fifty years, talked about the relationship between the various landmarks which he took to be the bounds, he knew them very well because he had walked them above forty times. He described to the court how he had learned the bounds from his father when he was a boy, and remembered the time when the annual perambulation was stopped during the reign of Edward VI, only to be resumed once again in 'Queene Maries daies'.[43] Importantly, his description of the boundary offers a further contextual layer to our interpretation of the 1589 map. Cosen recalled the perambulation route along the south part of the field of Thorpe, extending westward by Thorpe wood and by 'St Leonards to Byshopps gates' and from there northwards by 'Lathes Stoone' to another 'dole stoone' at the southeast end of 'Magdalen Chappell yarde' and from there 'assendinge upp to a hill in Ravensgate waie', proceeding eastward in another green way on the north side of 'St Willms in the Woode' towards a place or bound called 'the White Stake' and from there leaving the White Stake on the north part in the green way to a drove lane at the east end of a great close called 'Lumners', which he estimated to be 2000 acres.[44] During the perambulation, he recalled how the company often saw and met with the inhabitants of Postwick upon the heath.

The late sixteenth-century court records reveal how local memory, based upon practice, learning through observation and experience, gave tangible substance to the special status of Mousehold as existing outside the jurisdiction of the city authorities and manorial control. Concerning the extension of Blofield manor across the heath, sixty-three-year-old Thomas More, a clerk from Norwich, confirmed that for thirty nine years he was one of the 'greatest tenants' of the manor of Blofield.[45] He had never known, since the Bishop of Norwich was lord of the manor or during the time of Sir Thomas Paston, the inhabitants in any yearly perambulation fetch in any part of Free Mousehold as parcel of the limits and bounds of the parish of Blofield. He remembered perambulations often being made by the inhabitants of Blofield and Hemblington in their 'Rogacon Daies' and that they 'never went into Free Mushold'. When John Spencer, a gentleman, attempted to graze 500 sheep on that part of Mousehold, they were driven off by the inhabitants of Blofield and never came there again. He produced further written proof in the form of two ancient sealed deeds, one dating to Richard III and the other to the time of Henry VII, both of which mentioned Free Mousehold, where the inhabitants of Blofield, Hemblington, Burlingham St Andrews and South Walsham dug flags, felled ling and gathered bracken in diverse places.

Paston was accused of attempting to re-route the perambulation of Thorpe to take in part of Free Mousehold beyond the White Stake. Such activities, which denied the existence of commonly recognised and accepted landmarks, were intended to undermine the authority of custom invested in the material evidence of the past in the landscape.[46] Later documents reveal the longevity of the White Stake as an extant boundary mark. In their attempts to 'ascertain, fix and finally determine the boundaries of Thorpe', the enclosure commissioners recorded the White Stake as marking the point where the three parishes of Thorpe, Sprowston and Great Plumstead met.[47] For contemporaries minor place-names provided important clues to the past.

Alongside figures like Robert Kett, who was written into the great chronicles of the era, at the level of the everyday, there is evidence that local figures were no less audacious in their attempts to call to account the activities of those who governed. Andy Wood discusses the remarkable case of John Kettle, a basketmaker who was prosecuted for being 'rebellious against the city authorities' and threatening a second 'Kett's Camp'.[48] Our investigations in to the workings of local memory can be developed further than the realms of speech and oral tradition, to consider the ongoing engagement of people with the material environment of Mousehold Heath. In a less obvious case to that of Kettle, but no less revealing for offering an insight into the everyday politics of resistance in the late sixteenth century, several deponents remembered Old John Bussey, a brickmaker who actively resisted the manorial authorities by living according to an alternative spatial ordering of the landscape through his everyday actions.[49] Sixty-year-old husbandman James Churche of Blowfield confirmed that he had dug earth and made bricks upon Mousehold and related his experiences of working on the heath to the lives of other commoners, including 'olde Bussey' who dug earth there thirty years ago. Sixty-year-old yeoman Thomas Eden of Martham spoke of 'Olde John Bussey' of Blofield, 'beinge a stowte fellowe' who was well remembered in the locality for being punished in Blofield court yet never paying his fines: 'he never paid a penny for that he justified the lawfull doinge thereof by reason that the earthe was taken and digged upon Free Mussold'. Eden went on to say that he had heard the tenants of Blofield report 'that Bussey did saie that the heath was not part of the lord of Blofeild's soyle'. He also reported Bussey saying that he was 'soe harshlie delte with by the lord of Blofield with amercements and panes that rather he woold be so used he woolde carye his lorde his copie hold in a wallet being but half an acre for he said he cared not for the lord'. Thomas More, a clerk of sixty-three years of age, confirmed that he dug earth and made brick clamps on the heath, and how Old Bussey once demanded of him how he dared dig on Mousehold for fear of punishment in Blofield court, to which he answered that 'Blofeilde Courte had nothinge to doe there'. He reported that Bussey agreed, commenting that he had made 'the like answere for the diggine of his earthe'. In cases like this, we gain an insight into the how individual memories were explicitly employed to connect with the wider community in order to make sense of, and to lay claim to, tangible knowledge.

Material Memories

The history of the early modern English landscape has traditionally been told from the perspective of landowning elites and tenant farmers whose activities in enclosing and 'improving' have left a visible imprint on the landscape and archival record. Understanding enclosure is central, giving structure and rationale to the historical narrative of modernity. Scholars have shown how enclosure brought about physical changes to the landscape and new ways of seeing the land as alienable property, thus marking a shift from a former customary culture based upon notions of shared practice, neighbourliness and commonality to a system based upon individual property ownership. In recent years, writers have become resistant to the idea of closure, demonstrating instead the protracted complexity of enclosure and emergent notions of private property.[50] For the tenants and commoners of Mousehold, access to the heath, whether for work, subsistence or recreation, continued to be hotly contested well into the late nineteenth century. Proposals for the enclosure of Mousehold Heath were heard in the late eighteenth century, but were not fully realised until almost a century later.[51] The inhabitants of Pockthorpe laid claim to time immemorial access rights which were recognised and understood in the names and traces of activities left behind by past generations. In Tim Ingold's words:

> Every feature, then, is a potential clue, a key to meaning rather than a vehicle for carrying it. This discovery of procedure, wherein objects in the landscape become clues to meaning, is what distinguishes the perspective of dwelling. And since… the process of dwelling is fundamentally temporal, the apprehension of the landscape in the dwelling perspective must begin from a recognition of its temporality.[52]

Old landmarks, boundary features and place-names continued to give context to social and political gatherings and everyday activities on the heath.

By the nineteenth century, Mousehold was described by many as a wasteland, a landscape denuded by overgrazing and pock-marked by a long history of proto-industrial activities. A map made in 1730 shows the extent of enclosure, and also the continuity of features and use of resources since the sixteenth century at least, in the area of heath bordering Pockthorpe (Fig. 2). John Crome painted the heath in the early nineteenth century, but the painting remained unsold during his lifetime, his audience finding it abhorrent and at odds with their aesthetic taste for 'improved' landscapes.[53] One letter writer to the editorial pages of the

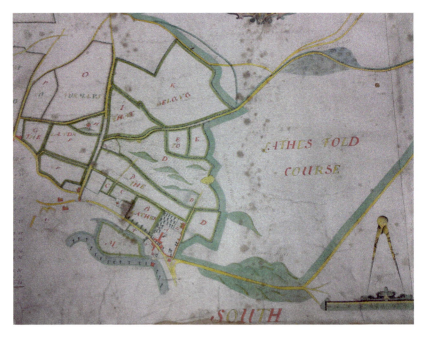

Fig. 2 Detail of a copy of a map of Mousehold made in 1730, following a survey of the lands belonging to the Dean and Chapter in 1718. Stone Mines is shown top right, St James Hill, gravel pits, lime and chalk kilns are also depicted. (NRO, MC3085/4: Reproduced with kind permission of Norfolk Museums Service (Norwich Castle Museum and Art Gallery))

Norfolk Chronicle in 1855 described how a very considerable portion of the heath had been enclosed which was considered a vast improvement, but in the remaining open and uncontrolled landscape: 'the promenade of the adult is frequently disagreeably checked by finding himself in rather too close propinquity to the noxious viper, and the gambols of the young' or in the event of one's walk being 'abruptly terminated by an involuntary somersault into one of the numerous gravel pits of the domain'. In the language of social description of the time, he referred to the aborigines of Pockthorpe and St Martin Oak, who were generally encountered on 'our native hills'.[54] By the late nineteenth century sentiment had changed, so that works being made to enclose and improve the heath were careful to preserve 'the natural wild beauty of appearance'.[55] The late nineteenth-century improvers imagined the heath transformed, the former traces of commoning and industry having been erased, lime and gravel pits filled in, the land covered with trees (which had the added benefit of reducing open space and thus preventing public meetings), with access being provided by new straight roads, and serpentine pathways designed for pedestrians to enjoy the clean air on the hills above the city of Norwich.[56]

The idea of Mousehold as a special place outside manorial and civic control remains evident in the nineteenth century, when the heath continued to provide a counter-space to the city where people could meet outside the control of the civic authorities, and outside conventional orderings of work time-discipline.[57] The heath was an apparently well-known location for public gatherings and political meetings, as well as being a place of work and recreation. The *Norfolk Chronicle and Norwich Gazette* records numerous public meetings on Mousehold. On 11 August 1839, for example, the Primitive Christian Society held a public prayer meeting on Mousehold Heath for the purpose of praying to 'Almighty God to undertake the cause of the poor and needy, to deliver them out of the hands of those who oppress them'. They apparently met 'in the valley where the Ranters commonly preach', suggesting a common location for such meetings.[58] A Chartists' meeting also took place the following year in the valley, where an overturned wagon provided a platform for the speakers.[59] Knowledge of Mousehold extended beyond the region with communities arriving from further afield to hold public meetings. On Saturday June 8 1822, five itinerant preachers or Ranters from Yorkshire, three men and two women 'held what they term a camp meeting, upon Mousehold Heath... many multitudes of people assembled to hear them, many of whom took provisions... and remained on the heath till evening'.[60] The evidence thus points to a continual process of social and political reconstitution of Mousehold as counter-space, where for some ordinary, everyday time might be suspended, sociability enjoyed and, when necessary, collective action taken.[61] This speaks to the ways in which recent writers have drawn on Ingold's discussion of landscape as 'task-scape'. Iain Robertson argues that 'performance and protest practices remained embedded within the "taskscape" to be remembered and drawn from generations after'.[62] Along similar lines, Katrina Navickas has shown how places of protest are not only made through symbol and ritual, but are reconstituted in everyday practices.[63] Drawing on this work, it is the deep temporality and multiplicity of attachments that are made foremost in everyday life that concern us here.

The apparent longevity of the association of Mousehold as an open-air public meeting place, was overlain and entangled with the continuing status of the heath as common land claimed by the community of householders living in the parish of Pockthorpe, a slum settlement outside the jurisdiction of the city. In an important discussion of the People's Park movement in Norwich in the late nineteenth century, Neil MacMaster provides a rich account of this later period of conflict over the enclosure and improvement of Mousehold Heath.[64] By this time very little survived of the former intercommon, with only a tract of 180 or so acres remaining unenclosed. The inhabitants of Pockthorpe relied on access to the heath for fuel, foodstuffs, grazing, quarrying and brickmaking, which formed a crucial part of their makeshift household economies. The interrelationship between settlement and heath was reinforced through everyday use of the commons, and was especially necessary during times of heightened tensions over rates of pay, particularly during the winter months when fuel was dear. In 1827, it was reported that 500 or 600 journeymen and weavers assembled on Mousehold Heath, in an explicit act of claiming the ground as an extension of their parish and place of dwelling. From Mousehold, they paraded through the streets with music and carrying poles, to one of which was affixed a loaf covered with black crape; to others papers were pasted with the words 'pay us for our labour' 'no Manchester low prices & co'.[65] They met again in December 1829, when it was estimated that upwards of 3000 unemployed joined them on Mousehold.[66] The heath held long-term associations as a resource for the poor. In the sixteenth century, it was reported that the 'poor folks of Norwich and of Pockthorp' asked leave to take furze or brakes for fuel growing on St James Hill among other places. In the nineteenth century, the city authorities made provision for the poor settled inhabitants of the city to cultivate areas of heath, in the expectation that they would be enabled by their own industry to make enough earnings to support their families. In 1826, seven acres was hired for the cultivation of potatoes 'with the spade'.[67] Flax was also considered to be an appropriate crop, suitable for the environmental conditions of the heath and in helping the poor cultivate better lives. In the latter part of the century, the rights of the poor to claim access to the heath was a vital part of the Pockthorpe campaign against the 'improvers'.

Faced with enclosure, the Pockthorpe people sought to defend what they claimed to be their ancient common rights to Mousehold and for over a quarter of a century they succeeded. In 1844, filling a void left by the collapse of manorial management in the early nineteenth century, they set up the Pockthorpe Committee to prevent the damaging exploitation of mineral resources on the heath.[68] Following years of protracted legal proceedings, which are well documented in the county record office, the city finally gained ownership of the heath in 1880 and immediately began work to transform the landscape into a People's Park. As with other similar schemes taking place around the country, the park was designed to be a recreational landscape which would be beneficial to the physical health and moral reformation of the people. The documentary material is fascinating not least for revealing the extent to which the inhabitants of Pockthorpe joined together to assert, sometimes aggressively, their claims to Mousehold Heath.[69]

The attempts of the city authorities in the 1880s to enclose and place Mousehold under the supervision and control of the Mousehold Heath Conservators was part of a broader and well-attested nineteenth-century improvement campaign concerned to bring about environmental reform and a moral cleansing of the working classes, and in so doing to restrict access to places of assembly. But for their aspirations to succeed the authorities set about erasing the physical evidence of practice and memory. They recognised the potency of the physical traces of the past in mobilising local inhabitants. Whether in a place-name, a physical feature, or memory of a past event, the material traces of the activities of past generations were part of everyday experience. In one such report made to the conservators in 1886, 195 men were employed 'in filling up holes breaking down the edges of the gravel pits taking away the roughness of various places, getting plots ready for planting, turfing banks etc. That day 352 men were at work that a new road 15 feet wide from the long slope was staked out.'[70]

This remaking of the Mousehold landscape, by reorienting movement and wayfinding, which was viewed as hugely beneficial for providing employment to the impoverished working classes, was met with sustained resistance. Newly instituted bye-laws for the use and enjoyment of the heath were routinely ignored. People were reported for not respecting the redesigned landscape, and keeping their usual entrances and old pathways across the heath. The banks of the new road were trampled and the heath was set on fire. Rangers were appointed and it was suggested that two police and one in 'plain clothes' should be enlisted to help maintain order. Barbed-wire fencing, hardly the aesthetic vision the conservators were aiming for, apparently proved a great success in protecting the banks from being trampled by trespassers.[71] Provisions were made to keep the site of St William in the Wood from being disturbed.[72] Thousands of trees were planted; however, not only were they pulled up, but the saplings were also affected by a summer drought. The environment, glacial gravel deposit and light sandy, easily leached soils, was not conducive to tree planting, and the Mousehold Conservators had to meet the costs of transporting gallons of water to the saplings.

Mousehold was a place where multiple memory communities drew meaning, whether through recreational activities, making a living from the resources provided by the heath, attending public meetings, or taking part in organised festivals and ceremonies. It is through this entanglement of meanings and the mobilisation of different histories in connection to the materiality of place that reproduced the political landscape over time. These different emphases reveal different ideas about what was worth remembering and commemorating about the past. Social groups mobilise different histories, but these are differentially empowered and often fragmented. The association with particular places and landmarks on the heath, some of which, like St James Hill, The White Stake, St William in the Wood, were old features that continued to frame people's movements and memories of the heath well into the nineteenth century. In one final example, concerning a festival to commemorate the life and work of George Borrow in 1913, further connections were made between Mousehold as a place to gather and make camp. The programme for Sunday included the following: 'The camping members of the Gypsy and Folk-Lore Club, together with the Caravan Club, and the Cycle Campers' Club will hold a Week-end Camp on Mousehold Heath'.[73] George Borrow was well known in the region for writing about his childhood experiences of Mousehold Heath and recording stories of gypsies and travellers with whom he met. Interestingly for our purposes, the organisers of the festival wished to use the 'Stone Pits' for their encampment. It is likely that this was the same area named on earlier maps as 'stone mine pits'. Given the location this proved to be contentious. Perhaps owing to its deep associations with the commoning landscape, and recent public disturbance, plans for the festival were restricted and the location moved to a nearby field and away from the material traces of the past.

Conclusion

One of the emergent themes of this chapter is the apparent lack of documentary evidence to suggest direct continuity in the remembrance of popular protests and resistance, and historical figures like Kett. In the nineteenth century, there is little direct evidence to suggest the Pockthorpe community were in any way inspired by the events of the mid-sixteenth century, although Kett was by then attached to the old site of St Michael's Chapel, which was known as Kett's Castle – also the name given to a nearby pub.[74] In the late sixteenth century, there again appears to have been little overt comment on the 'commotion time', and yet there are threads of meaning linking the past and present. The timespan discussed here is obviously vast, shifting from the sixteenth to the nineteenth centuries, and we should be cautious about assuming continuity of meaning that is somehow written into the landscape. Nevertheless, while substantial emphasis has been placed on the transmission of memory through relatively short-lived oral traditions, surviving for up to three generations or so after the event, we must also be careful not to bring closure by organising processes of memory into conventional chronological frameworks. Memories do not simply reside in the mind to be evidenced in the speech patterns of local people; rather, memories are made through routine practices and experiences of being in and making landscapes. Memories of Mousehold Heath operated at the level of the everyday, remembering past generations and, as in the case of Old John Bussey, the material work of day-to-day resistance. A landscape approach provides a useful methodological and conceptual framework for our understanding of the dynamic and contingent relationship between people and the material worlds in which they lived. Rather than assuming longevity of meaning, therefore, it has been our purpose to explore what this temporal connectivity meant in practice.

In attempting to elucidate the temporal and material dynamics in the process of making landscapes over time, the physical qualities and textures of everyday experience therefore should not be overlooked in the ways people interpreted and laid claim to Mousehold Heath. Nineteenth-century quarry workers and brickmakers, who were targeted in public notices produced by the city authorities, were working in a landscape created by the practices of early generations, stretching back to the sixteenth century and earlier. Industrial workings can be traced on early cartographic material dating from the late sixteenth century. The physical presence of old stone mines, clay, chalk, lime and sand pits and brick kilns provided context to everyday activities of dwelling. This interconnectivity between past and present and the idea of Mousehold as commons space influenced the decision people made to gather together for public meetings and recreational pursuits, and in their day-to-day practices of work and subsistence. On Mousehold Heath, meanings were made and remade through being in the landscape and engaging with and interpreting the workings of previous generations, and through those encounters knowing where to dig for gravel, where to gather furze, and where to meet. People in the past did not simply inherit a world of meaning rather, they inherited a world of traces and hauntings, and it was in the process of interpretation or misinterpretation that created the possibility of change.

As we have seen from the sixteenth to nineteenth centuries, Mousehold Heath was a contested landscape and claimed as a counter-space that worked in tension with other ideas and perspectives of landscape held by manorial and civic authorities. An appreciation of the workings of counter-space allows for alternative imaginaries and possibilities, in which the physical landscape, old monuments and natural features provide a prompt for reinterpretation and, occasionally, action. Landscapes, therefore, are not neutral backdrops. Across our period of focus, Mousehold was not simply an open, 'empty' space on the margins of the city and a convenient place for people to gather to meet for work and recreation. Nor was this landscape simply a repository of history and memory, its social and historical meanings simply known. In the sixteenth century and in the nineteenth century, similarities can be discerned in the ways practices of being in the landscape informed memory and renewed meanings which were made through interpreting the physical traces of the past in the landscape. In other words, people drew meaning from the landscape as it had been inhabited by former generations, the traces of which could be seen on the ground. For some manorial and civic elites, this led to the attempt to physically alter the past, by levelling landmarks and filling in gravel pits, and yet it was through such actions of destruction that the potency of the material evidence of the past was renewed by those who claimed the right to be in the landscape. Consideration of the interconnectivity between landscape and memory unsettles linear narrations of the past, by revealing the continuous reconfiguration of memory as material practice. It was the tensions between different users, between the imagined and physical landscape, that has created and reproduced Mousehold Heath into the twenty-first century.

Acknowledgements Research leading to this article has been supported by the European Research Council (ERC Grant Agreement no. 284085: 'The Past in its Place', with Professor Philip Schwyzer). I am particularly grateful to Briony McDonagh and Tim Cooper for their thoughts and comments.

NOTES

1. Erika Apfelbaum, 'Halbwachs and the social properties of memory' in Susannah Radstone, and Bill Schwarz (eds) *Memory: Histories, Theories, Debates* (Fordham University Press: 2010), 77–92; Maurice Halbwachs, translated by Lewis A. Coser, *On Collective Memory* (Chicago University Press: 1992).
2. James Fentress and Chris Wickham, *Social Memory* (Oxford, Blackwell: 1992), 135.
3. Henri Lefebvre, translated by Donald Nicholson-Smith, *The Production of Space* (Blackwell: 1991), 367, 380–3.
4. Pierre Nora, 'Between memory and history: Les lieux de mémoire', *Representations* 26 (1989), 7–25.
5. See, for example, Raphael Samuel, *Theatres of Memory: Past and Present in Contemporary Culture*, vol. 1 (Verso: 1994); Niamh Moor and Yvonne Whelan (eds), *Heritage, Memory and the Politics of Identity* (Ashgate: 2007); Paul Ashton and Hilda Kean, (eds) *People and Their Pasts* (Palgrave Macmillan: 2009).
6. Jay Winter, 'Sites of memory', in Radstone and Schwarz, *Memory*, 312–324, 313.
7. Moore and Whelan, *Heritage*; Ashton and Kean, *People;* Barbara Bender, *Stonehenge: Making Space* (Berg: 1998).
8. Susannah Radstone and Bill Schwarz, 'Introduction: Mapping Memory', in Radstone and Schwarz, *Memory*, 1–9.
9. David Cressy, *Bonfires and Bells: National Memory and the Protestant Calendar in Elizabethan and Stuart England* (Weidenfeld and Nicolson: 1989); Paul Connerton, *How Societies Remember* (Cambridge University Press: 1989), chapter 4.

10. Halbwachs, *On Collective Memory*, 235 and Lewis A. Coser, 'Introduction: Maurice Halbwachs 1877–1945', in Halbwachs, *On Collective Memory*, 2.
11. Adam Fox, *Oral and Literate Culture in England* (Oxford University Press: 2000); Andy Wood, 'Custom and the social organisation of writing in early modern England' *Transactions of the Royal Historical Society* (6th series) 9, 257–69; Adam Fox and Daniel Woolf (eds) *The Spoken Word: Oral Culture in Britain 1500–1850* (Manchester University Press: 2002).
12. For a useful introduction to approaches in landscape archaeology, see, for example, Wendy Ashmore, 'Social archaeologies of landscape', in Lynn Meskell and Robert W. Preucel (eds), *A Companion to Social Archaeology* (Blackwell: 2007), 255–272; J. C. Barrett, 'Chronologies of Landscape', in P. J. Ucko and R. Layton (eds) *The Archaeology and Anthropology of Landscapes: Shaping Your Landscape* (Routledge: 1999), 21–30; Bender, *Stonehenge*.
13. Doreen Massey, 'Places and their pasts', *History Workshop Journal* 39 (1995), 182–92.
14. Tim Ingold, 'The temporality of the landscape', *World Archaeology* 25:2 (1993), 152–74 and *The Perception of the Environment: Essays on Livelihood, Dwelling and Skill* (London: Routledge: 2000), 189–218.
15. For example, Andy Wood, *The 1549 Rebellions and the Making of Early Modern England*. (Cambridge University Press: 2007); Diarmaid MacCulloch, 'Kett's Rebellion in context', *Past and Present* 84 (1979), 36–59; Jane Whittle, *The Development of Agrarian Capitalism: Land and Labour in Norfolk, 1440–1580* (Oxford University Press: 2000); Jane Whittle, 'Lords and tenants in Kett's Rebellion 1549', *Past & Present* 207.1 (2010), 3–52.
16. See also Alun Howkins, 'The commons, enclosure and radical histories', in David Feldman and Jon Lawrence (eds) *Structures and Transformations in Modern British History* (Cambridge University Press: 2011), 118–141.
17. Mark Freeman, '"Splendid display; pompous spectacle": Historical pageants in twentieth-century Britain', *Social History* 38.4 (2013), 423–455; Paul Readman, 'The place of the past in English culture c. 1890–1914', *Past and Present*, 186.1 (2005), 147–99.
18. Norwich Green Party, 'A New Economic Story – The Courageous State', available at https://archive.is/20121224044335/http://www.greenparty.org.uk/localsites/norwich/News/a-new-economic-story-the-courageous-state1.html
19. Wood, *The 1549 Rebellions*, chapter 6, 257–264.
20. Ibid.; Francis Blomefield, *An Essay Towards A Topographical History of the County of Norfolk* Vol. 4, available at www.british-history.ac.uk; Holinshed's *Chronicles of England, Scotland and Ireland*, available at http://english.nsms.ox.ac.uk/holinshed/

21. Wood, *The 1549 Rebellions*, 228.
22. Andy Wood, '"Poore men woll speke one daye": Plebeian Languages of Deference and Defiance in England c. 1520–1640', in Tim Harris (ed.), *The Politics of the Excluded* (Basingstoke: 2001), 67–98; Andy Wood, *The Politics of Social Conflict: The Peak Country, 1520–1770* (Cambridge University Press: 1999); John Walter, *Crowds and Popular Politics in Early Modern England* (Manchester University Press: 2006).
23. Wood, *The 1549 Rebellions*, 106–7, 139–256.
24. Ibid., 251–2.
25. Ibid., 252.
26. Winter, 'Sites of memory'.
27. Wood, *The 1549 Rebellions*, 10.
28. TNA, MR52; NRO, MC 3085/1; see also NRO, MC3085/2.
29. For my earlier exploration of these ideas, see Nicola Whyte, 'The afterlife of barrows: prehistoric monuments in the Norfolk landscape', *Landscape History* 25 (2003), 5–16; 'Landscape, memory and custom: parish identities *c.* 1550–1700', *Social History*, 32:2 (2007), 166–186; 'An archaeology of natural places: trees in the seventeenth-century landscape' *Huntingdon Library Quarterly* 76:4 (2013), 499–518.
30. Alexandra Walsham, *The Reformation of The Landscape* (Oxford University Press: 2011), 515–530; Adam Fox, *Oral and Literate Culture in England 1500–1700* (Oxford University Press: 2000), chapter 4; Daniel Woolf, *The Social Circulation of the Past: English Historical Culture 1500–1730* (Oxford University Press: 2003), chapter 9.
31. TNA, REQ 2/18 (Court of Requests 1547–1553).
32. Keith Thomas, *The Perception of the Past in Early Modern England* (Creighton Lecture Trust: 1984); Daniel Woolf, 'Of Danes and giants: some popular beliefs about the past in early modern England', *Dalhousie Review* 71 (1991), 166–209; Fox, *Oral and Literate*; Walsham, *Reformation of the Landscape*, chapter 7.
33. See also Walsham's discussion in *Reformation of the Landscape*, 515–31, 524; Cressy, *Bonfires and Bells*.
34. Andy Wood notes the physical and ecological damage to Mousehold; a line of enquiry worth developing further (Wood, *The 1549 Rebellions*, 232).
35. TNA, E178/7153.
36. Wood, "Poore men woll speke one daye".
37. TNA, E178/7153.
38. Wood, *The 1549 Rebellions*, 252–256; see also Andy Wood, 'The place of custom in plebeian political culture: England, 1550–1800', *Social History* 22 (1997), 46–60; Edward P. Thompson, *Customs in Common* (Merlin Press: 1991).

39. Keith Wrightson, 'Mutualities and obligations: changing social relationships in early modern England', *Proceedings of the British Academy* vol. 139 (2005) and 'The decline of neighbourliness revisited', in Norman Jones and Daniel Woolf (eds) *Local Identities in Late Medieval and Early Modern England* (Palgrave Macmillan: 2007), 19–49; Christopher Rodgers, Eleanor Straughton, Angus Winchester and Margherita Pieraccini, *Contested Common Land: Environmental Governance Past and Present* (Earthscan: 2011), especially chapter 2.
40. On the concept of dwelling, see Tim Ingold, 'The temporality of the landscape', *World Archaeology* 25:2 (1993) and *The Perception of the Environment: Essays on Livelihood, Dwelling and Skill* (Routledge: 2000); Mitch Rose, 'Dwelling as marking and claiming', *Environment and Planning D: Society and Space* 30 (2012), 757–771; for my attempts at developing these ideas, see Nicola Whyte, 'Senses of time, senses of place: Landscape History from a British perspective', *Landscape Research* 40.8 (2015), 925–38.
41. TNA, E178/7153.
42. For an excellent overview, see John Wylie, *Landscape* (Routledge: 2007), chapter 5.
43. TNA, E178/7153.
44. TNA, E178/7153.
45. Ibid.
46. Whyte, 'Landscape, memory and custom'.
47. NRO, N/TC50/70.
48. Wood, *The 1549 Rebellions*, 247–8.
49. TNA, E178/7153.
50. Briony McDonagh, 'Making and breaking property: negotiating enclosure and common rights in sixteenth-century England', *History Workshop Journal* 76.1 (2013), 32–56; Nicola Whyte, 'The common fields and social relations', in Chris Dyer and Richard Jones (eds) *Farmers, Consumers and Innovators: The World of Joan Thirsk* (University of Hertfordshire Press: 2016), 63–76.
51. NRO, COL 9/74; Neil MacMaster, 'Mousehold Heath 1857–1884: "popular politics" and the Victorian public park', *Past and Present* 127 (1990), 117–154.
52. Ingold, *The Perception of the Environment*, 208.
53. http://www.tate.org.uk/art/artworks/crome-mousehold-heath-norwich-n00689; see also Ian Waites discussion of Crome's depiction of Mousehold in *Common Land in English Painting* (Woodbridge, Boydell: 2012), 64–66, 85–96.
54. *The Norfolk Chronicle and Norwich Gazette* (Norwich, England), June 13 1855; *British Library Newspapers, Part III: 1741–1950*.

55. NRO, N/TC 5-11, 78.
56. NRO, N/TC 5-11.
57. Edward P. Thompson, 'Time, work-discipline and industrial capitalism', *Past and Present* 38 (1967), *56–97.*
58. *The Norfolk Chronicle and Norwich Gazette* (Norwich, England), Saturday 17 August 1839, pg. 2; Issue 3609. *British Library Newspapers, Part III: 1741–1950.*
59. Ibid. Saturday 2 May 1840, pg. 2; Issue 3646.
60. Ibid. Saturday 8 June 1822, pg. 2; Issue 2725.
61. For a more extensive discussion of the nineteenth century context, see Katrina Navickas, *Protest and the Politics of Space and Place 1789*–1848 (Manchester University Press: 2015).
62. Iain Robertson, *Landscapes of Protest in the Scottish Highlands and After 1914: The Later Highland Land Wars* (Routledge: 2013), 155.
63. Katrina Navickas, 'Moors, fields and popular protest in South Lancashire and the West Riding of Yorkshire, 1800–1848', *Northern History* Vol. 46 (2009), 93–111.
64. MacMaster, 'Mousehold Heath', 117–154.
65. *The Norfolk Chronicle and Norwich Gazette.* Saturday 17 February 1827, pg. 2; Issue 2960.
66. *The Norfolk Chronicle and Norwich Gazette.* Saturday 12 December 1829, pg. 2; Issue 3106.
67. *The Norfolk Chronicle and Norwich Gazette.* Saturday 3 June 1826, pg. 2; Issue 2923.
68. MacMaster, 'Mousehold Heath', 131.
69. Ibid. On the idea of improvement, see also Sarah Tarlow, *The Archaeology of Improvement in Britain, 1750–1850* (Cambridge University Press: 2007).
70. NRO, N/TC 5-11, 25 February 1886.
71. NRO, N/TC/5/10, 28 July.
72. NRO, N/TC 5-11, 25 February 1886.
73 NRO, MS 11322.
74. *The Norfolk Chronicle and Norwich Gazette.* Saturday 12 August 1826, pg. 2; Issue 2933.

Landscape, Memory and Protest in the Midlands Rising of 1607

Briony McDonagh and Joshua Rodda

In the early summer of 1607, a large group of perhaps as many as a thousand men, women and children assembled at Newton (Northamptonshire) and began digging up hedges. The hedges surrounded enclosures recently put in place by the local landowner, Thomas Tresham of Newton, a cousin of the much more famous Sir Thomas Tresham of Rushton. Arriving at Newton on 8 June, the deputy-lieutenant of Northamptonshire, Sir Edward Montagu, twice read out a royal proclamation demanding the rioters disperse. When they did not, their forces charged the crowd. After initially putting up fierce resistance, the crowd fled as the mounted horsemen charged for the second time. Forty to fifty of the rioters were killed in the field and many more captured, some of whom were later to be executed and have their mutilated bodies displayed at Northampton, Oundle and other local towns.[1] The events at Newton were the culmination of more than a month of unrest in parts of Northamptonshire, Leicestershire and Warwickshire, much of it focused on the issue of agrarian change – specifically

---

B. McDonagh (✉)
University of Hull, Hull, UK

J. Rodda
University of Nottingham, Nottingham, UK

© The Author(s) 2018
C. J. Griffin, B. McDonagh (eds.), *Remembering Protest in Britain since 1500*, https://doi.org/10.1007/978-3-319-74243-4_3

the enclosure of common field arable land and its conversion to sheep pasture – and recorded either in government papers and letters or in subsequent court cases, many of them pursued in the court of Star Chamber.

Yet for all the bloodshed at Newton, the Midlands Rising has received surprisingly little in the way of modern critical analysis. There is no detailed study of the Rising and no more than a handful of articles and book chapters concerned with it.[2] As Steve Hindle recently put it, the Midlands Rising is 'all but forgotten, even amongst historians of early modern rebellions'.[3] This is all the more surprising in the light of a recent resurgence of interest among historians and historical geographers in early modern and modern protest more generally. Thus, early modern social historians have explored the local dynamics of enclosure and the significance of popular memory – and, in doing so, have done much to extend our understanding of how enclosure was negotiated and resisted on the ground – while historians of the later eighteenth and nineteenth centuries have recently produced a range of studies of popular collective action which variously draw our attention to the importance of space and place in shaping protest, to the moral ecologies of place and to the everyday politics of protest.[4]

Here we draw on these new histories and historical geographies of protest to examine the Midlands Rising afresh, paying particular attention to questions about how those involved in the Rising assembled earlier protest memories and how the Rising was mobilised in later incidents concerned with enclosure and common rights. In what follows, we frame memory as active and inherently political, as intimately bound up in the power and politics of landscape.[5] For if, as Andy Wood so eloquently put it, '[c]ustom wrote memory on to the land', that process of inscription – of assembly – was always ongoing, necessarily shot through with the concerns of the present.[6] Landscape was always in the making, a multiplicity of stories ever unfinished and constantly unfolding.[7] Thus, we focus here not on *recovering* memory per se but on the *mobilisation* of protest memories in the (historical) present. In drawing on these and other debates – including recent work on the uses of the past in the present – we aim to situate the events of 1607 within their longer-term historical context and wider landscape setting, to offer a grounded analysis which explores the complex enmeshing of landscape, memory and protest as it was enacted in early seventeenth-century Northamptonshire in particular. We thus examine the Rising not only as an event which sent waves of panic through the Westminster government – a theme very ably investigated by Hindle – but also as an episode in the history of the local landscape which was shaped by indigenous experiences as well as exogenous factors and given form and meaning by local people and communities. In other words, as an event in both the *national* and *local* politics of land. At the same time, we deliberately counter what we see in the existing literature as a tendency for the Rising to float free of its temporal context. Scholars draw comparisons with the 'Commotion Time' of 1549, but say little about the half-century of enclosures, enclosure disputes and legislation which preceded the Midland Rising.[8] This is in part an issue of sources, specifically the difficulties of working with the enormous collection of poorly catalogued Elizabethan Star Chamber records stored at The National Archives.[9] These have been little explored in relation to the Midlands Rising and we have – at least until now – known little about the nature and scale of enclosure rioting in the period between Elizabeth's accession and the 1590s, a decade for which the Inquisitions of Depopulation drawn up in the aftermath of the Rising provide some, albeit sporadic, evidence.[10]

In what follows we use the Elizabethan and Stuart Star Chamber records for the light they shed on the Midlands Rising and its prehistory. The chapter thus approaches the enmeshing of landscape, memory and protest in three registers. Firstly, it explores the long history of enclosure protest in the sixteenth-century Midlands, bringing to bear new evidence from the Elizabethan Star Chamber records. It does this specifically in relation to Northamptonshire, though parallel tensions were almost certainly evident in Leicestershire and Warwickshire. In doing so, it addresses the question of any upsurge in enclosure in the last decade of the sixteenth century, arguing that John Martin's assertion that that the Rising was preceded by – and in part a response to – a dramatic increase in enclosure activity in the last decade of the sixteenth century which 'reached its peak in the five years preceding the revolt' needs rethinking in the light of new evidence.[11] Secondly, the chapter examines the specific incidents of anti-enclosure protest reported in 1607, exploring the multiple points of connection between the riots of May and June that year and earlier unrest over enclosure and agricultural change in the county. Specifically, we examine how those participating in enclosure riots mobilised earlier disputes to give meaning and legitimacy to their actions. Thirdly, having investigated how the various incidents of anti-enclosure protest which made up the Rising each drew on earlier histories of dispute for their shape and meaning, the chapter also considers how the Rising itself was remembered. That is, how the Rising was in turn invoked and mobilised by litigants and protestors involved in struggles over land and common rights in the years immediately following 1607. The final section offers some concluding comments.

A History of Protest

There were enclosure disputes from Northamptonshire being litigated in the central equity courts at Westminster from the turn of the sixteenth century onwards. The principal complaint of more than a quarter of the surviving Henrician Star Chamber cases for the county relates to enclosure, common rights or land use change.[12] This included complaints about hedge-breaking and the physical occupation of land by large groups of people – for example at Finedon, Rushton and Barnack in the first few decades of the century – but also animal trespasses, where the town herd was turned into newly enclosed parcels of land, thus destroying the growing crop and thereby resisting attempts to remove land from the common field system. Thus, while landowners complained about the physical occupation of enclosed land with human and animal bodies, commoners argued that their animals (and sometimes also their children) had been beaten and the beasts impounded or otherwise driven off the land, sometimes with dogs.[13] Initial complaints about the depasturing, impounding and rescuing of animals are a good indication of tensions over enclosure and the conversion of arable land to pasture, even where hedge-breaking is not explicitly mentioned. Mass ploughings, park breaking incidents and assaults on warren and park keepers are also suggestive of opposition to the extension of private property rights in Northamptonshire, as elsewhere.[14]

Detailed work on the Elizabethan Star Chamber records suggests that a very similar range of complaints reached the court in the second half of the century. Hedge-breaking was recorded at Kings Sutton in 1567, at Finedon once again in 1576 or 1577 and at Guilsborough in the early 1580s.[15] In early August 1571, dogs were used to drive cattle belonging to the tenants of John Bedell out of the fields of Naseby.[16] A similar incident reached the Star Chamber in 1587 when the inhabitants of Syresham near Brackley complained that servants of the Earl of Derby had driven their cattle from the common with dogs.[17] At Braunston in the early 1580s, a group of women came together in order to pull down the frame of a house being constructed on the common. This was a clear attempt to resist encroachments on common rights and having pulled down the frame of the house, the women turned their animals on to the land, thus reasserting common grazing rights.[18] There were obvious tensions over enclosure at Duddington in the late 1570s when William Kirkham (the elder) of Fineshade was said to have blocked the perambulation route through his closes with a new hedge as well as removed merestones –

themselves important mnemonics within the landscape – marking the boundary between the two parishes and between Duddington and the lands of the former Fineshade Abbey which the Kirkham family acquired after the dissolution.[19] During Rogation Week in early May, the inhabitants alleged Kirkham had sent armed men to protect the hedge and closes, and to menace the locals.[20] At Benefield in the mid-1590s, inhabitants complained that they were unable to graze their cattle in a parcel of recently enclosed land, previously part of the wastes of the manor. They said that the cattle belonging to one Agnes Fowler had been wrongfully impounded by Richard Dale, despite Fowler's rights being proven in the Assize courts.[21]

Some of these disputes were admittedly relatively small-scale disturbances involving only five or ten individuals. Yet there were also a number of larger, more serious disputes in the county. At Adstone in September 1599 more than a hundred people, mostly women, were said to have driven their cattle into enclosed land owned by George Dryden, the brother of Erasmus Dryden, MP and 1st baronet of nearby Canons Ashby. On another occasion a week later, Dryden said they brought a minstrel to the land in question and there was wild Morris dancing in the town accompanied by gestures that were intended to mock him. This was clearly community retribution aimed at an unpopular landowner, perhaps inflected by issues around the marriage of Dryden to Katherine Harby (née Throckmorton), whose son Dryden blamed for stirring up ill-feeling in the neighbourhood. In a counter-suit in Star Chamber, the inhabitants accused Dryden of cutting new ditches in the fields as well as assaulting them when they tended their cattle in the common fields and driving the animals off the land with dogs. They said he had enclosed part of the common – justified by Dryden as part of an exchange of land – and converted land from arable to pasture intending eventually to depopulate the entire town.[22]

A decade or so earlier and five miles north, landowner Valentine Knightley complained that a large group of 60–80 inhabitants had interrupted his attempts to plough land in the manor of Badby and Newnham. He said they had sent secret messengers about the town 'in manner of a rebellion to raise the people'. They assembled together under the leadership of a mounted 'captain' named Anthony Palmer, described by Knightley as the 'chief ringleader' who commanded the crowd with watchwords and signals. The crowd spent all day in the field interfering with his servants' attempts to plough and remained there even after a local JP had arrived and commanded the crowd to disperse. The interrogatories drawn up for Knightley went as far as to claim that the defendants had continued in the field saying they would 'leese [their] lives before [they] would leese [their] land'.[23] There had been previous cases in Chancery and Queen's Bench about the land, which it appears Knightley had enclosed from the wastes and put down to a mixture of pasture and arable use, thereby extinguishing customary rights. While the defendants claimed they had exercised rights in the ground time out of mind, Knightley said they 'invented' new customs in order to vex him: a reminder once again of the ways custom and memory were – in Andy Wood's words – 'regularly rehearsed and argued over'.[24] Knightley later detailed a number of further incidents in the manor, saying that in May a large group of women had driven his beasts off the common and into his own planted enclosures, as well as turned their own cattle into his crops in August.[25]

These then were big gatherings of people – often including large numbers of women – led by acknowledged 'captains' of the crowd.[26] Many such incidents incorporated ritualised elements. Rioters occupying land at Oundle in 1611 were said to have been accompanied by the ringing of church bells, the playing of bagpipes and much shouting, just as the bells were also said to have been rung throughout the earlier hedge-breaking riot at Finedon.[27] An assembly about rights of access over enclosed land at Stowe and Litchborough in August 1591 (or possibly 1592) was accompanied by the blowing of trumpets and horns.[28] There are clear parallels here with the events of 1607: the size of the crowds in the individual incidents, their deliberate bodily (and noisy) occupation of disputed space, the presence of ringleaders or captains, and the refusal to disperse when commanded by a JP all prefigure events during the Midlands Rising. To put it another way, the events of the Midlands Rising were preceded by more than a century of small-scale, local unrest over enclosure, engrossing and associated agricultural change, which on occasion erupted into significant episodes of popular opposition to the activities of enclosing landlords like Valentine Knightley. Knightley, it is worth observing, would be on the list of those prosecuted for enclosure in aftermath of the Midlands Rising, though it is clear from the newly discovered Badby evidence that he was also the focus of highly organised anti-enclosure protest more two decades earlier.[29] Crucially, there is little here to bear out Martin's assertion that there was an upsurge in enclosure in the decade before 1607: instead we see an extended history of anti-enclosure rioting and other forms of direct action in Northamptonshire, with evidence of widespread tensions over enclosure which stretched back decades before 1607.

It was, moreover, a history of protest of which the common people were well aware, at least as far as it affected them and their customary rights. As was also typical in other early modern courts, litigants and deponents attempting to claim or defend common rights almost always asserted that they had exercised those rights 'time out of mind' or in the other recurrent formulation used in the records, 'time out of memory of man'.[30] In early modern England, claims to common rights were almost always based on the twin claims of antiquity and continued use.[31] More specifically, many litigants and deponents also narrated long histories of what they saw as ongoing threats to communal agricultural systems: that is, they (re)mobilised earlier disputes over common rights, enclosure and agrarian practice in order to frame their experiences in the present and add context and weight to their legal arguments. At Finedon in the 1530s, both parties articulated a long history of tension over enclosure between the lord and his tenants which stretched back to at least the 1490s.

At Papley (Fig. 1) in the first half of the sixteenth century, several deponents provided careful evidence about the enclosure and depopulation of the hamlet: there had previously been 14 houses and 10 or 12 ploughs working the fields, but there were now only three or four ploughs and two tenements, plus two abandoned houses which 'stand dyssolate [desolate] and no tenantes dwelling in them'. Other deponents in the case described the depopulation of nearby Lilford by the same landowner some years earlier and in doing so, mobilised both geographical parallels and historical warnings in an effort to protect common rights at Papley.[32] More generally, warnings of depopulation linked present threats with future consequences. Plaintiffs complaining that neighbouring landowners had stopped rights of way, enclosed land or extinguished common rights not infrequently floated the spectre of depopulation, as Francis Harby was to do at Adstone in 1599.[33] The forcible depopulation of settlements was illegal, if by no means unknown, in sixteenth-century England.[34] The residents of Northamptonshire villages were clearly alert to the possibility that depopulating enclosure might affect them and their livelihoods: as Martin points out, by the late sixteenth century large sheep flocks were increasingly being put to pasture on the sites of deserted settlements, both in the west of the county and also in rising numbers in the east.[35]

Fig. 1 1632 map of Papley (Northamptonshire) showing the enclosed and depopulated township. NRO, Map 2221. (Reproduced with permission)

The Year of the Rising

The small-scale anti-enclosure riots which characterised much of the sixteenth century continued into the first decade of the seventeenth century, with unrest over common rights and enclosures at Foscote and Abthorpe in 1603, hedge-breaking at Raunds in the same year and two hedge-breaking riots at Daventry in 1604.[36] In February 1607, a cottage on the common at Eye near Peterborough was pulled down in protest at recent assarting on the fen and in the same month a group of 21 husbandmen, labourers and weavers from Clopton – some twenty miles to the south-west – pulled down fences and filled in ditches around two parcels of land in neighbouring Titchmarsh.[37] Yet if these incidents directly echoed earlier outbreaks of anti-enclosure rioting, there was also a feeling that the scale of enclosure and associated conversion to pasture in the county was such that it was endangering the livelihoods of some. As John Martin demonstrated some years ago, sheep numbers grew considerably in the county across the second half of the sixteenth century and by 1600, half the parishes in the county had large sheep flocks grazing on enclosed pastures.[38] When James I visited the county in 1603, crowds met him to demand that recently enclosed commons should be laid open, the enclosures having been committed – according to one source – by 'wolfish Lords, that have eaten up poor husbandmen like sheep'.[39] A year later, Sir Edward Montagu reported further disquiet about enclosure in the county.[40]

More sustained anti-enclosure rioting was said to have started in Northamptonshire on the last day of April 1607, according to a letter written by Gilbert Talbot, Earl of Shrewsbury in early June that year, though he did not specify the towns and villages affected.[41] There were certainly enclosure riots at Northampton early in May and at Shutlanger and Stoke Bruerne in the middle of the month, when 200 inhabitants destroyed hedges, ditches and fences surrounding three pasture closes belonging to the local parson Richard Lightfoot and pulled down a house that he had built on the land, casting portions of it into a nearby river.[42] In his bill to the Star Chamber, Lightfoot claimed that the inhabitants had recently enclosed 'a great part' of the common fields with little in the way of recompense to him, though the inhabitants denied this and argued that it was Lightfoot who had wrongfully enclosed land. The Shutlanger hedge-breaking incidents are amongst the few from Northamptonshire in 1607 for which detailed court papers survive – because a case was quickly pursued in Star Chamber – and there is good evidence here both of the scale of crowds that might assemble to oppose enclosure and of the large sheep flocks enclosers might stock the fields and commons with: Lightfoot was said to have turned 200 sheep into the fields of Shutlanger, where he had right for only 40. Events at Shutlanger thus connected into both a local and national politics of land and resources: this was about Lightfoot overstocking the common and enclosing where he had no right, but also popular opposition to the growth of large sheep flocks in the county.

Ten days later, on Trinity Sunday (31 May), there were documented riots at Haselbech, Rushton, Newton and Pytchley as well as at least seven further sites in Warwickshire and Leicestershire, several of them very close to the Northamptonshire border.[43] There also seems to have been some disorder at Rothwell Fair on Trinity Monday, where the widow of Sir Thomas Tresham of Rushton later accused John Lambe of upsetting the stalls and general 'disorderlie behaviour'.[44] Sir Thomas had built the unfinished market house in the square in 1578, so Rothwell was key Tresham 'territory' and a very public site to articulate discontent with the Tresham family and their estate policy.[45] That so many riots took place within a few days of each other implies communication and coordination between different communities, as does the distance rioters were said to have travelled to take part in disturbances.[46] Little is known about how communities coordinated this weekend of action, but the diggers broadside penned by the 'poor delvers and day labourers' of Warwickshire and circulated early in the summer of 1607 was no doubt important in helping forge connections between communities.[47] As Hindle notes, it was probably sold in alehouses in the region and James I later referred to it as one of the 'wicked instruments' by which the Rising was organised.[48] The authorship of the broadside is unclear, but the supposed leader of the Rising – a tinker by the name of John Reynolds who came to be known as Captain Pouch because of the satchel he carried – may have contributed to it. Reynolds certainly played a role in coordinating the anti-enclosure protests in Northamptonshire and the nearby counties, and was said by followers to have claimed the authority to 'cut downe all enclosures betweene… Northampton and the cytie of Yorke'.[49]

The first riots were dealt with via the civil authorities, but by late May the government had recognised the scale of the problem and the king issued a proclamation to put down enclosure riots and other unlawful assemblies in the Midland counties.[50] By early June, the authorities were no longer prepared to tolerate the unrest.[51] Even taking into account that the size of the crowd at Newton was probably exaggerated by Shrewsbury and by later chroniclers, this was a much larger assembly than any of the earlier riots documented here and presumably represented the coming together of the individual companies involved in the past few weeks' rioting as well as the involvement of a significant number of townspeople from nearby Kettering.[52] The crowd at Newton had apparently been there several days by the time that the gentry forces led by Sir Edward Montagu and Sir Anthony Mildmay arrived at the site on the 8 June. Cutting down hedges, digging up their roots and filling in ditches was a time-consuming process: considerable time and concentrated labour was needed to cause lasting disruption and prevent a landowner swiftly stopping up gaps in a hedge and re-enclosing the land.[53] It seems probable that at least some rioters camped at the site, while others presumably made the three-mile trip back to Kettering at night. The size of the assembly – reminiscent as it was of the events of autumn 1536 and specifically 1549 – as well as the fact that it seems to have involved individuals from a number of surrounding villages and increasing urban participation helps to explain the reaction of the authorities and the significant violence and bloodshed which resulted.[54] The disorder was put down brutally in June.[55] John Reynolds was arrested at Withybrook in Warwickshire in early June and probably executed at Northampton, assemblies at Welham and Cotesbach (Leicestershire) were dispersed and arrests made, and news of the bloody end to events at Newton was probably enough to persuade other assemblies to disperse and head home.[56] By mid-July, the government had decided to commission inquisitions into 'unlawful enclosures' which were conducted in August and September.[57] A great deal of useful information was collected in this process even whilst the inquisitions actually did little to curb enclosure in the Midlands, it having been later ruled that the commission was not valid and the returns were therefore 'against law'.[58]

Yet while the scale of the unrest and the geographical mobility of the rioters distinguished events of 1607 from the earlier riots documented in the Star Chamber and elsewhere, the methods of protest adopted by the rioters and the grievances articulated by them were much the same, echoing concerns which had pushed communities across the region into action throughout the past century. Martin argues that the importance of Haselbech, Rushton and Newton stemmed from the Tresham family's recent and 'brutal' improvement activity in the area and their considerable unpopularity as a result.[59] Haselbech had been enclosed and the community evicted in the mid-1590s and both Sir Thomas and the only other major landowner in the parish, John Read of Cottesbrooke, were prosecuted in 1607. Both were dead by the time inquisitions were conducted, but it was said they had enclosed and converted 1600 acres, demolished 14 houses and evicted more than 70 people.[60] Enclosure was underway at Rushton by the 1540s if not earlier, and by the turn of the seventeenth century the whole parish was enclosed.[61] Sir Thomas also raised entry fines in both Orton-in-Rowell and Great Houghton, presumably with enclosure in mind. He sold Great Houghton to Ferdinando Baude in 1601 and 1604, and Baude had enclosed the parish by 1606, decaying 31 houses and evicted 240 people in the process.[62] It may have been here that the Northampton riots of early May were focused and there was certainly significant unrest here and in neighbouring Little Houghton in 1608.[63] Sir Thomas's cousin, Thomas Tresham, was responsible for the enclosure of Newton – where there were at least 650 sheep as early as 1564 and which seems to have been wholly down to grass by 1607 – and Pilton, ten miles to the east.[64] The Tresham properties known as Lyveden Old Bield and New Bield both lay within Pilton parish, the latter laid out on land probably enclosed under a 1540 licence to empark. Work started on the New Bield in the mid-1590s and it may be that the construction of this elaborate and expensive building provoked particular ire amongst local inhabitants.[65]

Thus, while the Tresham family were involved in a number of recent enclosures, it was not as if they and the other enclosing landlords had been previously unknown to the local authorities. Instead the Tresham family were involved in enclosure disputes for several decades before the events of 1607. Thomas Tresham of Newton – whose hedges the thousand people at Newton were breaking and who was prosecuted for enclosure in 1608 in the wake of the Rising – had previously been prosecuted for enclosures at Bletchingdon (Oxfordshire) undertaken before December 1592.[66] Sir Thomas Tresham of Rushton had also built a reputation for enclosing and engrossing. In the midst of a dispute over title of 1575 with one George Robins, Sir Thomas complained that the jury had been turned against him by use of a dire warning from Robins's coroner, who was said to have told the jurors:

> to loke unto yt lest the getting of the lande so should be a [pre]sident agaynst them and such as they and hym selfe were, saying further that yf the land should be so caried awaye then lett hym & them and such as they ar loke not to enioye that w[ch] their forfathers had left them, for yf (saith he) such as [Tresham] ys, that ys of power and welth, should take displeasure wth us or any such as we be… then some quarrell should be made to the tytle of

o[r] land & so to gett yt from us therefore... masters nowe yt standeth you upon to loke unto this, as you tender your owne estates, and your posteritie.[67]

The other landowner at Haselbech, John Read, was also a known encloser. He had been prosecuted in 1597 for enclosures in neighbouring Cottesbrooke as well as being implicated in the violent eviction of cattle from the common fields of Naseby almost three decades earlier in 1571.[68] Elsewhere in the vicinity of Haselbech, Robert Osborne of neighbouring Kelmarsh was named in the Inquisitions of Depopulation of 1608 as having enclosed several hundred acres in the parish. He had also been one of the defendants in a bill brought by the Attorney General in 1597.[69] When examined, Osborne essentially admitted that he had undertaken depopulating enclosures at Kelmarsh in the 1580s. He said that he had enclosed 800 acres in the parish and increased his sheep flock from 1400 to 2000 animals, and that the number of ploughs in the village had fallen from 25 to 15.[70] However you try to spin it – and he did try – this must have sounded to both the court and the local population like depopulating enclosure.

By contrast, William Belcher of nearby Guilsborough flatly denied having enclosed any land or in any way contributed to the depopulation of the village when he was examined in 1597 and 1608. As he stated in his answer in 1597,

> as to any inclosure made or houses decayed town depeopled or anie other matter whatsoever in the Information layed to be donne maytayned or committed by this defendant in the Towne of Gisborough in the county of Northampton... for full answer hereunto the defendant pledeth not guilty in such manner and forme as in the said Bill is alleged and prayeth thereof to be dismissed.[71]

Yet there were at least two hedge-breaking incidents in Guilsborough in the early 1580s, in the legal aftermath of which Belcher himself admitted that he had ditched a pasture and enclosed both a highway and an area of common land. He had provided another parcel of ground as an alternative, in part because the first was already so surrounded by enclosed land that the inhabitants could not get their cattle to common there.[72] Thus, the denials of 1597 and 1608 simply don't ring true: Belcher had been enclosing at Guilsborough since at least the 1580s, much to the annoyance of the inhabitants.

Elsewhere in the county, too, the enclosers of 1607 had long been at their game. The Humphrey family of Barton Seagrave are another example of repeat offenders. William Humphrey was prosecuted in 1608 when he was accused of wasting eight houses of husbandry in Barton Seagrave, each with near 100 acres, within the last twenty years.[73] The family held land at Barton since the mid-fifteenth century, but seem to have expanded their territorial ambitions a century later, rebuilding the manor house at Barton and acquiring manors in the neighbouring parishes of Isham in 1546, Burton Latimer in 1555 and Orlingbury at around the same time.[74] All four parishes bordered Pytchley, one of the known centres of anti-enclosure rioting in 1607. William was involved in an enclosure dispute in c.1574 concerning land at Orlingbury. The plaintiff William Tafte of Orlingbury complained that Humphrey had enclosed grounds called Battsaddle, previously subject to common rights, and employed men to keep Tafte's cattle out. There had been cases at the Assizes and in Chancery, but Tafte claimed that Humphrey had procured false testimony so that Tafte lost his cases.[75] Nor was William the only member of the family to come to the authorities' attention as a result of extinguishing common rights: one son, Richard, was named as an encloser in 1597 when he denied having enclosed land at Swepstone in Leicestershire and another son, Thomas, was prosecuted in 1608.[76] Barton Seagrave not only bordered Pytchley, but lay less than five miles south of Newton: it seems likely, therefore, that at least some of the men and women who assembled at Pytchley and Newton were drawn from the Humphrey family's lands at Barton and Orlingbury.

Thus, the connections between the events of 1607 and the earlier disputes go far beyond method and grievance. There is good evidence to show that those whose properties were the focus of the rioters' actions in May and June 1607 were serial offenders, men who had long been enclosing land to the great disapproval and disadvantage of local communities, and who were well known to the local and national authorities for doing so. Moreover, several of the sites at which protest was focused in 1607 were also places where the local communities had long histories of resisting enclosure and agricultural change. Rather than primarily being a response to events of the late 1590s as Martin argues, the new evidence from STAC 5 suggests that the Rising might be best seen as the outcome of several decades of enclosure activity in the vicinity, of long-running grievances and simmering resentment about the loss of common rights and family homes. Memories of these earlier enclosures, evictions and related legal proceedings were variously articulated in the later cases concerned with the Rising. Perceived injustices – both recent and decades-old – and popular memories of that which had been lost (or more precisely taken) clearly did much to mobilise those attending assemblies and breaking hedges in May and June. Here we can read the Midlands Rising not simply as a response to an unprecedented upsurge in the scale and frequency of enclosure in the English Midlands in the decade prior to 1607, but rather the most striking moment in an ongoing surge of discontent with enclosure which had been building at least through much of the previous reign.

That things came to such a dramatic head in the early summer of 1607 was probably the result of a combination of factors, not least the rising grain prices of the early years of the seventeenth century and fears about a poor harvest that summer.[77] Such grain shortages were, of course, in part precipitated by the conversion of arable land to enclosed pasture, as the Warwickshire diggers recognised.[78] One wonders too about the particular family circumstances of some of the big Northamptonshire landowners, especially the Treshams. Sir Thomas died in September 1605 and his son and heir, Francis Tresham died in the Tower of London just before Christmas that year after being implicated in the Gunpowder Plot. He was later attainted and his severed head displayed at Northampton.[79] The hugely indebted estate was inherited by Sir Thomas's son, Lewis Tresham, (1578–1639) who seems to have managed the estate with the help of his mother, Muriel.[80] After years of difficulties with the Crown, well-known indebtedness, the death of two heads of the family in three months and the public exhibition of (parts of) Francis's dead body, the Tresham family arguably looked weaker in 1606 and 1607 than they had for many decades.[81] It is tempting to think that this may have contributed to willingness of local communities – long disadvantaged as they were by the activities of the Treshams and their landowning peers – to rise up in resistance. That Sir Thomas was later posthumously convicted of the enclosure of 670 acres at Rushton was probably considered slim recompense by the communities and individuals most impoverished by his actions.[82]

Remembering the Rising

Just as the Rising grew from a long history of anti-enclosure rioting, it equally did not serve as an absolute end point to such protest. While the Inquisitions of Depopulation ultimately did little to rein in the actions of enclosing landlords, cases concerned with common rights and enclosure continued to reach the equity courts throughout the first few decades of the seventeenth century. But what about the events of the Midlands Rising was remembered and remobilised, and what forgotten or deliberately neglected? Hindle's excellent article covers some of this ground, though he primarily focuses on what we might identify as national narratives of the Rising. We may note too – as others also have – that the term 'diggers' was first coined in reference to the rioters of 1607 only to appear again in the late 1640s to describe Gerrard Winstanley's experiment on St George's Hill.[83] What we might think of as the enduring afterlives of rebellion are assuredly worthy of further research, but we focus here on the immediate aftermath of the Rising, and particularly on how the events of 1607 were used as an ongoing strategy to negotiate property and common rights in the law courts.

It is clear that in the decade following 1607, the events of the Midlands Rising continued to loom large in litigation from the county both as a warning of similar to come and, very occasionally, as an example to be followed. Litigants made frequent reference to the Rising in bills of complaint brought to the Star Chamber. For instance, in late 1608 and early 1609 anti-enclosure riots twice broke out at Little Houghton, just to the east of Northampton. The rioters in this case turned 200 cattle into an area of pasture, before later pulling up the hedges and turning ploughs onto the ground, presumably with the intention of converting it back into open-field arable. They claimed that these pastures had previously been common land, and that they had been wrongfully enclosed by the landowner, Daniel Ward. There were said to have been radical speeches: by Ward's report, the rioters said that they 'would have so done w[th] all inclosures & turne their plowes into pastures, & make all comon for corne, as though they had been owners or com[m]aunders'. Ward drew a clear line of connection between events in his own parish and those of 1607 which had, of course, involved rioting in the close vicinity: the Little Houghton rioters acted 'w[th]out any regard had of the late rebellion in thes[par]tes & of the punishment of the offenders in that kinde'.[84] Ward was seeking to underline the illegality of the crowd's actions but while he framed the incident as a riot, the constable and inhabitants claimed in their answers that the land had been wrongfully enclosed by Ward and that the boundaries and hedges had been removed in a peaceable manner. Ward had been subject to a prosecution for enclosure in 1608 as was his neighbour

Ferdinando Baude of Great Houghton – and the defendants carefully detailed the legal efforts they had made to preserve their common rights.[85]

In the summer of 1609 a dispute erupted over common pasture rights in Heath Hill Close in Moreton Pinckney, in the west of the county. The plaintiff in the ensuing Star Chamber case, Thomas Fusson, complained that rioters twice cut down the hedges and filled in the ditches of the close, driving their cattle into the land and assaulting one of Fusson's servants. In this, they 'did raise and sire a new rebellion in the said county of Northampton not much unlike the last rebellious tumult for inclosure'.[86] Other plaintiffs similarly frame their actions in terms of the dangers posed by open revolt. Daniel Deeve of Oundle complained that the occupation of his wheat field by rioters in October 1611 was intended to draw the whole population of Northamptonshire 'into a mutinye and rebellion'. According to Deeve, the defendants had occupied the field for 12 days, building 'cabbens and fortes' and using large dogs to keep the plaintiffs out. This was in part a family dispute about the ownership of the land, but events had many of the formal trappings of a larger anti-enclosure protest. On the twelfth day of their occupation, the defendants cut and carried away Deeve's corn:

> with bagg pipes playeing ringing of Belles by the space of one whole daye and a nighte wth holloweinge and throwing upp of hattes from the top of the Steeple and in other places and with outcryes and clamors to th greate terror and feare of the inhabitantes thereaboutes and the disturbance of yo[r] ma[tes] peace.

Deeve enlisted the help of JP and fellow encloser Gilbert Pickering to deal with the occupation of his land, but the incompetence (or deliberate foot-dragging) of the constable meant that warrants were not served against the rioters.[87] In the counter-suit, Deeve was in turn accused of leading a riotous occupation of the land: he and his men continued 'theire said riott & outrage wth shoutes & cryes by the space of twoe dayes at the least… to the great… terror of yo[r] highnes peaceable Subjectes'. The plaintiffs in this case did not make specific reference to the events of 1607, but they argued that in occupying the land and evicting the plaintiff's tenant, Deeve was 'making a scorne of Justice or of any Justice of the peace' and 'great uprore in the said Towne of Owndell to the greate disquiet of the said Towne and Inhabitantes thereof'.[88] The mutilated bodies of those executed for their involvement at Newton were displayed at Oundle in 1607, so the events of that summer were no doubt still written into everyone's consciousness in the town half a decade later.

In the aftermath of the Rising, warnings that an agricultural riot might set a dangerous example or precedent had clearly taken on greater weight. Even relatively straightforward property disputes might be framed in similar terms and direct reference to the Rising included to underline the supposed seriousness of what were, in reality, fairly trivial cases. At Middleton in 1613, a forcible dispossession was said in the bill of complaint to 'tend to the breach of yo[r] Ma[ties] peace', but also 'give occasions of insurrec[tion]s and the like incon[v]eniences'.[89] In much the same way, an assault and forcible dispossession at Grafton Underwood reported as part of a dispute between a widow and her stepson was framed with reference to the Rising. William Bate stated that his stepmother and more than twenty others had assembled at Grafton – which he described as lying within 'one myle of the place of rebellions and late insurrections… about the throwing down of hedges and ditches in the said county' – armed with weapons including bows and pike staves. There, they assaulted him, forced his cattle off the land and broke down the hedges, in part by driving the cattle over them.[90] At its heart this was a dispute about the inheritance of the estate, but Bate referenced those 'late insurrections' in a deliberate attempt to up the ante. In doing so, he demonstrated a fairly elastic concept of geography: Grafton Underwood was in fact more than four miles from Newton and five from Pytchley, rather than one!

Conclusions

In this short essay, we have employed a little-used set of records to throw fresh light on the Midlands Rising and its prehistory, as well as to reflect on the uses of the past – and specifically, past protest – in the (historical) present. The new evidence from the Elizabethan Star Chamber records provides little support for the argument that there was a dramatic upsurge in enclosure activity in the late decade of the sixteenth century and first few years of the seventeenth century which precipitated the Rising. Enclosure, engrossing and the loss of common rights were significant causes of complaint to the court from the early sixteenth century onwards and opposition to the extension of private property rights – articulated via litigation, hedge-breaking and animal trespasses amongst other methods – continued throughout the second half of the century. The events of the

Rising were preceded by more than a century of small-scale, local unrest over enclosure and agricultural change which at times erupted into significant episodes of popular opposition to the activities of enclosing landlords, as, for example, at Badby and Newnham in the 1580s. The inhabitants of Northamptonshire parishes were very well aware of these histories: litigants and deponents in the Star Chamber offered detailed narrations of what they saw as ongoing threats to communal agriculture, mobilising earlier disputes over common rights, enclosure and depopulation as a way to add context and weight to their legal arguments. In other words, they repeatedly put the memory of the people to use in defending common rights and resisting change that they saw as detrimental to their livelihoods, using earlier histories of litigation and protest to give meaning and legitimacy to their actions.

Here we situate the Midlands Rising as an episode in the local as well as the national politics of land, arguing that understanding the Rising requires us to ground the events of 1607 in both their wider landscape and their longer-term historical context. There were clear continuities between the Rising and the earlier riots, mostly notable in the grievances aired, the methods used and the individuals whose estates were targeted. Many of the enclosing landlords whose properties were targeted in 1607 – and who were named subsequently in the Inquisitions of Depopulation – had also been the subject of the earlier enquiries. Several were named in the inquisitions of the early 1590s and some had been brought before the Star Chamber and other central equity courts as long ago as the early 1570s when they were accused of enclosing land and engrossing farms. In other words, they were serial offenders well known to the local and national authorities and deeply unpopular amongst their tenants. The complex enmeshing of landscape and memory was central here, so that perceived injustices over the loss of land and rights within local communities eventually provided the touchpaper which ignited wider regional unrest. Crucially, while the events of 1607 undoubtedly carried echoes of the Commotion Time of 1549, each of the individual episodes of unrest which made up the Rising were nevertheless rooted in their community and landscape.

At the same time, the Rising also had a complex afterlife – or, more properly, afterlives – at the local level. Northamptonshire communities continued to mobilise accounts of injustice and the loss of common rights in resisting further agrarian change – as for example, at Little Houghton – while plaintiffs complaining to the court about crowd action which threatened enclosures often framed their arguments in terms of the dangers of open revolt. This approach is evident too in the bills of those plaintiffs like William Bate who referenced the 'late insurrections' as a means of underlining the riotous example set by his opponents and, he hoped, winning his rather more straightforward property dispute. In doing so, Bate and others mobilised the Rising as a means of stifling dissent and shutting down opposition to enclosures and the extension of private property rights. Here we see memories of protest utilised in multiple ways: as an important moment in the development of local landscapes and a hook on which popular memory could be hung; as a reminder of common rights extinguished and livelihoods lost, which might on occasion be used to reanimate resistance; and conversely, as an example of the dangers posed by popular disorder, a spectral presence which could be mobilised in heading off future unrest. In remembering rather than forgetting the Rising, landowners and enclosers thereby pushed forward the emerging logic of private property, even whilst they also left open the possibility of alternative, altogether more disruptive ways of remembering and remobilising the events of 1607.

Acknowledgements Research for the chapter was undertaken as part of a project entitled 'Experiencing the landscape: Popular geographical imaginations in the English Midlands, 1450–1650' and funded by the British Academy (Small Grant no. SG140176). We are especially grateful to Amanda Bevan and staff at The National Archives who were kind enough to make a working database of parts of STAC 5 available. We are also grateful to all those who offered comments on earlier versions of the paper including the audience and speakers at the International Conference of Historical Geographers held in London in July 2015.

Notes

1. For a summary of the events at Newton, see Steve Hindle, 'Imagining insurrection in seventeenth-century England: Representations of the Midlands Rising of 1607', *History Workshop Journal* 66 (2008), 21–61, especially 21–3. For events at Newton, John Nichols, *The History and Antiquities of Leicestershire* (London: 1795–1815), Vol. VI, part I, 83. For the places of execution, see *The History and Antiquities of Northamptonshire. Compiled from the manuscript collections of the late learned antiquary, John Bridges, Esq. By the Rev. Peter Whalley* (Oxford: 1791), Vol. II [not I as given in Martin], 206.

2. John Martin, *Feudalism to Capitalism: Peasant and Landlord in Agrarian Development* (Palgrave Macmillan: 1983), 161–215; Roger B. Manning, *Village Revolts: Social Protest and Popular Disturbances in England, 1509–1640* (Clarendon Press: 1988), 229–46; Steve Hindle, 'Imagining insurrection'. See also John Walter, '"The pooremans joy and the gentlemans plague": a Lincolnshire libel and the politics of sedition in early modern England', *Past and Present* 203 (2009), 29–67 on a libel sent in the aftermath of the Rising.
3. Hindle, 'Imagining insurrection', 23.
4. Readers interested in this work might start with Andy Wood, *Riot, Rebellion and Popular Politics in Early Modern England* (Palgrave Macmillan: 2001); idem, *The Memory of the People: Custom and Popular Senses of the Past in Early Modern England* (Cambridge University Press: 2013); Nicola Whyte, *Inhabiting the Landscape: Place, Custom and Memory, 1500–1800* (Oxford: 2009); Carl J. Griffin, *Protest, Politics and Work in Rural England, 1700–1850* (Palgrave Macmillan: 2014); Katrina Navickas, *Protest and the Politics of Space and Place, 1789–1848* (Manchester University Press: 2015).
5. Here the work of cultural geographers and anthropologists has been influential in our thinking: see, for example, Tim Ingold, 'The temporality of the landscape', *World Archaeology* 25.2 (1993) and *The Perception of the Environment: Essays on Livelihood, Dwelling and Skill* (Routledge: 2000); Barbara Bender, *Landscape: Politics and Perspectives* (Berg: 1993), and with Margot Winer (eds) *Contested Landscapes: Movement, Exile and Place* (Oxford: 2001); Don Mitchell, *The Lie of the Land: Migrant Workers of the California Landscape* (Bloomsbury: 1996); Doreen Massey, *For Space* (Sage: 2005); Mitch Rose, 'The Seductions of Resistance: power, politics, and a performative style of systems', *Environment and Planning D: Society and Space* 20.4 (2002), 383–400 and 'Dwelling as marking and claiming', *Environment and Planning D: Society and Space* 30 (2012), 757–71.
6. Andy Wood, *The Memory of the People*, 15.
7. On our reading of landscape, see Briony McDonagh and Stephen Daniels, 'Enclosure stories: narratives from Northamptonshire', *Cultural Geographies* 19.1 (2012), 107–21.
8. For discussions of the Midlands Rising and the commotion time of 1549, see Hindle 'Imagining insurrection', 23 and 26; Martin, *Feudalism to Capitalism*, 161; Andy Wood, *The 1549 Rebellions and the Making of Early Modern England* (Cambridge University Press: 2007), 239. See also L. A. Parker, 'The agrarian revolution at Cotesbach', *Leicestershire Archaeological Society* XXIV (1949), 41–75 on the sixteenth- and early seventeenth-century enclosures there which precipitated the Rising, though he says little about events of 1607 themselves; and Steve Hindle, 'Self-image and public

image in the career of a Jacobean magistrate: Sir John Newdigate in the Court of Star Chamber', in Michael J. Braddick and Phil Withington (eds), *Popular Culture and Political Agency in Early Modern England and Ireland: Essays in Honour of John Walter* (Boydell and Brewer: 2017), 123–44, 128 on 'simmering tension over common rights' which existed at Chilvers Coton from the early 1590s.
9. While the sizeable collections of Henrician and Stuart records are well catalogued, the Elizabethan records are not: there is no effective place, county or subject index for the estimated 38,000 documents in STAC 5 and the main catalogue and finding aids list cases by the surnames of the first plaintiff and defendant only.
10. Eric Kerridge, 'The Returns of the Inquisitions of Depopulation', *English Historical Review* 70.125 (1955), 212–228; John Martin, 'Enclosure and the Inquisitions of 1607: An examination of Dr. Kerridge's article 'The Returns of the Inquisitions of Depopulation'', *Agricultural History Review* 30.1 (1982), 41–8.
11. Martin, *Feudalism to Capitalism*, 164. See too Manning, *Village Revolts*, 82 who argues that the incidence of enclosure riots almost doubled in the 1590s compared to the 1570s and 1580s. Note, however, that only three of his Elizabethan cases came from Northamptonshire, Leicestershire and the other East Midlands counties, once again underlining the need for more research on the Star Chamber records for those counties most affected in 1607.
12. Briony McDonagh, 'Making and breaking property: negotiating enclosure and common rights in sixteenth-century England', *History Workshop Journal* 76.1 (2013), 32–56.
13. The National Archives [hereafter TNA], STAC 2/27/111 (Barnack); 2/23/34, 2/23/39, 2/28/111, 2/28/119 and 2/28/126 (Rushton); 2/17/396, 2/26/250, 2/26/359, 2/30/138 and 2/32/70 (Finedon); 2/19/160, 2/17/221 and 2/24/362 (Whitfield); 2/20/364, 2/20/357 (Cold Ashby); 2/23/29, 2/33/66 and 2/19/28 (Papley and Warmington).
14. See, for example, TNA, STAC 2/7/4-14, 2/30/80 and 2/25/299 (Kingsthorpe and Moulton); McDonagh, 'Making and breaking', 16–19.
15. TNA, STAC 5/K6/21, 5/K3/16, 5/C51/7, 5/B83/31 and 5/B70/40.
16. TNA, STAC 5/B88/25.
17. TNA, STAC 5/D23/23.
18. TNA, STAC 5/J10/37. This is wrongly catalogued on Discovery as Jenkyns v. Brewer, 28 Eliz.
19. TNA, STAC 5/H6/36, 5/H81/36, 5/H20/12 and 7/23/40 and 41; *An Inventory of the Historical Monuments in the County of Northamptonshire, Volume 6, Architectural Monuments in North Northamptonshire* (Her

Majesty's Stationery Office, London, 1984), 61–3. On the importance of boundary stones in disputes over custom and common rights, see Nicola Whyte, 'Landscape, memory and custom: parish identities c. 1550–1700', *Social History* 32.2 (2007), 166–86; William D Shannon, 'Adversarial map-making in pre-Reformation Lancashire', *Northern History* 47 (2010), 329–42.
20. TNA, STAC 5/H6/36 and 7/23/40.
21. TNA, STAC 5/H13/31.
22. TNA, STAC 5/H48/4; 5/H17/13; 5/D19/13.
23. TNA, STAC 5/K6/19. To 'leese' here means to deliver or release (OED. com).
24. TNA, STAC 5/K13/10; Wood, *The Memory of the People*, 2 and 14.
25. TNA, STAC 5/K1/16 and K13/10.
26. Crowds involving large numbers of women were also noted at Finedon in 1576 (TNA, STAC 5/C51/7) and Braunston in 1571 (STAC 5/J10/37). See too STAC 8/147/19 in which women (and men dressed as women) gathered to block and dig up transport routes at Milton and Cherry Orton in 1614.
27. TNA, STAC 8/94/4 and 8/121/20. See the note above on Finedon.
28. TNA, STAC 5/G38/19. See too STAC 5/F16/2 for riotous entry into a wood in Furtho accompanied by a drummer.
29. TNA, STAC 8/15/21.
30. On women as deponents in the central equity courts, see Nicola Whyte, 'Custodians of memory: women and custom in rural England c.1550–1700', *Cultural and Social History* 2.8 (2011), 153–173. On the 'male erasure of the memory of women's words and deeds', see Wood, *The Memory of the People*, 305–7.
31. McDonagh, 'Making and breaking', 8; Edward P. Thompson, *Customs in Common* (London: 1991), 97; Wood, *The Memory of the People*, passim.
32. TNA, STAC 2/23/29.
33. TNA, STAC 5/H48/4.
34. Joan Thirsk, 'Enclosing and Engrossing', in Joan Thirsk (ed.) *The Agrarian History of England and Wales IV 1500–1640* (Cambridge University Press: 1967), 200–55, especially 213–35.
35. John Martin, 'Sheep and enclosure in sixteenth-century Northamptonshire', *Agricultural History Review* 36.1 (1988), 39–54, especially 53.
36. TNA, E 134/1Jas1/Hill; STAC 8/159/16; STAC 8/145/7.
37. TNA, STAC 8/170/16; 8/231/25; 8/244/14.
38. Martin, 'Sheep and enclosure', 53–54.
39. Charles Harding Firth, *Stuart Tracts, 1603–1693* (E. P. Dutton: 1903), 40 and 42.

40. Historic Manuscripts Commission, *Report on the Manuscripts of Lord Montagu of Beaulieu* (London: 1900), 42 [available online https://archive.org/stream/cu31924028044992/cu31924028044992_djvu.txt]; cited in Hindle, 'Imagining insurrection', fn. 27.
41. British Library [hereafter BL], Lansdowne MSS 90/23.
42. BL, Add MSS 11,402, folio 127 (for Northampton); TNA, STAC 8/198/21 (for Stoke Bruerne and Shutlanger). There was a second hedge-breaking incident at Stoke Bruerne on 9 June (ibid.).
43. TNA, C 205/5/5 (Haselbech, which details the almost total enclosure of the parish and refers to a highway stopped 'until of late it was throwne down by those that made the late insurrection'); Bridges and Whalley, *Northamptonshire*, II, 206 (Pytchley, Rushton and Newton); Nichols, *Leicestershire*, VI.I, 83 (Newton); see Martin, *Feudalism to Capitalism*, 164–7 on Warwickshire and Leicestershire. The Earl of Shrewsbury was clear that he considered the disorder to have started in Northamptonshire and later spread to the other counties (BL, Lansdowne MSS, 90/23).
44. TNA, E 134/7JasI/19.
45. List of Buildings of Special Architectural and Historic Interest.
46. See Martin, *Feudalism to Capitalism*, 165 for a map showing where the rioters were recruited from. Note too that the rioters in the Shutlanger hedge-breaking riot in mid-May were said to have travelled to Towcester to 'procure assistance' (TNA, STAC 8/198/21 esp. the interrogatories).
47. BL, MS Harley 787/11. Note a similar sentiment here to that Knightley attributed to the rioters at Badby: the Warwickshire diggers professed, 'wee for our partes neither respect life nor lyvinges; for better it were in such case we manfully dye, then hereafter to be pined to death for wante of that which these devouring encroachers doe serve theyr fatt Hogges and Sheep with all'.
48. Hindle, 'Imagining insurrection', 26.
49. TNA, STAC 8/221/1. Cf. TNA, STAC 8/295/22 where the landowner and plaintiff Daniel Ward claimed that the defendants had broken hedges and ploughed up land 'saying that they would have soe done w[th] all inclosures & turne their plowes into pastures, & make all comon for corne, as though they had beene owners or com[m]aunders'.
50. Martin, *Feudalism to Capitalism*, 166; BL, Add MS 11,402, folio 127 (29 May 1607) for the general proclamation covering Leicestershire, Warwickshire, Worcestershire and Gloucestershire.
51. Compare the attitudes to the rioters in BL, Add MS 11,402, folio 127 of 11th May and BL, Lansdowne MSS 90/23 of 2nd June, where the Earl of Shrewsbury commented that 'his Majestie is nothyinge well pleased with the remiss course that both the sheriff and Justices of peace have taken in that matter, and also the deputy lieutenant… for his Majestie expected,

that so soone as suche insolent numbers hadd been gathered together, the sheriff & justoces sholde have prepared them selves with posse comitas to have gon against them, and to have apprehended some of the chefest of them, to have sent some of thos up hither, and to have committed others (in good numbers) to the Gaioles'. Shrewsbury laid out the course of action for dealing with any further unrest: if persuasion failed, they were to assembled 40 or 50 horse to 'run over, and cutt into peeces a thousand of suche naked roges as thos' are'.

52. On this, see Martin, *Feudalism to Capitalism*, 165 and 201. Shrewsbury's advice of 2 June (written several days before events at Newton) refers to cutting down a 'thousand of such... roges' as a means to end the disorder, perhaps implying his estimate of the numbers assembled there was as much informed by rhetoric as a first-hand estimation of the numbers involved.
53. On this, see McDonagh, 'Making and breaking', 6. Parker, 'Cotesbach', 74 notes that due to the destruction of fences, common grazing arrangement were temporarily reinstated in Cotesbach for a few years after the Rising, although final enclosure followed before 1612.
54. Large assemblies of 3000 and 5000 individuals were also reported at Hillmorton (Warwickshire) and Cotesbach (Leicestershire), respectively.
55. A note below BL, Add MS 11,402, folio 127 (29 May 1607) suggests it was 'The middest of June before all... was quieted'. Martin, *Feudalism to Capitalism*, 167 suggests Northamptonshire, Leicestershire and Warwickshire all 'remained in a disturbed condition until the end of June'.
56. Hindle, 'Imagining insurrection', 26; Parker, 'Cotesbach', 72–3.
57. BL, Add MS 11,402, folio 128 (23 July 1607); TNA, C 82/1747 (formal order, August 1607) and C 205/5/5.
58. E. F. Gay, 'The Midland Revolt and the Inquisitions of Depopulation of 1607', *Transactions of the Royal Historical Society*, New Series 18 (1904), 195–244, specifically 218–19 and the letter cited by Gay on 219, n. 2.
59. Martin, *Feudalism to Capitalism*, 184.
60. TNA, C 205/5/5; Northamptonshire Record Office [hereafter NRO], WY16/(a) (for the enclosure agreement). Sir Thomas's son, William, was married to John Read's daughter, Theodosia (NRO, L(C) 1609).
61. TNA, STAC 2/23/34, 2/23/39, 2/28/111, 2/28/119 and 2/28/126; McDonagh, 'Making and breaking', 11–12; Martin, *Feudalism to Capitalism*, 185.
62. Martin, *Feudalism to Capitalism*, 183–4. See too TNA, E 163/16/19 on a petition the Orton tenants sent to the king about entry fines and Sir Thomas Tresham's actions in response.
63. TNA, STAC 8/295/22.
64. Martin, *Feudalism to Capitalism*, 185.

65. List of Building of Special Architectural and Historic Interest; see also Royal Commission of Historical Monuments England, *An Inventory of the Historical Monuments in the County of Northampton* (London: 1975), Vol. 1, 72–4.
66. TNA, STAC 5/A13/36 (contained in STAC 5/T8/31-40).
67. TNA, STAC 5/T10/3 and 5/T7/14. The case related to land in (Great) Houghton.
68. STAC 5/A13/36 and 5/A56/24 (for 1597 prosecution and Read's answer); 5/B88/25 (for the *c*. 1571 interrogatories and depositions).
69. TNA, STAC 8/18/12; C 205/5/5 (where local husbandmen claimed Osborne had pulled down 'cottages, barnes and stables… and the number of two hundred persons or thereabouts depopulated'); STAC 5/A13/36.
70. TNA, STAC 5/A13/36.
71. TNA, STAC 5/A11/27 and 5/A13/36; 8/18/12.
72. TNA, STAC 5/B70/40; 5/B83/31.
73. TNA, STAC 8/16/12.
74. VCH Northants III, 177 and 183; IV, 191 and 206.
75. STAC 5/T34/23. The Chancery case is TNA, C 3/175/17. William Humphrey was also involved in a number of Star Chamber cases relating to the tithes and tithe wood of Barton Seagrave, where he was lessee of the rectorial tithes, in the later 1570s (STAC 5/H17/21, 5/H33/27 and 5/H73/35). See too C 3/172/6 for a Chancery case of *c*. 1563 involving William Humphrey about title to two closes of pasture in Shangdon, Leicestershire.
76. See STAC 5/A13/36 which names Richard Humphrey and 5/A11/30 for the denial in the Swepstone case (dated 11 Feb 1598); for Thomas's conviction see TNA, C 82/1759 (cited in Martin, 'Enclosure', 42).
77. Martin, *Feudalism to Capitalism*, 161–3.
78. Martin, *Feudalism to Capitalism*, 163 too makes this point. See too the grievances analysed by Hindle, 'Imagining insurrection', 28–30.
79. Mark Nicholls, 'Francis Tresham', *Oxford Dictionary of National Biography* (Oxford University Press, 2004; online edn, Jan 2008) [http://www.oxforddnb.com/view/article/27708, accessed 10 March 2017].
80. On the Tresham debt, see Mary Finch, *The Wealth of Five Northamptonshire Families 1540–1640* (OUP for Northamptonshire Record Society: 1956), 76–92.
81. Julian Lock, 'Tresham, Sir Thomas (1543–1605)', *Oxford Dictionary of National Biography* (Oxford University Press: 2004; online edn, May 2009) [http://www.oxforddnb.com/view/article/27712, accessed 10 March 2017]. The family's indebtedness stemmed from both recusancy fines and the large portions paid for the ambitious marriages of Sir Thomas's daughters.

82. On the posthumous conviction, see Martin, *Feudalism to Capitalism*, 185.
83. Hindle, 'Imagining insurrection', 24; John Gurney, *Brave Community: The Digger Movement in the English Revolution* (Manchester University Press: 2007), 123. On the Diggers' occupation of common land and its relations to earlier repertoires of protest, see B. McDonagh and C. J. Griffin, 'Occupy! Historical geographies of property, protest and the commons, 1500–1850', *Journal of Historical Geography* 53 (2016), 1–10.
84. TNA, STAC 8/295/22.
85. Joint answer in TNA, STAC 8/295/22; 8/18/12 for the prosecution. See too STAC 8/221/1 for another instance of the Rising as an example to be followed.
86. TNA, STAC 8/148/7. Manning, *Village Revolts*, 83 also discusses this case as an example of a complainant who 'sought to discredit enclosure rioters' by associating them with the events of 1607.
87. TNA, STAC 8/121/20. On foot-dragging as a form of protest in itself, we are influenced by James C. Scott, *Weapons of the Weak: Everyday Forms of Peasant Resistance* (Yale University Press: 1987) and *Domination and the Arts of Resistance: Hidden Transcripts* (Yale University Press: 1990). See also Jeanette M. Neeson, *Commoners: Common Right, Enclosure & Social Change in England, 1700–1820* (Cambridge University Press: 1993).
88. TNA, STAC 8/94/4.
89. TNA, STAC 8/121/15.
90. TNA, STAC 8/61/33.

Relating Early Modern Depositions

Heather Falvey

On 17 June 1643 at Westminster 28-year-old Robert Freeman made a deposition to representatives of the House of Lords. He related the extreme measures that had perforce been taken at Whittlesey, in the Isle of Ely, to suppress the fenland riots that had erupted there just over a month earlier. On 16 May, Freeman explained, he had accompanied his master, George Glapthorne, JP, on the 14-mile journey to Wisbech to request the assistance of Parliamentary troops who were stationed there temporarily. When the two men returned to Whittlesey, Freeman saw

> diverse of the sayd ryottours upon the topp of the rick of Hay of John Newtons neere Lipny Hill in the sayd Fenns. and did see them throw the same into the Dykes there. And further saith that he did see to the number of foure or five hundred of the sayd riottours gathered together the next morning being wensday morning by the ringing of a Bell, ready to come downe to the said Fenns, had not the Parliament forces come and prevented them.[1]

When reconstructing micro-histories of protest and unrest in early modern England depositions such as that made by Robert Freeman are the principal sources which scholars have exploited. Even in this brief

---

H. Falvey (✉)
Institute of Continuing Education, University of Cambridge,
Madingley Hall, Cambridge, UK

© The Author(s) 2018
C. J. Griffin, B. McDonagh (eds.), *Remembering Protest in Britain since 1500*, https://doi.org/10.1007/978-3-319-74243-4_4

extract Freeman not only relates his memories of the violent protests on 16 May and of the planned riots on 17 May, but also locates those memories securely in the landscape of the Whittlesey fens. This was no landscape unchanged since time immemorial; rather, it was one that had recently been transformed by technologies of drainage and cultivated according to 'improved' agricultural methods. Indeed, by infilling dykes with hay protestors were not only destroying produce from one of the farms recently established in the drained fen but also blocking the watercourses of the new drainage network.[2]

To reconstruct past protests, such as those at Whittlesey, historians are reliant on the memories of witnesses – on their memories of the locality, events and participants. For obvious reasons, defendants (as the alleged protestors) were reluctant to admit their involvement. On the other hand, it is likely that many witnesses were themselves actors in the alleged events since their recollections are often highly detailed.[3] By definition, memories were passed down orally, thus by transliterating these memories recorded depositions provide glimpses of past scenes that would otherwise remain obscured by the curtain of time. Furthermore, those who remembered protest frequently justified events in terms of defending local custom thus inadvertently exposing details of past customary practices.[4]

Depositions have been used not only to offer plausible narratives of what may or may not have happened in any given episode, but also to reconstruct past landscapes and to identify the protagonists and the loops of association which drew them together in those landscapes. The genesis, nature and significance of depositions have on occasion been assumed without questioning their authenticity. In some large-scale projects social historians have 'mined' numerous depositions to produce studies of early modern attitudes and behaviour but, by their very nature and purpose, such studies have not always contextualised those depositions. This chapter takes the opposite approach by uncovering what can be learned through close reading and contextualisation of depositions and various associated documents. By considering a handful of early modern protests which are exceptionally richly documented this chapter offers a more nuanced understanding of depositions both as a genre and as a specific stage in due process. The purpose is not to denigrate large-scale studies of memories to reconstruct past landscapes and past protests, but rather to offer a discussion of the evidence for the identity of those whose memories have been recorded. Indeed, as we shall see, in addition to named deponents there were many others – some now impossible to identify – who had recounted their memories to the authorities.

Having outlined the relationships between depositions and the questions (formally known as 'interrogatories') which prompted them, and between those interrogatories and evidence collected earlier in the legal process, this chapter then argues that interrogatories themselves can profitably be used in the historical reconstruction of popular protest. Furthermore, rather than asking whether it is possible for the historian to determine if deponents really did 'declare the truth and [their] knowledge' of the matters in dispute,[5] it discusses specific episodes where conflicting 'relations' of the same events can be compared and contrasted, and in the process offers a typology of witnesses' modes of response to interrogatories.

The nouns 'relationships' and 'relations' are used intentionally here. In her ground-breaking analysis of narrativity in seventeenth-century publications and legal records, Frances Dolan has demonstrated the complex and ambiguous nature of 'relations' as forms of testimony and evidence.[6] The three relevant definitions of the verb 'to relate' given by the *Oxford English Dictionary* are: (1) To recount, narrate, give an account of (actions, events, facts, etc.); (2) To have some connection with; to stand in relation to (something); (3) To understand or have empathy for; to identify or feel a connection with (people).[7] Dolan argues that historians (and literature scholars) rather than focusing simply on what was being related, should also analyse the relationships between the narrator and the events that they related, and the narrator and the person who recorded their relation. But before considering the relators, their relations, and relationships, it is necessary to outline how, when and why depositions were elicited from them.

DEPOSITIONAL EVIDENCE

When riots or other forms of protest were alleged, the usual mode of prosecution and investigation was known as the 'English bill process'.[8] After initial bills of complaint had been submitted by the plaintiff and answers provided by the defendant, and a subsequent round of replication and rejoinder by each party, the court might proceed to the examination of defendants and/or the deposition of witnesses. Testimony of this kind was usually solicited on behalf of the complainants, often the landowner(s) whose property had been invaded or destroyed.[9] But inhabitants might also act as complainants: for example, bringing suits over the stopping up of rights of way, the loss of common rights or the erection of enclosures.[10] Depositions of witnesses – that is, answers to various interrogatories relating to the suit – and, on occasion, examinations of defendants, were made under oath, certified as to their authenticity and returned to the court that had originally commissioned the enquiry. Such depositional evidence survives in varying quantities in the archives of a number of jurisdictions. For historians of protest, the most relevant central courts are those of the Exchequer, of the Duchy (of Lancaster) Chamber, and of Star Chamber.[11] These were 'courts of conscience', rather than criminal courts, and as such 'applied the spirit of justice not the letter of the law'.[12] The examination of witnesses took place either in Westminster or in the locality of the dispute, the latter being preferred if the distance from London was over ten miles and/or the number of witnesses was great.[13] Depositions taken 'in the country' were collected by commissioners who were usually men of standing in the county wherein the dispute was located, but who did not live close enough to be involved directly. If the matters being investigated were considered sufficiently serious, however, deponents might be summoned to Westminster, regardless of the distance that they needed to travel. In their depositions, witnesses to the contested events – whether participants, observers or victims – related in varying degrees of detail what they had seen or heard, who had been involved and, occasionally, their understanding of the causes of conflict.

There can be no denying the historical appeal of the voices 'heard' in depositions of this kind. At a time when many legal records were still written in Latin or Law French, the everyday, even earthy, English recorded in depositions lends an aura of authenticity and immediacy to testimony. Thus, it can be argued, we actually 'hear' the recollections of ordinary – and often illiterate – men and women: people who might have left no other mark in the historical record. It is unsurprising, therefore, that social historians have made extensive use of depositional evidence when attempting to reconstruct not only the everyday but also the extraordinary in early modern England.[14] Handling of such 'evidence' nonetheless requires considerable care and caution. Although Natalie Zemon Davis' seminal analysis of pardon tales is based upon French jurisdictions that have no direct English equivalent, numerous historians of early modern England have followed her advice on dealing with 'fiction in the archives'; namely, that when evaluating such evidence, historians should allow for the fact that the circumstances and purpose of its creation shaped its form and content.[15] These difficulties notwithstanding, virtually every commentator on this problem concedes that depositions reveal far too much to be relegated to the 'discard pile'.[16] G. R. Quaife notes, for example, that witness testimonies 'recapture (even through the legalistic verbiage) the atmosphere of the particular situation and of the period in general'.[17] Furthermore, as Peter Marshall notes, 'the "fictions" of the courtroom had to be thoroughly plausible ones in order to deliver the desired results, and this means that they have the ability to offer unrivalled insight into attitudes, values, and usually unspoken assumptions about the world'.[18] Andy Wood and Nicola Whyte have even felt sufficiently confident to treat depositions as 'memory texts'.[19] In sum, various social and cultural historians have strenuously acknowledged the dangers of uncritical reliance on depositional evidence, and then proceeded nonetheless to rely heavily on it without considering fully issues of authenticity.

Legal historians, on the other hand, are less than happy with social historians' apparently carefree approach to depositional evidence.[20] This scepticism as to the value of depositional evidence has deep roots: the legal commentator W. S. Holdsworth dismissively argued as long ago as 1926 that 'a more futile method of getting at the facts of the case… never existed in any mature legal system'.[21] Depositions were nevertheless fundamental to the English legal process from the sixteenth to the nineteenth century, which means that, for all their faults, there are no viable alternatives for historians seeking the authentic witness experience. Indeed, even the legal historian W. H. Bryson concedes that each set of depositions 'gives an incident or vignette of life in England… Here is a fertile field from which can grow many things besides stubble and thorns'.[22]

While social historians of the law and legal historians have disputed the plausibility of depositions, the question of how witness testimony was actually generated has attracted rather less attention. The taking of depositions was, in fact, only one stage in a much longer process of collecting evidence. Bryson helpfully sets the scene in which depositions were secured.[23] Two or more of the commissioners met at a pre-arranged place and time – often a local inn – whither witnesses were summoned. Each witness gave evidence in private to the commissioners, in the presence of a clerk, the witness having sworn to tell the truth and not to publicly reveal their answers before the depositions were published. The interrogatories were read to the witness one question at a time and their answers were recorded on paper. After all of the witnesses had been examined, the clerk engrossed the depositions on parchment. When depositions were taken at Westminster, they were also taken in private, but in that case before one of the judges of the court.[24] On these occasions, the original paper depositions were submitted rather than being engrossed and the deponent signed or marked at the end of their deposition, and occasionally at the bottom of each sheet.[25]

Some of the conventional reservations regarding the authenticity of depositional evidence concern the relationship between the witness and the clerk, or, more precisely, between what was related by the witness and what was actually written down by the clerk. As Dolan notes, some historians have tried to account for this by concluding that clerks wrote down evidence 'more or less verbatim' or 'more or less accurately'.[26] But either something is 'verbatim', or 'accurate', or it is not. Focusing on church court depositions, in particular, Dolan suggests a more positive relationship between the clerk and a deponent: the two were not necessarily antagonistic. Indeed, this was a period in which there was widespread participation in the law: the deponent was not necessarily cowed by his or her situation, indeed the act of relating their version of events might frequently have been empowering.[27] The clerk's main function was to convert into writing the words that had been spoken by the deponent, rendering them in the third rather than the first person, and, as we shall see, where necessary adding legal phrasing derived from the interrogatory itself. Evidence given in a Duchy of Lancaster suit in 1633 indicates that at the end of the process the recorded deposition was read back to the deponent.[28] Furthermore, examinations conducted at Westminster in 1664 indicate that deponents might have the opportunity to review and amend what the clerk had written.[29] In these particular documents, the paper depositions have been altered and subsequently signed, or marked, by each deponent, to acknowledge that the written words (eventually) recorded what they had said. Thus, while depositions were indeed filtered through the clerk's transcription, the written deposition bears a direct relationship with the words that were related orally to the commissioners.

Depositions and Their Corresponding Interrogatories

Given that interrogatories were drawn up to elicit answers sought by one or other of the parties, depositions should ideally be read in conjunction with the relevant interrogatories. This is often impossible, however, because of the ravages of archival attrition: survival of both interrogatories and depositions in the same action is patchy. When, as in the most common scenario, only depositions survive, historians are by definition ignorant of the precise questions to which witnesses were responding. We may have their recorded testimony, but equally, their answer may simply be a repetition or distillation of a question which the historian can neither see nor hear. Consider, for example, the interrogatory (number 7) to which Robert Freeman gave the answer with which this chapter opens:

was not the sayd ryott soe dangerous as that there was noe meanes to remove it but by a parte of the Parliament Armye and what number of souldiers were necessarily drawne thither to remove the saide ryott and force and did they not threaten to come againe after the souldiers should departe?[30]

In answer to this particular question about the quelling of the riot, another deponent, James La Roue, related that

> the sayd ryott was soe Dangerous as that there was noe meanes to remove it but by sending for a part of the Parliaments Army; wich were sent for, and there came about the number of a hundred men or thereabouts, purposed to remove the said riottours and forces, but did not heare any of them threaten to come againe after the said Souldiers should departe.[31]

On the other hand, Lewis Randall, a 23-year-old carpenter, who had been suspiciously close to the action, related that

> the ryott was soe dangerous as that there was noe meanes to remove the same but by sending for a parte of the Parliaments Army wich was done accordingly and there came about the number of a hundred men and upwards wich yet remaine in the said Towne of Whittlesea to there greate Charge but did not heare any of the sayd riottours say they would returne as soone as the said souldiers should depart.[32]

In the first and last sections of their testimony, both deponents apparently repeated parrot-fashion part of the text of the question they had been asked. But are these engrossed statements likely to be the actual words spoken by La Roue and Randall? Rather than repeating the entire question verbatim, each of them almost certainly said 'Yes' to the first section; then estimated the number of soldiers involved; and finally said 'No' to the last part. In each case, the text of the interrogatory was probably inserted by the clerk to clarify their responses.[33] Randall also added specific and unsolicited information that the soldiers remained in the town, at the expense of the inhabitants, to keep the peace. Other witnesses went further in the provision of unsought information. As we have seen, Robert Freeman related in detail the summoning of the troops, the destruction of John Newton's hayrick and the gathering next morning of a crowd some 400 to 500-strong.

Close reading of interrogatories and of corresponding depositions therefore indicates that while some witnesses offered their own version of events and might provide detailed descriptions of what had happened in their presence, or to their knowledge, other witnesses were recorded as simply restating, or negating, the question that they had been asked. Deponents in this latter group of witnesses were, it seems, not necessarily *remembering* what they had seen but may have been merely *relating* the party line of those on whose behalf they had been summoned to provide evidence. Such 'recollections', repetitious as they often are, raise fundamental questions concerning the source of the 'memory' on which the historian is relying. Were the words recorded in the deposition those of the witness, or those of the interrogatory?[34] We might, accordingly, develop a typology of witnesses' proximate responses to interrogatories. As the three different responses to the seventh Whittlesey interrogatory indicate, a deponent might simply agree, or disagree, with the question; they might agree, or disagree, and then relate something else that they had remembered individually; or might provide an entirely 'unscripted' answer. There is also, of course, a fourth alternative: they might not answer a question at all, either because they knew nothing about its subject, or because it was not specifically directed towards them. During the enquiries into the Whittlesey riots, for example, all nine of those deposed offered answers to question 7 but only one of them answered question 6, which was very specific and significant (and to which we shall return).

This raises in turn the question of how interrogatories were themselves constructed. Of course, the questions asked of witnesses were fashioned to suit the interests of the parties concerned, but how and by whom was it decided precisely what should be asked? Initial general questions, such as the length of the deponent's acquaintance with the parties, or the degree of their familiarity with the locale, were posed in order to establish that the witness might have relevant knowledge. Subsequent and more specific questions, however, might relate to particular events, practices, customs or activities, or might be framed to establish the credentials of individuals connected with the suit. But where, exactly, did the assumptions that underlay this agenda originate? It might be supposed that interrogatories were constructed by legal counsel for the party concerned, and that therefore when deponents agreed to the text of the question as all or part of their answer, they were literally having words put in their mouths to serve the interests of that party. But how would counsel know what *specific* questions to pose? At the very least it seems likely that some interrogatories were framed in conversation with relevant parties who might themselves subsequently become witnesses to whom those interrogatories were put. More specifically, the occasional survival of preliminary documents in the legal process reveals that affidavits made by victims or witnesses could often be the source material for subsequent interrogatories. The particular wording of interrogatories was not therefore necessarily a matter of the plaintiff's invention: the choice of questions was based on *someone's* relation of the events being investigated.[35] It is not insignificant, moreover, that recollections recorded in affidavits had been taken under oath. What, then, might an analysis of the relationship between affidavits and interrogatories disclose about the witness testimony offered in depositions?

Evidence Related by Witnesses in Affidavits

The evidence generated during the investigation of the Whittlesey riots of 1643 is instructive in this regard. Complaints about the rioting in the fens around Whittlesey were presented to the House of Lords by the earls of Bedford and Portland, who owned the adjacent manors of Thorney and Whittlesey and held land in the drained Whittlesey fens.[36] The bundle of documents in the Parliamentary Archives relating to the riots includes an affidavit by John Newton, gentleman, of Whittlesey.[37] This sworn statement was taken on 29 May 1643, less than a fortnight after the rioting had occurred. When his affidavit is compared with the various papers generated during the suit, it becomes clear that it was Newton himself who had identified the men subsequently hauled up before the House and imprisoned in the Fleet. Robert Freeman's deposition indicates why Newton was selected: Newton's property had been attacked during the riots and as a victim he was well placed to give an account of events. Firstly, Newton gave a general outline of events on 15 May: about 100 persons, mostly armed with agricultural implements, had destroyed dykes, pulled down houses and cut down crops of coleseed and rapeseed. But he then related a very specific incident that also occurred on that same Monday:

> George Glapthorne Esqr' a Justice of the Peace came there and required the said persons to bee obedient to the Lawes of the Realme and to depart thence in a peaceable manner, whereupon the afore named Jeffery Boyce, James Boyce, and William Mash held pitchforks against the said George Glapthorne and told him that hee was noe Justice, for hee was against the King, and was all for the Parliament and that they would not obey him nor any Law, and many of the Company whose names this deponent knoweth not cryd out and sayd that shortly hee would bee served as Felton served Buckingham.[38]

From Freeman's own deposition we already know that on the Tuesday Glapthorne had gone to Wisbech to seek assistance from Parliamentary troops who happened to be stationed there. From Newton's affidavit, it is clear that on the Monday, Glapthorne, the local JP, had failed to disperse the rioters. In fact, as a leading proponent of drainage in the area, Glapthorne leased many acres of improved land and had developed significant rental property on that land; his position therefore antagonised those whose access to the former common fens had been curtailed.[39] This particularly vivid section of Newton's affidavit was subsequently converted into the sixth interrogatory, the only difference being that the names of the alleged offenders were requested rather than stated. Only one of the nine deponents answered this particular question: Newton himself. Tellingly, however, he now backtracked and watered down his testimony, which was much more circumspect in his deposition than it had been in his affidavit less than three weeks previously:

> [A]mongst the whole assembly of the said riottours one Jeffrey Boyce by name, and named a defendant in this suite, having a pitchfork in his hand did say unto this deponent that Mr Glapthorne was noe Justice of the peace for that he was against the king and was all for the Parliament, therefore hee the said Boyce would not obey him or any orders or lawes from him; but whether any of the said riottours did cry out that the said Mr Glapthorne would be served as Felton served Buckingham or not, this deponent cannot depose.[40]

Now Newton related not that three named men had threatened a magistrate with pitchforks, but that only one man had been involved and that he was simply holding a pitchfork in his hand while speaking with Newton. The change implies a significant reduction in the degree of confrontation related between the 'rioters' and the JP. Threatening a JP with a dangerous weapon was a serious offence; on the other hand, in 1643 a political declaration in support of the king was still acceptable. Perhaps Newton had been 'got at' by locals between the submission of his affidavit and the taking of his deposition and so he backpedalled on this particular aspect of the riots.

The contents of Newton's affidavit, therefore, suggest that other such documents would be invaluable to historians reconstructing protest. During the 1640s people in many areas 'took advantage of the times'[41] to break down enclosures in former common lands in forests, fens and elsewhere.[42] Aggrieved landlords who were members of the House of Lords addressed petitions to their peers for orders for 'quieting of their possession'. Many of these petitions survive in the Parliamentary Archives: a survey of the appendices of the fourth, fifth and sixth reports of the Historical Manuscripts Commission, which calendar the papers of the House of Lords in the 1640s, and of the online catalogue of the Parliamentary Archives, produces 62 such petitions. Most were acted upon, and preserved with them in the archive are the documents generated during subsequent legal proceedings. Of these 62 bundles, 21 include affidavits, and it might be hoped that they could be compared with subsequent interrogatories and depositions; in fact, the Whittlesey episode of enclosure rioting is the only one for which this specific combination of sources survives.[43] The Whittlesey papers are, therefore, highly significant because of what they uniquely reveal about the collection of evidence and the construction of interrogatories.[44]

Evidence Related by Defendants in Affidavits

In the matter of the Whittlesey enclosure riots, those who gave evidence in response to interrogatories were deposed as witnesses rather than examined as defendants. It would be appropriate to consider whether the relationship between affidavits, interrogatories and depositions applied equally for defendants as for witnesses. Documents generated in 1633 during the course of a protracted dispute in Duffield Frith (Derbyshire) are instructive in this respect because the archive includes an initial witness statement around which interrogatories were subsequently framed. In July 1632, 34 leading commoners in the three wards of the former royal forest of Duffield Frith had signed agreements consenting to the partition and enclosure of the wards.[45] There then followed the process of dividing the wards and marking out the new enclosures. For this the Duchy of Lancaster employed the surveyor William Jordan, who commenced work in March 1633.[46] On 20 September 1633, two of the commissioners charged with overseeing the partition reported on its progress.[47] It appeared that Jordan had been impeded by local people determined to prevent the marking out, let alone the enclosure, of the divisions. John Lane the younger, one of the men appointed to assist Jordan, provided the commissioners with a detailed 'memorandum', identifying by name four men and four women who had been disrupting the work and threatening the surveyor.[48] There are significant alterations and insertions to the text of the memorandum which cumulatively imply that Lane went to considerable lengths to ensure that it precisely reflected his recollection of events. The memorandum is subscribed with a clerk's note 'by mee John Lane the yonger'; and signed by the commissioners themselves who acknowledged that the 'Informacion' had been delivered to them by Lane.[49] The Duchy Council was sufficiently outraged to summon the four men to Westminster for questioning and the examinations of three of them survive.[50] A reading of John Lane's relation of events alongside the interrogatories administered to these putative miscreants shows that four of the eight questions (numbers 5, 6, 7 and 8) were based squarely on Lane's account. When his 'memorandum' is compared with the men's answers material and revealing discrepancies in the testimonies become clear.

Within his lengthy information John Lane had related that 'some of the women gathered up stones & some toke away the meare stones wich were left for markes' and that as he was riding off to report events to the commissioners, one 'Richard Tayler did sweare he would kill him & when John Lane was ridden [that is, was riding] away Richard Tayler Ronn to the workemane and offered to strike him with his bill slandring them for theeves'. These specific recollections subsequently formed part of Interrogatory 7:

> did not yow or some one or more of yow gather upp Stones, and take away the meere markes and Stones and pull upp the Stakes and did not yow or some of yow pursue and follow after the said workmen or those that weere imployed in this worke, or came along to assist him. Did not yow sweare that yow would kill him the said Surveyor or some of them. Did yow not call them or some of them Theeves.

Richard Taylor, an ebullient 70-year-old, responded

> That neither hee this Deponent nor any of [the defendants] named did gather upp any stones or tooke awaye the Meere Markes and stones or pulled upp the stakes or followed or pursued the workemen that were soe sett on worke as afore said, Or threatened to kill the said Surveyour or called him or any of the workemen theeves But saith that there were fower or five women wich this Deponent thinketh did pull upp the stakes wich the said workemen had sett…

Taylor denied threatening to kill the surveyor and did not mention threats made to anyone else, but he did allege that those responsible for disrupting the survey were married women: individuals who could not, by definition, be prosecuted in law because they were the legal responsibility of their husbands.[51] Indeed, the examinations of all three defendants demonstrate that there was local knowledge concerning the position of married women before the law, each of those accused laying the blame exclusively on the women and distancing themselves from their activities. Tellingly, although Lane's affidavit had not just referred to female involvement but had actually named individual women, the interrogatories made no reference whatsoever to female participation. This issue was only (re-)introduced by the male defendants themselves, each of their answers to the eighth interrogatory naming the female activists. The strategies employed by both sides therefore imply clear recognition of this notorious blind spot in the law.[52]

The survival of John Newton's affidavit in the House of Lords Main Papers and of John Lane's information in the Duchy commissioners' papers not only provide historians of protest with detailed eye-witness accounts of events at Whittlesey and Duffield, but also furnish highly revealing evidence of the way in which interrogatories might have been constructed. This suggests that an analysis of affidavits and their related interrogatories and depositions in Exchequer suits should be equally instructive. TNA's online research guide to the Exchequer archive suggests, however, that a search for this specific combination of sources would be difficult, if not impossible. But the poor survival rate of affidavits notwithstanding, a far more important conclusion might be drawn about the origins, nature and significance of interrogatories: even where affidavits do not themselves survive, it is clear that interrogatories must have been based upon some form of witness recollection. Interrogatories therefore assume just as much significance as depositions in the narrative reconstruction of popular protest.

Evidence Related by the Complainant

Of course, not all interrogatories were informed by prior affidavits. Some questions, as has already been noted, simply requested basic information to establish a deponent's relationship with the parties and places in dispute. Furthermore, logic dictates that other interrogatories would be based on the recollections, or knowledge, of the complainant himself.[53] Surviving documents relating to a Star Chamber suit in the 1570s confirm this deduction and demonstrate not only the relationship between the bill of complaint and the interrogatories on behalf of the complainant, but also how that bill had itself been constructed.[54]

In the early summer of 1575 Godfrey Bradshaw alleged that 44 named men had broken down enclosures in Chinley in the High Peak of Derbyshire. Relevant papers in the archive of the Elizabethan Star Chamber comprise only Bradshaw's bill of complaint and the answers of six of the alleged rioters.[55] It is relatively straightforward to reconstruct Bradshaw's version of events from his bill of complaint. Perhaps unsurprisingly, the rioters' answers to that bill denied any involvement whatsoever. There are, however, additional relevant documents surviving in Bradshaw's personal papers held in the Sheffield Archives: an earlier draft of his bill and a set of interrogatories that he wanted to be administered to witnesses and defendants.[56] Although no corresponding depositions have survived, the 30 interrogatories fill in the outline sketched in Bradshaw's bill. Admittedly, the absence of depositions means that witnesses' versions of events are lacking, but since the interrogatories greatly embellished Bradshaw's original allegations they can be analysed to show what the rioters were alleged to have done, both in general and in particular. Alongside the 'usual' allegations of pulling down hedges and ditches by force and with arms, some allegations of rather more heinous criminal behaviour were made. Did Edward Kyrke try to hire someone to burn down Bradshaw's house?[57] Did certain people give land to William Beard so that he 'shuld from tyme to tyme send them ydll [that is, idle] ryotouse persons to assyste them in there yll doinge'?[58] Did Reynold Kirke meet with Master Bircles of the county of Chester 'concerning prophesies by noble men' and were 'Bookes of prophesye' consulted?[59] Clearly, Bradshaw was keen to implicate his opponents in considerably more serious crimes than 'mere' riot: incitement to commit arson; procuring or supplying disinterested but disorderly persons; dabbling in prophecy, a treasonous activity in the aftermath of the Northern Rebellion.[60] Analysis of these interrogatories in and of themselves, even without any depositions, allows a detailed reconstruction of the somewhat bitter social relations in the Chinley area at that time.[61] Questions, therefore, are in many ways just as revealing as answers.

Falsification of Evidence

We have already identified four possible modes of answering an interrogatory. In the light of other evidence, two further possibilities suggest themselves. Fifthly, the deponent's answer might actually be falsified, or at least altered materially, by the clerk, possibly under pressure from one of the parties to the suit. Deponents 'in the country' answered in private before the commissioners and the clerk present wrote their answers on paper, subsequently engrossing all deponents' answers on parchment; thus, any crossings out, insertions or alterations would be made *before* the depositions were engrossed. Although emendations of this kind would generally be very difficult to detect, it should nevertheless be acknowledged that depositions returned to Westminster might differ from testimony as it was originally related to the commissioners. The survival of an affidavit preserved in the Duchy of Lancaster archive confirms this possibility.

On 3 October 1633 an affidavit made by several commissioners was returned to the court of the Duchy Chamber, protesting about malpractice by some of their fellow commissioners and the defendants' clerk.[62] On 1 October, they had been part of a commission to examine witnesses in the suit *Jane Lyvesaye* v. *John Crosse* and others.[63] Edward Gelibrond, gentleman, had given a 'full & plaine answere' to the thirteenth interrogatory for the defendants but

> Henrie Walmsley gentleman (whoe was Clerke for the defendantes) fraimed the deposicion Contrarie to the meaning & likeing of the said deponent, whereupon the deponent tooke him self the paper, whereon the deposicion was writt as aforesaid, & altered the same, according to his owne Mynd, & would then have subscribed his name.

Two of the commissioners told Gelibrond that he should not alter the record of his deposition, which, they declared, must stand as it was a true account of what he had said. He refused to sign the original as a true record, whereupon those commissioners, together with the clerk, suddenly left the room, taking with them the amended deposition. The three refused to continue on the commission. Later on, those commissioners and the clerk brought in the engrossed depositions, including Gelibrond's, affixed to the interrogatories, and demanded the other commissioners certify them. It was clear to them all not only that the other commissioners had engrossed the statement which Gelibrond had wanted to alter, but also that they had inserted various words and sentences which 'were never uttered, nor spoken by the said deponent, nor sett downe in the paper deposicions'. Consequently, the commissioners concurred with Gelibrond's request not to certify the depositions. Aside from the detailed insights into the workings of a commission of enquiry that this incident reveals, it also provides a cautionary tale of what might happen behind the scenes when paper depositions were engrossed: some of those sitting on that particular commission were not as impartial as they should have been and the defendants' clerk was less than scrupulous, removing the paper depositions and engrossing onto parchment the (unaltered) statement that *he* wanted to have presented to the Duchy Chamber. Of course, such activities would be very difficult to detect from this distance in time, but nevertheless the possibility of falsification needs to be acknowledged.

Truth and Lies

A sixth possible answer to an interrogatory is an untruth, which, given that testimony was given on oath, amounted to perjury (itself still underexplored in the historiography). Of course, detecting perjury would have been difficult for contemporary authorities, let alone for twenty-first-century historians. An interrogatory might ask explicitly whether a named person had said or done XYZ. In such instances, that person would often be one of the deponents or defendants to whom that question was posed. If the deponent or defendant denied that they had done or said XYZ, who is to say, from this distance in time, whether they were lying? Given that the interrogatory was based on *someone's* version of events, it may be that initial relation was untrue. Or perhaps what had actually happened lay somewhere in between.

If we return to Duffield in the 1660s we can hear defendants contradicting specific allegations made against them and we can propose several possible scenarios that might explain their outright denial. In November 1662, Sir William Smith and Sir Thomas Hooke the current owners of the enclosed parts of Duffield Frith sought an injunction against commoners who had thrown down recently-erected fences.[64] Unconvinced by the commoners' claims that they could not be bound to honour an enclosure agreement which they had not personally signed, the court decreed that Smith and Hooke should enjoy 'full, quiet and peaceable possession' of their estates.[65] Unsurprisingly, the commoners breached the injunction and pulled down fences, driving cattle, sheep and horses into the enclosures. In April 1664, four men were hauled up to Westminster to answer for their contempt. The paper interrogatories contain some additions, and the defendants' examinations are heavily altered, with deletions and insertions (Fig. 1).[66] The questions and answers focus specifically on the serving of the injunction on the four men by Francis Blood, whose testimony informed the interrogatories. The men were questioned about their reaction to being served with the injunction and about the words they had spoken to Blood. Comparing the reported speech in the interrogatories (in both cases, inserted into the interrogatory in a different hand) with the deponents' versions provides very different relations of their responses.

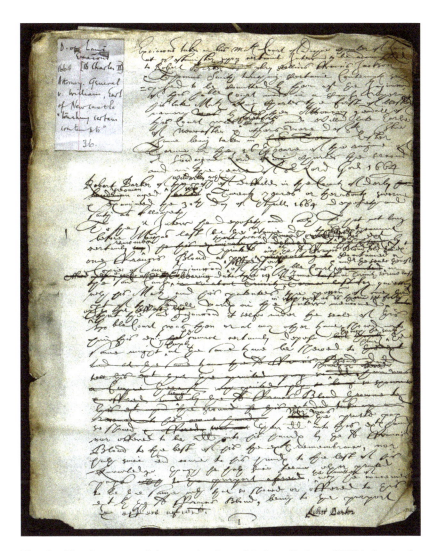

Fig. 1 The first page of the examination of Robert Barker of Wilderley in the parish of Duffield, ~~husbandman~~ yeoman, aged about ~~27~~ 26. (Source: TNA DL4/108/36, p. 1 (Photographed by TNA) (Duchy of Lancaster copyright material in The National Archives is reproduced by permission of the Chancellor and Council of the Duchy of Lancaster))

Had Robert Barker said 'that [he] cared noe more for the said Injuncion then [he] did for the stone that was under [his] foote, or wordes to the like effect'?[67] Initially, Barker denied that he had spoken these words but claimed that, on being told that the injunction was from the king, he had 'prayed God to bless his Majesty and the Royall Family and all his Courtes of Justice'. Inserted into his deposition were also the following words: 'and haply he might further say that [the injunction] did no more concerne him then the stone under his Foote', or words to that effect, since neither he nor anyone he claimed under were party to the original enclosure agreements.[68] Had Francis Jackson said that he 'vallued noe more the said Injuncion then [he] did a paper to wipe [his] Breech, or wordes to that effect'?[69] Jackson denied using 'the reproachfull words in this Interrogatory recited or any words to that effect', but insisted that his reply had been simply to the effect that 'he conceived he was not concerned in the said Injuncion he having no way disturbed the right of any therein'; in any case he too had not been party to the original enclosure agreements.[70]

Which account of the response to the serving of the injunction is more plausible? That of the man attempting to serve the injunction, or that of men invading enclosures on former commons? If the depositions alone had survived, the evidence available would only comprise the commoners' somewhat bland responses. The relevant interrogatories, however, suggest rather more graphic responses in the heat of the moment. But there is at least one other possibility: that Francis Blood had exaggerated their reaction because he had actually failed to serve the injunction on the men – and because the men (as they admitted in their examinations) had been splitting hairs over whether Blood had attempted to serve the original injunction or a printed paper copy. It was the severity of contempts reported in the interrogatories that had caused the men to be taken before the court. It is entirely possible that not only the commoners but also Blood related versions of events designed to put themselves in the best light. Thus, the relationship between opposing testimonies requires consideration: the 'truth' being sought lay somewhere on the spectrum between the two extremes related to the court.

Conclusion: Relating Memories of Protest

Historians of early modern protest are naturally drawn to the voices of deponents relating, apparently in their own words, their recollection of contested events. Yet, as has been suggested here, the reconstruction of those events from such narratives is not unproblematic. As Dolan observes, surviving depositions are merely the clerk's record of what the witness observed and related – but those relations were prompted largely by the questions put to them by investigating commissioners.[71] From this perspective, depositions are merely the final stage in a protracted process of investigation and litigation that might be taking place (either simultaneously or sequentially) across a number of jurisdictions. This chapter has argued that reconstructing the various phases of litigation can shed light on the relationship between depositional evidence and testimony generated earlier in the investigative process. It has also demonstrated how and why certain individuals were questioned in certain ways; how their testimonies were recorded; and how historians might interpret them. Although witness depositions have generally been the star attraction for the micro-historian of protest, it is clear that interrogatories are no less significant for the narrative reconstruction of popular protest, not least since they too were prompted by witnesses' recollections. Above all, given the demonstrable relationship between earlier witness testimony and subsequent interrogatories, where they survive, affidavits constitute the most immediate – and therefore the most revealing – source for the study of early modern protest.

Whether the legal archive survives in full – as for the riots in Whittlesey's fens or for the more subtle protests within Duffield Frith at the time of Jordan's survey – or is piecemeal as at Chinley, such documents allow the reconstruction of protest in those landscapes through the memories recorded therein. This detailed analysis, however, provides a cautionary tale. While the record of his deposition states that 'Lewies Randall of Whittlesea Carpenter aged 23 yeares and upwards' gave the ensuing answers, suggesting that the historian has access to the memories of a young, landless artisan unlikely to appear in other contemporary records, in fact, as we have seen, some of Randall's evidence simply concurred with that of John Newton 'gentleman aged about 44 yeares'. But for the social historian keen to hear the recollections of the 'lower sort' of men and women, this is not the dampening revelation that it might at first seem, apparently privileging the memories of the better sort. The point is not that Randall's voice is now partly drowned out by Newton's, but rather that Randall's was required to be heard confirming, or negating, Newton's original voice. Whether because he was an actor in the riots, or because he might be able to supply further information about events and protagonists, the authorities considered it worthwhile questioning the carpenter after the gentleman's affidavit had been related.

Acknowledgements As ever, I am especially grateful to Steve Hindle for his insightful comments and guidance, and for his patience on being confronted yet again by the activities of the inhabitants of early modern Duffield and Whittlesey: when I first selected these communities for study, I had no idea just how fruitful the surviving material would be. I am also very grateful to Tim Stretton who introduced me to the work of Frances Dolan. Both Steve and Tim made extensive comments on earlier drafts of this chapter; any remaining errors are my own.

NOTES

1. Parliamentary Archives [hereafter PA], HL/PO/JO/10/1/152, 19 June 1643–29 June 1643, bundle dated 26 June 1643, draft order and judgment in the case between the Earls of Bedford and Portland and the inhabitants of Whittlesey, plus 11 documents annexed, deposition of Robert Freeman, 17 June 1643.
2. For the economy and demography of early modern Whittlesey, see Heather Falvey, 'Custom, resistance and politics: local experiences of improvement in early-modern England' (unpublished PhD thesis, University of Warwick: 2007), chapter 3; Heather Falvey, 'Assessing an early modern Fenland population: Whittlesey (Cambs)', *Local Population Studies* 92 (2014), 7–23.
3. See, for example, the discussion of the evasive answers given by defendants following accusations of riot on 3 July 1620 at Berkhamsted (Herts) in Heather Falvey, 'Crown policy and local economic context in the Berkhamsted Common enclosure dispute, 1618–42', *Rural History* 12 (2001), 123–58, and the discussion of the detailed depositions of Anthony Lawe and Lewis Randall of Whittlesey in Heather Falvey, 'Voices and faces in the rioting crowd: identifying seventeenth-century enclosure rioters', *The Local Historian* 39:2 (2009), 137–51. For Randall, see also below.
4. The relationship between custom, memory and writing has been discussed by many early modern historians. See, for example, David Rollison, *The Local Origins of Modern Society: Gloucestershire 1500–1800* (Routledge: 1992): 12–15; Adam Fox, 'Custom, memory and the authority of writing', in Paul Griffiths, Adam Fox and Steve Hindle (eds) *The Experience of Authority in Early Modern England* (Palgrave Macmillan: 1996), 89–116; Heather Falvey, 'The articulation, transmission and preservation of custom in the forest community of Duffield (Derbyshire)', in Richard W. Hoyle (ed.) *Custom, Improvement and the Landscape in Early Modern Britain* (Ashgate: 2011), 65–100.
5. The National Archives [hereafter TNA], E 134/1659/East27, interrogatories and depositions for the plaintiffs and the defendants in the matter of Lord Fleetwood, late Lord Deputy of Ireland and Edward Cooke esquire *v.* 77 named defendants. The demand follows five of the interrogatories for the defendants.

6. Frances E. Dolan, *True Relations: Reading, Literature and Evidence in Seventeenth-Century England* (University of Pennsylvania Press: 2013).
7. *OED, sub* 'relate', definitions 2a, 6a, 9 [online edition].
8. The best summary of the process for Equity suits is the research guide published on TNA's website: http://www.nationalarchives.gov.uk/help-with-your-research/research-guides/equity-proceedings-court-exchequer/ [accessed 16/08/16].
9. The Crown (or its representatives) might also act for the landowner. There might be interrogatories and depositions for the defendants as well as for the plaintiffs. Some deponents might give evidence for both sides in a dispute.
10. See Briony McDonagh, 'Making and breaking property: negotiating enclosure and common rights in sixteenth-century England', *History Workshop Journal* 76 (2013), 32–56.
11. For the records of these courts and the survival of the various classes of records, see, for example, W. H. Bryson, *The Equity Side of the Exchequer: its Jurisdiction, Administration, Procedures and Records* (Cambridge University Press: 1975); Henry Horwitz, *Exchequer Equity Records and Proceedings, 1649–1841* (Public Record Office: 2001); William D. Shannon, '"On the left hand above the staire": accessing, understanding and using the archives of the early-modern Court of Duchy Chamber', *Archives* xxxv no. 123 (2010), 19–36; John A. Guy, *The Court of Star Chamber and its Records to the Reign of Elizabeth I* (HMSO: 1984); Thomas G. Barnes, 'The archives and archival problems of the Elizabethan and Early Stuart Star Chamber', *Journal of the Society of Archivists* 2 (1963), 345–60.
12. Shannon, '"On the left hand above the staire"', 23. This article is the only lengthy published discussion of the workings of the Court of the Duchy Chamber.
13. The prescribed procedure for taking depositions is described in detail, with examples, in Bryson, *Equity Side*, 138–43.
14. For example, see the extraordinary and the everyday revealed in the depositions relating events in 1572 in Nantwich: Steve Hindle, '"Bleedinge afreshe"? The affray and murder at Nantwich, 19 December 1572', in Angela McShane and Garthine Walker (eds) *The Extraordinary and the Everyday in Early Modern England: Essays in Celebration of the Work of Bernard Capp* (Palgrave Macmillan: 2010), 224–45. See also, for example, Falvey, 'Voices and faces in the rioting crowd'; Steve Hindle, 'Beating the bounds of the parish: order, memory and identity in the English local community, c. 1500–1700', in Michael J. Halvorson and Karen E. Spierling (eds) *Defining Community in Early Modern Europe* (Ashgate: 2008), 205–28; Bill Frazer, 'Common recollections: resisting enclosure "by agreement" in seventeenth-century England', *International Journal of Historical Archaeology*, 3 (1999), 75–99; Nicola Whyte, 'Landscape, memory and cus-

tom: parish identities c.1550–1700', *Social History* 32:2 (2007), 166–86; Andy Wood, 'Custom, identity and resistance: English Free Miners and their law, c.1550–1800', in Griffiths, Fox and Hindle *The Experience of Authority*, 249–86.
15. Natalie Zemon Davis, *Fiction in the Archives: Pardon Tales and their Tellers in Sixteenth Century France* (Stanford University Press: 1987). See, for example, Tim Stretton, 'Social historians and the records of litigation', in Solvi Sogner (ed.) *Fact, Fiction and Forensic Evidence* (University of Oslo: 1997), 15–34; Adam Fox, 'Oral and literate culture in early modern England: cases from legal records', in Sogner, *Fact, Fiction*, 35–52; Malcolm Gaskill, 'Reporting murder: fiction in the archives in early modern England', *Social History* 23 (1998), 1–30; Malcolm Gaskill, 'Witches and witnesses in Old and New England', in Stuart Clark (ed.) *Languages of Witchcraft: Narrative, Ideology and Meaning in Early Modern England* (Palgrave Macmillan: 2001), 55–80.
16. Stretton, 'Social historians', 28.
17. G. R. Quaife, *Wanton Wenches and Wayward Wives: Peasants and Illicit Sex in Early Seventeenth Century England* (Croom Helm: 1979), 5.
18. Peter Marshall, *Mother Leakey & the Bishop: A Ghost Story* (Oxford University Press: 2007), 15.
19. Andy Wood, *The Memory of the People: Custom and Popular Sense of the Past in Early Modern England* (Cambridge University Press: 2013); Nicola Whyte, *Inhabiting the Landscape: Place, Custom and Memory, 1500–1800* (Windgather Press: 2009); Nicola Whyte, 'Custodians of memory: women and custom in rural England, c.1550–1700', *Cultural and Social History* 8 (2011), 153–73. See also, for example, Jonathan Healey, 'The political culture of the English commons, c.1550–1650', *Agricultural History Review*, 60 (2012), 266–87.
20. There seems to be a distinction between legal historians and social historians of the law. It would have been instructive to have the views of the late Professor Chris Brooks on the value of depositional evidence, but his work focused on early modern lawyers themselves rather than those who came before them and what they said.
21. Christine Churches, '"The most unconvincing testimony": the genesis and historical usefulness of the country depositions in Chancery', *The Seventeenth Century* 11:2 (1996), 209–27, 209, quoting from W. S. Holdsworth, *History of English Law*, vol. 9 (Methuen: 1926), 353.
22. Bryson, *Equity Side*, 143.
23. The following is taken from Bryson, *Equity Side*, 139. Shannon, '"On the left hand above the staire"', 24–9, outlines the procedures of the court of Duchy Chamber; see 26–7 for commissions of enquiry.
24. In the case of the Exchequer, before one of the barons of the Court. See Bryson, *Equity Side*, 135–38.

25. Bryson, *Equity Side*, 136.
26. Dolan, *True Relations*, 120; citing Garthine Walker, 'Rereading rape and sexual violence in early modern England', *Gender & History* 10 (1998): 1–25, 8; Laura Gowing, *Domestic Dangers: Women, Words and Sex in Early Modern London* (Clarendon Press: 1996), 46.
27. Dolan, *True Relations*, 121.
28. TNA, DL 9/7, bundle dated Michaelmas Term 1633, document dated 3 October 1633. Issues raised by this particular document are discussed below.
29. TNA, DL 4/018/36. These documents are discussed in more detail below.
30. PA, HL/PO/JO/10/1/152, 26 June 1643, interrogatory 7 administered to witnesses.
31. PA, HL/PO/JO/10/1/152, 26 June 1643, James La Roue's answer to interrogatory 7. La Roue was a Walloon settler who cultivated land in the drained fens at Whittlesey and lived in one of the new houses erected on that land. For the Walloon community in the fens, see Heather Falvey, 'Interpreting the Instrument of Government: objections to the 1654 election in the Isle of Ely', *Parliamentary History* 31 (2012), 133–51.
32. PA, HL/PO/JO/10/1/152, 26 June 1643, Lewis Randall's answer to interrogatory 7.
33. I owe this suggestion to Tim Stretton. In this particular instance, how and why would a foreigner and a lowly carpenter remember the convoluted wording of the question?
34. A preliminary discussion of this issue is in Falvey, 'Voices and faces in the rioting crowd'.
35. Although some interrogatories might, of course, have been framed in relation to the initial bill of complaint; these *would* give the plaintiff's version of the alleged events. This is discussed below in the matter of Godfrey Bradshaw and the neighbours of Chinley.
36. For details of the riots see: Falvey, 'Custom, resistance and politics', chapter 5. The earls brought their complaint brought to House of Lords because they were peers, but Portland was in prison for much of early 1643.
37. PA, HL/PO/JO/10/1/152, 26 June 1643, affidavit of John Newton, 29 May 1643.
38. PA, HL/PO/JO/10/1/152, 26 June 1643, affidavit of John Newton. That Clapthorne might 'bee served as Felton served Buckingham' can be construed as a threat by the rioters to kill the JP just as the duke had been assassinated by Felton in August 1628. For a discussion of Felton's actions, see Thomas Cogswell, 'John Felton, popular political culture, and the assassination of the Duke of Buckingham', *Historical Journal*, 49 (2006), 357–85.
39. For Glapthorne, see Falvey, 'Interpreting the Instrument of Government'.

40. PA, HL/PO/JO/10/1/152, 26 June 1643, deposition of John Newton, 16 June 1643.
41. Historical Manuscripts Commission, *Appendix to the 5th Report: Calendar of the House of Lords' Papers* (HMSO: 1874; reprinted 1979), 82, affidavits of John Parish and John Flaske, 25 April 1643.
42. See, in particular, Buchanan Sharp, *In Contempt of All Authority: Rural Artisans and Riot in the West of England, 1586–1660* (University of California Press: 1980); Keith Lindley, *Fenland Riots and the English Revolution* (Heinemann Educational Ltd.: 1982); Andy Wood, *Riot, Rebellion and Popular Politics in Early Modern England* (Palgrave Macmillan: 2002). See also discussions of the activities of 'the Diggers', for example in *Winstanley and the Diggers, 1649–1999*, edited by Andrew Bradstock (Frank Cass: 2000).
43. A search of the PA's online catalogue (on 20 April 2016) between 1640 and 1650 on 'affidavit(s)' and 'interrogatory/ies' and 'deposition(s)' revealed that only six other sets of papers include affidavits, interrogatories and depositions within the PA, and these during the period 1641–1644.
44. It may be that it was the political content of the affidavit itself that ensured its retention in Parliament's archive.
45. The 'agreements' were the result of protracted wrangling and were signed by fewer than 10 per cent of the legal commoners. The agreements are in TNA, DL 44/1117. For details of the enclosures and subsequent objections to them, see Falvey, 'Custom, resistance and politics', chapter 4.
46. For an account of Jordan's work in the Frith, see Heather Falvey, 'Marking the boundaries: William Jordan's 1633 pre-enclosure survey of Duffield Frith (Derbyshire)', *Agricultural History Review* 61 (2013), 1–18.
47. The commissioners' report is in TNA, DL 44/1127.
48. TNA, DL 44/1127, memorandum of John Lane the younger, 18 September 1633.
49. The memorandum is recorded in the third person and does not state that it was given under oath.
50. TNA, DL 4/85/64.
51. The significance of this is discussed in detail in Falvey, 'Marking the boundaries', 13–15. John Lane had identified the women by name: Alice Taylor, wife of John; Ellen Webster, wife of William; Grace Webster, wife of Thomas; and Joan Osbaldeston, wife of John, a tailor (TNA, DL 44/1127, memorandum of John Lane the younger). The three defendants, John Taylor, William Webster and Thomas Webster, also identified the four women by name (TNA, DL 4/85/64, depositions of Taylor, Webster and Webster).
52. For women's involvement in protest, see, for example, Steve Hindle, 'Persuasion and protest in the Caddington Common enclosure dispute 1635–1639', *Past & Present* 158 (1998), 37–78; Ralph A. Houlbrooke,

'Women's social life and common action in England from the fifteenth century to the eve of the Civil War', *Continuity & Change* 1 (1986), 171–89; Briony McDonagh, 'Subverting the ground: private property and public protest in the sixteenth-century Yorkshire Wolds', *Agricultural History Review* 57 (2009), 191–206; John Walter, 'Grain riots and popular attitudes to the law: Maldon and the crisis of 1629', now reprinted in John Walter, *Crowds and Popular Politics in Early Modern England* (Manchester University Press: 2006): 27–66; Wood, *Memory of the People*, 297–315.

53. Or, indeed, of the defendant where interrogatories for that side survive.
54. See also the discussion of the preparation of a Star Chamber brief in Steve Hindle, 'Self-image and public image in the career of a Jacobean magistrate: Sir John Newdigate in the Court of Star Chamber', in Michael J. Braddick and Phil Withington (eds) *Popular Culture and Political Agency in Early Modern England and Ireland: Essays in Honour of John Walter* (Boydell Press: 2017), 123–44.
55. TNA, STAC 5/B93/31, bill of complaint of Godfrey Bradshaw and answer of Edward Kirke et al.
56. Sheffield Archives [hereafter SA], BD 102 and 103, Godfrey Bradshaw's draft bill of complaint (the folios that comprise the draft bill are interspersed with the folios of another document); SA, BD 101, interrogatories to be administered on behalf of Godfrey Bradshaw, undated, but early 1576.
57. SA, BD 101, interrogatory 17. For the horror of arson in the context of early modern communities, see Bernard Capp, 'Arson, threats of arson and incivility in early modern England', in Peter Burke, Brian Harrison and Paul Slack (eds) *Civil Histories: Essays presented to Sir Keith Thomas* (Oxford University Press: 2000), 197–214.
58. SA, BD 101, interrogatory 15.
59. SA, BD 101, interrogatories 27 and 28.
60. For the significance of prophecy as a catalyst for dissent, see Krista Kesselring, 'Deference and dissent in Tudor England: reflections on sixteenth-century protest', *History Compass* 3 (2005), 1–16, especially 7–11; Tim Thornton, *Prophecy, Politics and the People in Early Modern England* (Boydell Press: 2006), 24–25.
61. The events at Chinley are examined in Heather Falvey, 'The politics of enclosure in Elizabethan England: contesting "neighbourship" in Chinley (Derbyshire)', in Jane Whittle (ed.) *Landlords and Tenants in Britain, 1440–1660: Tawney's Agrarian Problem Revisited*, (Boydell Press: 2013), 67–84.
62. TNA, DL 9/7, bundle dated Michaelmas Term 1633, document dated 3 October 1633.
63. It is likely that documents generated later in this dispute are in TNA, DL 4/88/20, *Lyvesay* v. *Crosse and Lyvesay*, 11 Charles I.

64. TNA, DL 5/36, ff.198r–198v, *Attorney General* v. *the duke of Newcastle et al.*, 21 November 1662 (summarising events).
65. TNA, DL 5/36, ff.256v–257v, 4 June 1663.
66. TNA, DL 4/108/36, interrogatories to be administered to Robert Barker, Humphrey Collins, Francis Jackson and Thomas Smyth, and answers of the same men, examined on 30 April 1664.
67. TNA, DL 4/108/36, interrogatory 3.
68. TNA, DL 4/108/36, deposition of Robert Barker.
69. TNA, DL 4/108/36, interrogatory 6.
70. TNA, DL 4/108/36, deposition of Francis Jackson.
71. Dolan, *True Relations*, 121.

Remembering Protest in the Forest of Dean, c.1612–1834

Simon Sandall

On 12 August 1831, Warren James appeared before the Assize sessions at the Shire Hall in Gloucester charged with leading disturbances in the Forest of Dean earlier in the summer. The first of the two indictments, relating to a charge of felony grounded in the Riot Act of 1715, declared that 'Warren James, together with divers other unknown evil disposed persons to the number of 100 or more, with force of arms did unlawfully, riotously, routously and tumultuously assemble together to the disturbance of the public peace'.[1] The dispute related to a perceived breach of the terms under which the forest had been 'settled' in 1668. The seventeenth-century Dean Reafforestation Act stated that half of the 22,000 acres of Dean's central demesne lands could be enclosed to allow for the re-growth of trees planted, replacing those depleted by industrial practices and other uses. In 1831, the area that had been enclosed for the previous twenty years was due to be laid open in accordance with the Act of 1668. When it became apparent that this was not going to happen Warren James wrote to Edward Machen, deputy surveyor of the Forest, informing him that the controversial hedges, banks and fences would be removed. By this point, the banks and hedges had become well established in the local landscape. When no

S. Sandall (✉)
University of Winchester, Winchester, UK

further action was proposed on the matter, James decided to publicise his plans for the commonalty of Dean to 'open the Forest' of their own accord.

James was the son of a free miner and this piece explores the significance of his parentage in relation to these disturbances. Following the prolonged episode of crowd activity and James' prosecution, those that had been involved clearly pointed to the loss of Dean's Mine Law Court and its records in 1775 as the cause of their vulnerability to encroachment on the customs and traditions which had sustained their ancestors' livelihoods since a 'time out of mind of man'. As we shall see, the free miners of Dean had been the key focus and leaders of physical resistance to such encroachment since the early seventeenth century. On another level, the documentation accrued in their body of legal records had successfully repelled attempts by external interests to gain a foothold in the Forest until the demise of their occupational court in 1775. This chapter looks back from the early nineteenth century, exploring the disturbances of 1612 and 1631, as well as the nature of the court's operation in the intervening period, to understand why the loss of the Mine Law Court was so lamented by protestors in the 1830s.

At the beginning of June 1831, Warren James distributed notices to be pinned to trees throughout the area. These notices announced a meeting of the free miners of the locality 'for the purpose of opening the forest, and their right of common to the same'.[2] Despite the rudimentary nature of his call to action, he received overwhelming support for removing enclosures which had transformed the local landscape. As this chapter demonstrates, James was able to draw his authority from deep-seated cultural memories, drawing on the locally metonymic phrase 'open the Forest' as a representative of the free-mining community. Dean's free miners had claimed customary rights since 'time out of mind of man' which had permitted them to sink pits anywhere within the Hundred of St Briavels, the boundaries of which were roughly coterminous with the extent of the forest's mineral reserves, particularly coal. The free miners were dependent not only upon rights to mineral resources, but also upon many of the same customary rights to pannage, estovers, and grazing as the rest of the Forest commonalty. Defence of their rights, therefore, meant the defence of practices and an 'open' Forest which sustained many poorer inhabitants in Dean.

Although estimates of the numbers involved in the disturbances may be hyperbolic, fears expressed in a letter from concerned magistrates to the Home Office suggest that up to 3000 people were eventually recruited to

Warren James' project. Shortly after the disturbances, in 1838, Dean's free miners were required to register their occupational status in the written records of the Deputy Gaveller. By the end of November 1839, 827 miners had been recorded which suggests that Warren James' call to action had exercised influence far beyond those directly employed in the industry.

The customary law which underwrote the free-mining industry and, by extension, wider commoning traditions in the Forest of Dean was regulated through the Mine Law Court. The written collection of records and decrees, known locally as the 'Book of Denis', upon which miners' legal defence had come to rest was apparently stolen in 1775 and the court was subsequently discontinued. As described, the Commission conducted in the wake of the Warren James 'riot', which gathered testimony from those connected with the free-mining industry, suggests that memories of the loss of the Mine Law Court evoked feelings of vulnerability to outside interests and the forces of a market economy. Regarding the discontinuance of the court, the miners claimed:

> That the foreigners finding the Mine Law Courts an insuperable obstacle to their success, and more particularly that by the orders last quoted of 1775, there was no chance for their being permitted to work in the mines, found that the only means by which they could hope for success was to destroy the Mine Law Courts.
>
> That the documents of this court were always kept in the Speech House in the Forest of Dean, but that after the conclusion of the last court in 1775 some person or persons broke open the chest in which they were contained and removed them.
>
> That the free miners from that period to the present have made repeated applications to the wardens and the gavellers respecting these orders and documents, but that the wardens and gavellers, while they declared that they could not hold the Mine Law Courts as usual without these documents, at the same time denied all knowledge of their existence.[3]

It seems sensible to concur with many of those questioned in the 1832 Commission when they suggested that the loss of the Mine Law Court, 47 years previously, had rendered the forest and its resources increasingly vulnerable to the encroachments of 'foreigners' and private interest. The general reply of the free miners to the 'Honourable Commissioners of Inquiry' forcefully made the point that 'the Mine Law Courts were in active working during a period of time beginning far beyond the memory of man and extending down to the year 1775, during which their rules and regulations, under the sanction and authority of the Crown, strictly checked and prevented all intrusion into the mines by foreigners'.[4] The sentiments of many among the community were reflected in the testimony of John Worgan, a 57-year-old free miner of Five Acres within the Forest of Dean. He suggested that 'free miners are imposed upon very much by foreigners', adding that he, himself, was 'turned away to make room for a Bristol man, and we cannot remedy ourselves, unless our Mine Law Courts be revived'.[5]

The cultural and occupational orientation of Warren James and the community of free miners made them particularly suitable agents for the organisation and articulation of collective grievances of propertyless inhabitants, many of whom were dependent on rights to common in the forest. At the same time, the feelings of vulnerability were clearly focused on the loss of the Mine Law Court in 1775, a generation earlier. This chapter explores the relationship between the free-mining community, their court, and the wider Forest commonalty with a view to understanding why this loss was still so keenly felt in 1832.

Mining industries have long preoccupied historians of industrialisation. Extant documentation of the early coal-mining industries has encouraged examination of both innovation in extraction processes, and the role of large-scale capital investment in funding development and expansion.[6] More recently, historians of the early modern period have demonstrated a concern, not solely with the history of industrial development, but also with ways in which this intensification affected the social structures and cultures of mining communities.[7] Anthropologists and sociologists have made significant contributions to understanding the types of community and belief systems engendered by the specific conditions that characterise mining operations.[8] Martin Bulmer explains that 'settlements based on coal-mining' are widely regarded as being strong in 'community feeling', 'community solidarity', 'community spirit', or in having 'a sense of community'.[9] Suggesting that 'the location of mineral deposits in inaccessible areas gives rise to relatively self-contained communities', Richard Godoy neatly summarises anthropological and sociological contributions:

> a combination of low wages, coercive organisation, dangerous but autonomous working conditions, the economic leverage of miners flowing from the importance of mining exports to the health of the national economy, and the physical and social isolation of many mining enclaves underwrites the formation of intense forms of worker solidarity and radical labour movements as well as the growth of new forms of political consciousness.[10]

Godoy discusses radical movements in modern mining cultures but, while Dean's free miners were not subject to the same pressures of coercion, many of the characteristics that he describes do reflect their conditions during the late sixteenth and seventeenth centuries. He notes that 'mining communities tend to integrate surrounding regions into a single economic sphere', an observation which illuminates the miners' centrality to popular senses of this region during the early modern period.[11] Mining and its related industries were integral to the Forest as an economic unit. Propertied and propertyless, rich and poor, 'ancient' inhabitants and recent migrants were all dependent in many ways on the activities of the mining community.[12]

This chapter argues that, in addition to their economic influence, this occupational group had long been integral to resisting encroachment upon local and 'ancient' rights to resources in the Forest. The following section outlines the nature of the protests that clearly were remembered by the Forest community in 1832, while the third considers the social, cultural and political dynamics of the Mine Law Court itself and the way that this institution came to embody resistance to external encroachment in the minds of many in the nineteenth-century Forest of Dean.

Free Miners and Protest in the Early Seventeenth Century

On his accession to the throne in 1603, James I inherited severe fiscal difficulties from the regime of his predecessor. As part of an early Jacobean drive to tighten the use of royal demesne lands, many foresters were made to feel increasingly insecure over their common rights. Post-Conquest forest law had been upheld by the Justices in Eyre, a triennial circuit made by royal courts. Since the decline of these sessions in the fourteenth century, royal forests were increasingly managed through an array of swanimotes and local courts which operated under the influence of local gentry. Peter Large concludes that 'the progressive weakening of the Crown's administrative hold during the sixteenth century had effectively handed over the control of many royal forests to their inhabitants'.[13] Many legal records from Dean reflect this shift away from the protection of Crown interests by the first half of the seventeenth century.[14]

From the perspective of the Jacobean government, this relative autonomy had allowed rent on Crown estates to remain at lower and outdated levels, avoiding the vast upheavals in land ownership and inflationary growth of the sixteenth century. Richard Hoyle warns against simplistic readings of the efficacy of Elizabethan land sales, arguing that these make 'no allowance for inflation; in real terms the value of the estates was progressively reduced'.[15] In May 1602, Lord Treasurer Buckhurst had implored that 'it was fittest to have peace with Spain before we be too far spent, for he [Spain] hath a spring that yieldeth continual supply, his Indies, & we are like a standing water, which war will exhaust & make dry & barren'.[16] The economic situation was evidently becoming very alarming and James I's administration was left with the task of attempting to squeeze more income from lands which had effectively had the terms of their tenure frozen by the Elizabethan government. Uninterrupted use had 'anciently' justified customary access to forest resources, but now attention turned to undermining this security of tenure. Many private men of no particular qualification were recruited to carry out searches of 'concealments' which, generally, consisted of land that had been assarted from royal forest without disclosure. In 1613, John Sallens of Blakeney informed the Court of the Exchequer that he had been 'lawfullie seised in his demeasne... time out of mind' and thus had rights to common in the forest.[17] These usages were in dispute following a royal grant of forest resources made to William Herbert, the third Earl of Pembroke, a prominent figure in this episode. Despite protestations to the contrary, Otho Nicholson claimed that these lands had been assarted but Sallens and his co-plaintiffs still submitted 'themselves & theire estate to his mercy'. Nicholson, the most notorious of these searchers, had apparently promised 'the said Inhabitants that compounded' that they would not lose 'theire Commons, estovers, botes profits or commoddities within the said Forrest'.[18] The quest to uncover defective titles clearly promoted uncertainty. The authority of these searchers was often questionable and regularly in conflict with the interests of other private men. For complex and often-contradictory reasons, these areas were increasingly subject to the scrutiny of the Crown and private speculators at the beginning of the seventeenth century.

The seventeenth century, then, witnessed a two-pronged assault on Dean's customary traditions from both changing Crown policies and novel opportunities for private projectors, several of whom were members of the local gentry. As suggested above, these encroachments not only impeded the exercise of mining custom, but also disrupted common rights to grazing and fuel. As foresters, the miners were as dependent on access to these resources as their right to mine for coal and ore. Two of them, Christopher Bond and Thomas Worgan, were arrested following the 1612 disturbances, which are discussed below. As they languished in the Gatehouse jail in Westminster, their plea for an expeditious hearing centred on concerns that 'their harvest & other affairs were lying all to losse & spoile for want of their libertie'.[19] This reliance, and their symbolic position within the Forest commonalty, it is argued, foreshadows their heavy involvement in organising resistance to the enclosure and privatisation of forest wastes.

The early-seventeenth-century assault on custom and consequent insecurity over long-established rights, then, forms the backdrop to the Earl of Pembroke's royal grant in 1611. Under the terms of his grant, Pembroke was allowed 12,000 cords of wood and £33.6 s.8d. per annum towards enclosing this area for 22 years. Nobody was to take ore, coal, wood, timber or cinders from the Forest without the earl's permission.[20] This encroached upon local custom at all levels of the social scale and, quite predictably, generated considerable tensions in Dean. In 1612, the Earl of Northampton, as lord lieutenant of Gloucestershire, reported the disorder caused by Pembroke's grant. This mining and cutting, he said, had caused 'some fifteen desperate knaves' to set fire to piles of cordwood, after which they danced around the fire crying 'God save the King'.[21] He explained that:

> they still walk the wood with weapons and oft I hear weak shot; they call their neighbours cowards for not assisting them; they give out that they look for more help; the Justice has given order for their apprehension but the country favour them.[22]

Northampton stressed the benefits of local gentry regaining control from the 'odious' Pembroke. These forest residents, he suggested, were more capable of tempering the 'wild humores of those Robin Hoodes'.[23]

Roger Manning and Cyril Hart agree that these 'Robin Hoodes' were probably members of the free-mining community.[24] As mentioned, two of those arrested for these disturbances, Christopher Bond and Thomas Worgan, were certainly free miners. An Exchequer suit of 1613–14 lends further credence to this interpretation by confirming antagonism between free miners and the recipients of royal grants. An order issued by the court in January 1613 had dealt a potentially devastating blow to the mining community, confirming their custom only 'of charity and grace, and not of right'.[25] The Earl of Pembroke's complaint suggests that the miners' immediate reaction was to continue working. He was aggrieved that the miners had 'by pretence of title of common and of Estovers in the said

Forrest' and directly against the terms of his grant, 'taken libertie to themselves to cut down, waste and spoil his Maiesties wood... at their wills and pleasures'. Worse still, according to Pembroke, they had 'wrongfully entered the said Forrest' and 'unlawfully... digged and gotten great store of iron mynes, ore and sinders'. He suggested that iron and coal had been 'taken and carried to the rivers of Severn and Wye to be transported into the realm of Ireland and to divers ironworks and other places without the licence or consent of your Suppliant and against his will'.[26]

The miners replied with a comprehensive account of their ancient rights which, they asserted, had 'been allowed unto them... by all the time whereof the memory of man is not to the contrary' and had also 'been allowed before the Justice in Eyre and also at the Courts of Justice holden in King Edward the Thirds tyme before the Constable of the said Forrest and Steward of the Castle of St Brevells'. In a more immediate defence, they countered accusations that they had been evading the terms of the grant to sell their product in Ireland, explaining that they 'would starve if they were to rely on the custom of Pembroke's works'. These free miners claimed that they were:

> able by their labours to get sufficient iron ore and myne for the complainants works within half a year which the complainants forges and mills will hardly spende and work out within one year after as the other half year your defendants and the rest of the mynors shall be voyde of worke and thereby have not means to maintain themselves and their charges.[27]

Pembroke's royal grant caused considerable disruption to Dean's traditional customary practices. The 'timeless' custom which had allowed miners to seek coal and ore in different parts of the royal demesne lands was incompatible with the earl's attempts to control mining and the flow of trade in and out of the forest. The occupational flexibility and independence which had apparently been theirs for centuries was stifled by Pembroke's directives. This was not only a concern in respect of their occupation, the miners pleaded, but their families and dependants were also endangered. The grant thus had a social as well as an economic impact, as its implications extended into households and domestic contexts which points to the symbolic resonance of the free-mining community as a focus for resisting encroachment, not only on mining rights, but also on the broader web of customary perquisites which sustained many amongst the Forest commonalty.

A further controversial royal grant of Dean's mineral resources, this time to Sir Edward Villiers in 1625, set in motion a far larger series of physical protests which culminated in the Skimmington riots of 1631. These riots serve as another reminder that ideological opposition to 'improvement' and privatisation of the wastes and external encroachment was very much cemented in the material conditions of Forest life.[28] Dean supported many employment opportunities related to the coal and iron industries. The 1608 survey of Able and Sufficient Men in the Forest lists miners, colliers, oresmiths, apprentices, nailers, cutlers and pinners as well as many other occupations derived from exploitation of the Forest's wood and timber.[29] This activity was recorded throughout Ruardean in related place names such as 'Turner's Tump', 'Cinder Hill', 'Nailbridge', 'Smith's Way' and 'The Pludds'.[30] Thirsk warns against regarding such industrial occupations as by-employment, arguing that 'they were not accidental or subsidiary, secondary or a miserable makeshift. They were an integral part of the pastoral way of life.'[31] It would appear that the large numbers of poorer inhabitants in the Forest did not represent a group which had been entirely alienated from their means of production. These areas could sustain large communities of poorer, landless inhabitants through trades and occupations which did not entail direct subordination to wealthier employers. Records also imply relatively free access to pasture on Dean's commons and wastes, conditions which indicate a relatively autonomous and assertive commonalty. Furthermore, these groups, alongside the miners, depended upon common access to 'open' forest and the various resources which, protesters claimed, had been regarded as collective property since 'time out of mind'. Again, as had been the case in 1612, it was this 'open' forest that was under threat by the royal grants to Sir Edward Villiers in 1625.

At 10 a.m. on the morning of 25 March 1631, Villiers' agent, Robert Bridges, sat at home with his family in Bicknor, an industrial village towards the north-east of the Forest of Dean. He described how their house was marched upon by a group of inhabitants from their village and from Stanton, Newland and Coleford. The band numbered at least 500 and 'did march with two Drummes two Coulers and one Fife and in a warlike and outragious manner did assemble themselves together Armed with gunnes, pykes, halberds and other weapons'.[32] After threatening to 'pull downe Bridges' howse', they 'went into the ground called Mailescott, and there did extreamly beate certain Colliers being in the said Grounds and one other person being a Strainger'.[33]

The context of this disturbance tells us much about the dynamics of community in the Forest and the role of the free miners as a focus for these relations. As mentioned, Bridges was an agent of the Villiers family, favourites of the Caroline court who, in 1625, had been granted mineral rights in Mailescott Woods, an area of Dean adjoining Bicknor. Disregarding 'timeless' Forest custom, this royal grant aroused great anger. Under the terms of the 1625 grant, Villiers gained 500 acres known as Mailescott Woods in the Forest of Dean 'for good services done'.[34] The grant of Forest resources to an outsider would have been an unpopular proposition in any situation, as was evident from the disturbances that followed Pembroke's grant. Yet Villiers' grant was particularly inflammatory. Not only was it made to an outsider to be 'held as of his Mannor of Eastgreenewiche'[35] in Kent but, upon the death of Sir Edward, the land fell under the administration of Sir Giles Mompesson who was acting on behalf of Lady Barbara Villiers. Mompesson was a projector who had 'acquired a very evil reputation' through what his adversaries described as his 'reckless audacity'.[36] He appears to have wasted no time in enclosing the land at Mailescott and setting men to work in digging or sinking coal pits.

An Exchequer decree of 1628 further granted quiet possession of Mailescott to Lady Villiers and had, significantly, distinguished formal rights related to property tenure from the less formal custom of the propertyless.[37] Privileging exclusive ownership attached to the enclosure of common land, this decree hardened lines of division between private interest and common right in the Forest. A large proportion of this community stood to lose essential resources if the 'open' forest were to be enclosed. Once again, evidence implies that resistance to this privatization was led by free miners.

In direct violation of the 1628 decree, and exercising Forest custom, a number of inhabitants continued to mine and to pasture cattle on this land. Buchanan Sharp notes that at their prosecution:

> all of the defendants, as inhabitants of the hundred of St Briavels, asserted that they had the right to common of pasture *and the right to mine in the wastes of the forest*... [stating] flatly in their answer to the Attorney General that they would not be bound by an Exchequer decree that recognised *the right of the King and his grantees* to enclose Mailescott and other lands in Dean.[38]

Mailescott and other lands named in the 1628 decree had their enclosures destroyed during protests associated with the loss of mining rights in this part of the Forest. Before the enclosures could proceed, Lady Villiers had to make one concession – to 'permit the mining of iron ore in Mailescott Woods as freely as before the decree of 1628'. This concession did not bring these disturbances to a close, but it seems that once the miners' demands had been satisfied only minor riots persisted.[39] This bears two interpretations; either anger at the enclosures had dissipated or, more likely, the mining community had been the organisational focus of larger-scale resistance. The larger-scale incident at Bridges' house is significant in this context. Among the marching group was John Williams, who was also known as the mysterious Skymington, an alias that, as will become clear, appears to have held great regional significance. His occupation was recorded as 'labourer', a description which was interchangeable locally with the term miner.

During March and April 1631 in Dean, enclosed lands were thrown open by large numbers of rioting commoners led by John Williams. In 1612, the Forest's 'Robin Hoods' had been careful to accompany their 'disorderly' actions with shouts of 'God Save the King', thus aligning themselves with the best interests of the Jacobean commonwealth. In 1631, the direct interests of the Crown, together with those of local landowners and industrialists, were generally avoided, which further suggests efforts to maintain the legitimacy of these actions.

The level of support for those involved in the 1631 disturbances was clearly demonstrated by fierce animosity borne towards those responsible for Williams' arrest. Williams was 'finally captured sometime in March of 1632 by William Cowse, one of the King's forest officers'.[40] On Sunday 8 April, both Cowse and his accomplice, William Rolles, were leaving church in Newland when they were assaulted by a large group of parishioners. During this affray, both pistols belonging to Cowse and his contingent were discharged. Three Justices of the Peace, Sir Richard Catchmay, Sir Robert Cooke knight and Charles Bridgeman esquire, professed that:

> Wee coulde by no means discover what was the first occasion of the Affraye, whether the under sorte of people were provoked by seeing those twoe persons in the Company of Mr Rolls & Mr Cowse whoe had done the good service of apprahending him whome they commonly called Skymington, or that they were provoked by these wordes uttered by Mr Rolls cominge out of Church (where are the Hawkins-es the Ryoters).[41]

These Justices were unsure whether the anger of parishioners had been provoked merely by the presence of Williams' captors or by the fact that they had attended church in hope of apprehending more suspects as they worshipped. Whatever the precise catalyst, the arrest of Williams was evidently a deeply unpopular act. Cowles and Rolles implicitly acknowledged this, arriving at church prepared to defend themselves against the parishioners of Newland. According to the local JPs, these parishioners had simply 'repayred to Church in an orderly manner to heare devine service without any expectacion of meeting as is Conceived with Mr Rolls Mr Cowse & the rest of their Companye'.[42]

The anger in this parish suggests a keenly felt sense of collective interest in this forest community. The difficulty encountered by forest authorities also points to the neighbourly relations that informed the moral economy of Dean, certainly when this way of life seemed to be threatened.[43] In November 1631, the sheriff of Gloucestershire wrote to the Attorney General, describing problems entailed in recruiting the local population to his searches for 'John Williams called by the name of Skymington'.[44] The opening passage of the sheriff's account is worth quoting at length. Upon receiving a warrant from local Justices:

> to apprehend some of the late Riotors in the Forrest of Deane wheruppon my undershereife with 120tie men by me provided, passed over the River of Sevearne late in the night with an Intent to take the said offendrs, and for that purpose watching all night, repaired (before the breake of the day) towards the howse of one John Williams called by the name of Skymington, thinkinge to have caught him in his bedd, But beinge discovered by some of the Inhabitants of that place, they only apprehended two of the offendors, and soe retired for that tyme, which with a woman brought in at the next Sessions, was all the Service could be done upon that warrant.[45]

Neither the sheriff nor his men were comfortable searching in this terrain. Faced with the opaque nature of this region, the sheriff noted that due to its landscape of 'hills, woods myne pitts and colepitts where they dwell the apprehending of them becomes very difficult and must be effected only by policy and never by strength'. Until the efforts of Cowle and Rolls bore fruit a few months later, it seems that this policy had been unsuccessful. The sheriff ordered a 'Callinge together of the Trained bondes of the Forrest' in the hope that he could arrest those suspects known to be trained soldiers. He also tried to entice Williams' neighbours with the promise of a large reward, but the foresters were reluctant to betray the leaders of these riots, often tipping them off in advance of his searches. The sheriff complained that he had searched from 'place to place that day, parte of that night, and the next day where the Riotors dwell', but upon arriving at their respective homes he had been informed that they had fled into Herefordshire and Monmouthshire.[46]

Returning to the main disturbances themselves, the symbolism invoked by the 'rioters' suggests much about solidarities and conflicts within this forest community. As rioters attempted to pull down the fences erected by Mompesson, they acted 'by sound of drum and ensigns in most rebellious manner, carrying a picture or statue apparelled like Mompesson and with great noise and clamour threw it into the coalpits that the said Sir Giles had digged'.[47] Given the nature of these disturbances, it is no surprise that the leader or leaders were commonly referred to as 'John' or 'Lady Skymington'. This action was, it seems, framed in the idiom of popular shaming rituals.[48] David Underdown notes that a skimmington was also 'a ritual action against the chosen target: to "ride skimmington" was to take part in a demonstration against the skimmington in the pejorative sense'. Like the folk hero Robin Hood, however, the name skimmington had a variety of meanings within early modern popular culture. It could refer to the target of a shaming ritual, the act itself or, as in the case of Dean, to the leadership of a protest. This ambivalence allowed separate risings to subsume themselves as part of a wider and more general action and, importantly, it obscured identities. The rioters in Dean, it seems, were riding Skimmington against the particular interests of the Villiers family. Invoking customary social roles, the Skimmington rioters foregrounded a hierarchy of use rights that had been jeopardised by the 'improvement' of the forest. In this hierarchy, different social groups had always occupied different rungs but they were, at least, on the same ladder. As the 1628 decree concerning Mailescott drew a distinction between informal usages and private property rights, so too did it drive a wedge through this sylvan culture. The skimmington seems to have been an appropriate response to this violation of Forest custom just as the mining operations and miners themselves were a particularly apposite focus of organisation that underpinned this resistance.

Free Miners, Popular Litigation, and the Mine Law Court

In his work on collective cognition, Paul Dimaggio considers the relation between institutions and the capacity for agency, thereby shedding light on the role of the Mine Law Court in coalescing action in the interests of the broader Forest community. 'Culture is fragmented among potentially inconsistent elements', he suggests, describing how this limited coherence can inhibit collective activity. Dimaggio claims that the capacity for agency of any given community or social group is, to a large degree, dependent on the 'thematization of clusters of rituals and schemata around institutions'.[49] He thus outlines a functional aspect of institutions in generating interpretive schema which allow for a broad coherence of meaning and, thereby, the motivation for action in a collective context. He describes these 'institutional logics' as 'sets of "material practices and symbolic constructions" which constitute "organising principles" and are "available to organisations and individuals to elaborate"'. DiMaggio adopts Friedland and Alford's taxonomy of institutional practices, including those of capitalism, the state, democracy, family, religion and science, noting that 'each entails a distinctive logic'.[50] Friedland and Alford suggest that these institutional logics are 'symbolically grounded, organizationally structured, politically defined and technically and materially constrained'.[51] In the Forest during this period, it seems that the institutional logic of action pertaining to nascent capitalism and the state, both of which shared many features, were incompatible with that of the free-mining community and their court. In contrast to the abstracted axioms, linked routines and rituals of these external institutions, the logic and symbolic constructions of the Mine Law Court were embedded in popular life within the Forest, as demonstrated by the rituals and symbolism of the Skymington riots.

In this generalised sense, the Mine Law Court offered a coherent expression of interest for Dean's commonalty whose lives and subsistence strategies depended on the preservation of 'open' Forest and an oral legal culture which underwrote the impenetrability of local industry and direct access to local resources. This was clearly inimical to the logics of external capital interest, which were defined by privatisation, the certainty of the written legal record, and a preference for an increasingly proletarianised and, thus, mobile labour force. The following section explores the ways in which the Mine Law Court was partially transformed through an engagement with these interests, designed to preserve the customary and small-scale nature of the mining industry. In doing so, it is argued, the court was still able to retain its position in representing the institutional logics of both the free-mining community and the Forest commonalty.

From the late sixteenth century, equity litigation had been increasingly sought as an avenue of dispute resolution in the Forest. In many respects, this marked a shift away from the physical nature of testimony which had apparently characterised the legal culture in late medieval Dean. As I have argued elsewhere, these embodied methods of determining local customary rights drew on a mnemonically inscribed landscape, the demonstration of uninterrupted and continuous practice and the spoken testimony of older, predominantly male, foresters.[52] Extant documentation of the late Elizabethan Exchequer court, however, reveals significant continuities between the central written record and traditional legal practice. Rather than demonstrating the supercession of orality by more formal documentation, these records reveal the complex interplay of spoken and written evidence as the testimony of local inhabitants was captured in bills and depositions.

The most noticeable aspect of the depositions taken by commissioners for the Court of the Exchequer is the increasing numbers of cases being brought to this stage during the late sixteenth and early seventeenth centuries. Only two cases directly relating to the Forest of Dean were brought to deposition during the last two decades of Elizabeth's reign, compared with five during that of James I. Ten cases were addressed by commissions under Charles I and, following the turmoil of the 1640s, this legal avenue was quickly re-established as depositions were recorded for two cases; one in 1652 and the other in 1653. Six cases were tried between 1660 and 1683. A cursory analysis of these proceedings demonstrates that most of these actions, during the late sixteenth and seventeenth centuries, were brought by the Attorney General against local industrial gentry or resulted from disputes over competition for concessions to the region's material resources. An analysis of deponents supports Andy Wood's suggestion that the process through which more traditional methods of local dispute settlement such as the local court system, neighbourhood pressures or the physical petitioning of riot and other ritual demonstrations were displaced by an increasing recourse to equity courts could also result in a narrowing of the common voice of the 'countrey'.[53] In other words, as the legal processes and governing principles for this region gradually started to become external to the forest community, the voice of the poorest inhabitants of this region was no longer given the consideration that it had been when litigation had been more embedded in day-to-day activities.

Among the 59 deponents called upon during Elizabeth's reign, 45 were recorded as yeomen or husbandmen while 4 of the remaining 14 were miners. This group also contained two gentlemen. Those recorded during the reign of James I were taken from a very similar group, the majority of which were yeomen and husbandmen but also several miners and carpenters. By the time Charles I took the throne, the increasing business received by the Court of the Exchequer is plain to see, as is the greater variety of occupations listed for each deponent. This group was still composed, primarily, of those described as yeomen, husbandmen and gentlemen, but now included many in trades that might be considered artisanal, such as blacksmiths, dyers, joiners and carpenters. The mining community was also well represented amongst these deponents and, in fact, constituted 4 out of the 13 questioned during the 1650s. Between 1660 and 1680, of the 40 deponents traceable from the 1672 hearth tax returns for Gloucestershire, only 14 were rated on one hearth while none of those traceable appeared on the lists of exclusions on grounds of poverty. While these deponents were evidently still being chosen for their relevance to the case, it seems that the testimony of the poorest inhabitants was not sought by the commissioners. The most important exception to this narrowing of participation was the mining community which still remained vocal in this respect. Their engagement with this central court, however, while aiming to preserve Dean's industrial and occupational traditions, helped to render their operations and the practices of the wider forest community legible to outsiders.

The nature of the Mine Law Court records further emphasise further the increasing legibility of this region's industrial operations. By comparison with the paucity of information from previous centuries, increasing documentation gives the impression that this mining community steps into the light during the later seventeenth century. This was also the period during which Mine Law Court sessions became fixed permanently in one location. Until 1680, the Mine Law Court had no settled meeting place and had been held in different parts of St. Briavels Hundred. In 1625, Anthony Callowe had deposed that 'this court has been usually kept in some open place of the forest, for that there is no house or certain place appointed for the same', suggesting the court's more fluid engagement with the mining industry and the spatial relations which governed its operation.[54] While Townley has suggested that many sessions had been held at 'Hill Pytt' near Lydney, in 1656 the court was held at Littledean and it later convened at Clearwell, Coleford, Mitcheldean and Ruardean. In 1680, the court was held at the Speech House which became the fixed location until its discontinuance in 1775.

In his analysis of Ancient Law, Henry Maine observed that 'When primitive law has once been embodied in a Code, there is an end to what may be called its spontaneous development. Henceforward the changes effected in it, if effected at all, are effected deliberately and from without'.[55] From Maine's comments, Jack Goody concludes that 'after the code comes into existence, "legal modification" can be attributed to the "conscious desire for improvement"'.[56] These observations are pertinent to perceptions of mining custom following the civil wars of the 1640s and the Protectorate of the 1650s. Records of the Mine Law Court from February 1676 reflect this process of conscious 'improvement'. These records appear to reflect and emulate the codification and written preservation of the equity court to which the free miners had resorted with the aim of preserving their occupational custom. It is recorded that:

> Att this Court 12 out of the 48 Jurymen whose names are undernamed have been elected and chosen to consider of such Orders as have heretofore been made for the better ordering and management of the concerns of the Myners, and to consider which of them are fit to be made void and revoked and what Orders are fit to be continued and remain.[57]

The paucity of Mine Law Courts records from before 1656 makes it impossible to be certain regarding many changes or continuities in operations other than the court's increasing tendency towards documentation and its fixed location. It does seem, however, that the impact of writing would have been deeper than the mere recording of information. This shift would surely have been qualitative as well as quantitative. The 'conscious desire for improvement' outlined by Goody implies an analogy between the rationalisation of land management use and the codification of legal practices current in the Forest. This was particularly true of those governing extractive industries. That both imply a shift from legitimation grounded firmly in the material past to a more abstracted and self-reflexive worldview that oriented itself towards future 'progress' suggests a change in the way that the free miners were beginning to understand themselves. This change can be attributed not only to external pressure but also to an increasing engagement with the written record. As has been suggested, the miners appear to have adopted the written record in an attempt to preserve the traditional protectionism of their small-scale industry.

The 'Order made 18th of March 1668' which had prohibited any 'Foreigner living out of this hundred' from transporting or carrying coal 'contrary to our custom' also placed a check on the potential manipulation of iron-ore prices by making all bargaining the responsibility of 'six men (being free myners) chosen by the Company of Myners'. The same order stipulated that:

> No one of the said six men shall hereafter make any bargaine for any Iron myne without it be with the consent of the said six Bargainers or the major parte of them notwithstanding the Company of Miners (if they find just cause) with mutuall consent may alter or change the said Bargainers at their wills and pleasures.

This document also restricted the amount of coal that could be transported by each free miner to that which could be carried by 'four Horses Mares or Mare foals'.[58]

This documentation, generated in an attempt to protect customary mining rights, then, rendered the operations of the industry more legible to outside parties. It was not only the central equity courts and the written record that increased the vulnerability of the trade. In the eyes of some, external investment was deemed necessary to finance expensive machinery which could reach coal seams that had previously been beyond traditional small-scale customary mining operations. Increasingly sophisticated drainage equipment was brought into use within the Forest during the later seventeenth century and, notes A. R. J. Jurica, 'much mining was on a larger scale than had been permitted by ancient custom'.[59] Mine Law Court orders were evidently aimed at restricting the scale of these operations and preventing the apparent inward flow of those seeking to earn a living from this region's increasingly lucrative industries. These orders reveal various pressures on the miners to account for local needs while attempting to maintain the smaller scale of their traditional trade. An order of 1668 confirmed their exclusive privilege of supplying iron ore and coal outside of St Briavels Hundred. This, however, was rescinded in 1674 as it was imposing on the interests of several powerful parties, including the constable of the hundred in front of whom, of course, the Mine Law Court was held. By 1687, the situation had again reached crisis point as it was noted that the increased demand for coal was depriving local residents of adequate supplies.[60]

Even while the local mining industry reacted, as a whole, to the potential for profit through an increased demand, the court was still concerned not to alienate other residents who constituted the wider Forest community of which they were a part. In 1687 the court ordered:

> That all ordinances and orders made since the happy Restoration of his late Majesty King Charles the second of ever blessed memory that doe anyway relate unto the settling of rates and prizes of Oare and Lime coal to any the furnace or other place whatsoever or that doe nominate and appoint Bargainers for the same be from henceforth totally repealed and made void and of none effect to all intents and purposes as if the same had never been made and that all miners be left at liberty to sell carry and deliver their Oare and coale to whom where and at what reates and prizes they can best agree for without incurring any penalty or forfeiture for so doing.[61]

In rescinding its previous ordinances the court also ordered that the residents of the Forest were to be loaded before colliers as:

> complaint hath been made that the Inhabitants of the Hundred of Saint Briavells cannot have their Horses and other Carriages laden with fire Coale for their owne private uses at the several Cole Pitts within the same Hundred until the Collyers belonging to the said Pitts have first laden their owne horses with Coal to transport and carry the same out of the said Hundred whereby the Horses and other Carriages of the said Inhabitants are many times forced to stay at the said Pitts all day and sometimes to come home again unladen to the great prejudice of the said Inhabitants.[62]

The mining community thus demonstrated their concern to compensate for the loss of local protectionism. The court was keen to adopt innovatory practices, keeping pace with commercial opportunities offered by the national market for coal, but was also careful to minimise impact on the local community within which they lived and worked. As sessions and orders become more thoroughly documented, a clear picture emerges of the Mine Law Court's pivotal position in negotiating the conflicting pressures of the local and national coal trades.

As it attempted to retrench its hold on the regulation of the mining industry while still accounting for a necessarily increasing labour force, the court explicitly recorded and implicitly legitimated many instances which appeared to contradict the customary ideal of this small-scale operation. While primarily intended to secure the miners' own capacity for self-definition, these acknowledgements could substantially undermine perceptions of these rights as the prerogative of those born into the occupation with Dean. At the same time as the order of 1668 declared that 'noe younge man shall or may hereafter worke att myne or Coale (although he be borne within this hundred) if he hath not worked lawfully twelve months and one day', it also conceded that exception could be made if 'he be bound apprentize unto a Free Myner and lawfully serve him as an apprentize for the tearme of five years under the pennalty as in the former article expressed'. This penalty had been set at the rate of 'one hundred dozen of good sufficient oare or coale the one halfe to be forfeited to the Kings Maiestie and the other halfe to the myner who shall sue for the same'.[63]

Tightening the definition of those eligible to mine, the court evidently needed to allow additional workers necessitated by the growth of the industry. This, once again, weakened the literal interpretation that this occupation was open only to those born within St Briavels Hundred as the son of a free miner. In a somewhat radical departure from traditional mining custom, migrants that had been the source of so much concern or those who had simply not been born into the trade were allowed access provided that they fulfilled certain criteria. At this session in 1668, the court decreed that:

> noe person whatever that was borne upon the waste soile of the Forest as a Cabenner shall work at Myne or Coale or shall or may transport or carry the same with any manner of carriage except he hath lawfully worked for the space of seaven yeares already under the penallty as aforesaid.[64]

This stipulation was evidently insufficient as other Mine Law Court orders went further in defining and formalising this process of apprenticeship. In April 1680, it was explained that this court:

> for the better reforming and preventing of the inconveniences hapning amongst the said Myners by the many young men and boys that contrary to former usage have of late tymes set up for themselves to worke at and carry Myne and Cole not renting Land and keeping house as by the custome they ought Doe now order and ordayne That noe person shal bee reputed or taken to be a free Myner within the precincts thereof or shall keep horses for carrying any Oare or cole untill every such person shall have lawfully served in the art or mistery of Myning by the space of five years as an Apprentice to bee bound by Indenture to his father (being a free Myner) or to some other person that is a free Myner and shall attain to and bee of the full age of one and twenty years.[65]

Restricting encroachment, the Mine Law Court simultaneously opened a legitimate channel through which those not born in to the trade could attain the right to sink pits within those areas of the forest not subject to the rotational enclosure ratified by the Dean Reafforestation Act of 1668.

While miners accepted that outsiders were necessary within this context of expansion, they also understood the importance of maintaining control of those entering the trade. Increased regulation and written prescription helped to restrict entry, but the 'ancient' and quasi-familial structure of this group helped to perpetuate inner coherence during a time of considerable change. Entry was to be gained only under the extensive supervision of existing miners while seventeenth- and eighteenth-century Mine Law Court proceedings demonstrate that grievances were often argued, not between individual miners, but between a miner '& his verns', a term which had long been used to connote the sense of brotherhood or fraternity from which this community derived its fiercely resistant collective identity. Both this self-reflexive process of assimilation and the construction of a popular corporate identity were crucial to the 'butty system' which predominated in the face of large externally-funded mining operations of the eighteenth century.[66] Despite a tendency towards the reification and abstraction of regulatory codes, this system remained integral to the capacity for self-organisation through which Dean's miners were able to resist proletarianisation to a greater degree than workers in many other industries during this period. This resistance was clearly also aided by the idiosyncracy of this environment and the nuanced sense of place that was central to successful mining operations.

Mine Law Court records also suggest that the reification of occupational identity generated tension between traditional practices and the more formal nature of this trade as it developed during the eighteenth century. Increased documentation and written recollections of past activity apparently expunged many ambivalences and ambiguities which had been a characteristically functional element of the industry since the twelfth or thirteenth centuries. In February 1676, William Adams complained to the court that George Lodge had been 'following two professions and callings, a Myner and Collyer and a quarryman contrary to our Law and Custom'. Lodge answered that, yes, he had followed 'sometimes one Calling and sometimes the other calling as other men do and is not contrary to the Custome'.[67] By 1719, it was evidently deemed necessary, not simply to be known as a miner by others within the community, but for this status to be recorded in official court proceedings. This was the case with John Goding of English Bicknor who, it was recorded at the session held on Tuesday 13 May 1719, prayed:

> leve to prove himself a free Miner which was graunted him and upon the oath of one Witnese and his owne who both swore that he had Lawfully wrought a Yeare and a day at Cole. And thereupon he was adjudged a Free Miner as any other in the Forest of Deane.

George Churcham of Stanton was similarly confirmed as a free miner of Dean during this session.[68]

The list of those fined two shillings for etiquette of procedural breaches during the court session of 13 May highlights the visible nature of the mining community and the relatively formal nature of legal proceedings by the early part of the eighteenth century. We are told that three people were fined for 'talking in Court', six for otherwise 'disturbing ye Court' whilst Richard

Goding and Edmund Symons were fined for not appearing to 'serve on ye Jury'.[69] The 1719 proceedings were significant in another, more profound sense that seems to be linked to the efforts of central government to make its presence more keenly felt in this industry. This session occurred during a period in which Gloucestershire Quarter Sessions were involved with a 1716 'enquiry into poor relief' in Dean and the payment of relief, in 1729, to poor pensioners of St Briavels Hundred who were sustained out of the county stock because there had been no local provision for them. In a context of increasing poor law hegemony, William James and Richard Machen were named as 'Deputies to the Right Honorable James Earle of Berkley', 'Lord Chiefe Steward of his Majesties Court Leetes Court of Pleas and of the Mine Law Courts within the said Forrest'.[70] The 1719 sessions, then, marked increasing central influence over the proceedings of this once fiercely autonomous occupational court. As early as 1694, the jury had agreed that they were to emulate the method and usage of other courts of law. In 1754, this jury took the apparently unprecedented step of admitting more than twenty free miners into their trade in one session. Many of these newly constituted free miners were either from outside Gloucestershire or from outside the traditional free-mining community. Among them were the Right Honorable George Augustus Lord Dursley, Charles Wyndham of Clearwell Esq., Reverend Reynor Jones of Monmouth, Kedgwin Hoskins the elder of Clearwell, William Probyn of Newland, and Kedgwyn Webley of London, the latter three being described as gentlemen.[71] Christopher Bond, a prominent member of a local gentry family, had already been confirmed as a miner in 1737.[72] It appears that during the course of the eighteenth century, the institutional logic of mining operations in the Forest were becoming more closely aligned with both the elite culture of the local industrial gentry and the equity courts of central government. Despite this, it is clear from the 1832 'Memorials' that the court was still viewed as a bulwark against the encroachment of external capital interests, the loss of which had left the Forest commonalty dangerously exposed.

Conclusion

The testimony gathered by commissioners following the Forest of Dean 'riots' in 1832 demonstrates the social force of popular memory in two important senses. In the first, miners and other foresters recalled memories of the Mine Law Court as a bulwark against external capitalist encroachment. In the second, it is clear that collective memory of the community acting in defence of Forest custom cemented their hegemonic position and underpinned the power of this court. As the Mine Law Court had grown from mediating disputes that related to the regulation of custom and competition over resources within this sylvan culture, its institutional logic bore many similarities to patterns of life and work in the Forest. The core stipulation governing entry to, and membership of, the free-mining community was that a miner was to have been born within the hundred of St Briavels, to have been the son of a miner, and to have worked in the mines for a year and a day. This legal perspective lent itself to preserving the localism and protectionism that lay at the heart, not only of this industry, but also of the customary traditions which had mediated access to Forest resources since a 'time out of mind of man'.

From the end of the seventeenth century, and into the eighteenth, the practices of the Mine Law Court underwent various shifts to take account of the increasing currency of written legal codes and the expanding labour force necessary for a growing industry. The court adapted itself to preserve the customary practices of the free-mining community, but continued to act in strictly regulating any encroachments on these traditions. While the Mine Law Court was operational, then, free miners still had control over their industry and, by extension, access to Forest resources more broadly. Underpinning the power of the court, besides its jurisdiction, were collective memories of the free miners and their traditional role in organising physical and legal resistance to encroachments on local custom. While ultimately, of course, it was the loss of written legal records – known as the 'Book of Dennis' – which caused the dissolution of the court, it was undoubtedly oral traditions and tales of the mining community which gave them such cultural significance within the Forest commonalty. They were remembered for organising resistance to the Earl of Pembroke's grant in 1612, for the leadership of John Williams a.k.a. 'Skimmington', in the disturbances of 1628–31, and for the litigation which sought to preserve Forest custom during the seventeenth and eighteenth centuries. When Warren James, as the son of a free miner, called upon Dean's commonalty to 'open the Forest' in 1832, he was drawing on a popular history of resistance focused on the mining community in whose name he acted.

Notes

1. TNA, (CL) Assizes 5/151 pt. 1.
2. TNA, (CL) Assizes 6/2 pt. 29.
3. Cyril Hart, *The Free Miners of the Royal Forest of Dean and Hundred of St. Briavels* (Newton Abbot: 1971), 299–303.

4. Hart, *Free Miners*, 294.
5. Hart, *Free Miners*, 270.
6. Cyril Hart, *The Industrial History of Dean; with an Introduction to its Industrial Archaeology* (David & Charles: 1971); John Langton, *Geographical Change and Industrial Revolution: Coalmining in South West Lancashire, 1590–1799* (Cambridge University Press: 1979); James A. Jaffe, *The Struggle for Market Power: Industrial Relations in the British Coal Industry, 1800–1840* (Cambridge University Press: 1991); Colin C. Owen, *The Leicestershire and South Derbyshire Coalfield 1200–1900* (Moorland: 1984); William Ashworth, Roy A. Church, Michael W. Flinn, John Hatcher and Barry Supple, *The History of the British Coal Industry* (Oxford University Press: 1984–7).
7. David Levine and Keith Wrightson, *The Making of an Industrial Society: Whickham 1560–1765* (Clarendon Press: 1991); Andy Wood, *The Politics of Social Conflict: The Peak Country, 1520–1770* (Cambridge University Press: 1999).
8. Clarke Kerr and Abraham Spiegel, 'The interindustry propensity to strike: An international comparison', in Arthur Kornhauser, Robin Dubin and Arthur Ross, *Industrial Conflict* (McGraw-Hill: 1954); Seymour Lipset, *Political Man: The Social Bases of Politics* (Doubleday & Company: 1963); Martin Bulmer, *Mining and Social Change* (Croom Helm: 1978); Ricardo Godoy, 'Mining: anthropological perspectives', *Annual Review of Anthropology*, Vol. 14 (1985); June Nash, *We Eat the Mines and the Mines Eat Us: Dependency and Exploitation in Bolivian Tin Mines* (Columbia University Press: 1979); Dennis Warwick and Gary Littlejohn, *Coal, Capital and Culture: A Sociological Analysis of Mining Communities in West Yorkshire* (Routledge: 1992); Bill Williamson, *Class, Culture and Community: A Biographical Study of Social Change in Mining* (Routledge: 1982); Martin Bulmer, 'Sociological models of the mining community', *The Sociological Review*, 23 (1975); Norman Dennis, Clifford Slaughter and Fernando Henriques, *Coal is Our Life* (Tavistock Publications: 1956).
9. Martin Bulmer, 'Social structure and change in the twentieth century', in Bulmer, *Mining*, 15.
10. Godoy, 'Mining', 207.
11. Ibid.
12. Cyril Hart, *Royal Forest: A History of Dean's Woods as Producers of Timber* (Clarendon Press: 1966); Cyril Hart, *The Free Miners of the Royal Forest of Dean and Hundred of St. Briavels* (Lightmoor Press: 1953); Buchanan Sharp, *In Contempt of All Authority: Rural Artisans and Riot in the West of England, 1586–1660* (Breviary Stuff: 1980); Chris Fisher, *Custom, Work and Market Capitalism: The Forest of Dean Colliers, 1788–1888* (Breviary Stuff: 1981).

13. Peter Large, 'From swanimote to disafforestation: Feckenham Forest in the early seventeenth century', in Richard W. Hoyle (ed.), *The Estates of the English Crown, 1558–1640* (Cambridge University Press: 1992), 389–417, 389.
14. Whilst the 'Speeche Courte held at Little Deane' on 20 July 1637, for instance, records only prosecutions for offences against the wood of the forest, Star Chamber cases such as that relating to yeoman 'Robert Yearesly of Highemeadows within the parish of Newland and divers others to the number of five persons at the least' for killing deer 'riotously', suggests that 'poaching' was becoming the responsibility of a centralised legal authority. This case also provides some idea of local tensions which could be behind the recourse to central courts in such prosecutions. It notes that Yearesly had attempted to undermine the local system by telling people that 'William Wyntour of Colford', 'Deputie Constable of your highness Forrest of Deane' and 'Judge of your maiesties courte of St Brevells' was biased and had showed favouritism in his judgements (TNA, E146/3/29, STAC8/304/4). For more examples of this shift, see TNA, STAC8/280/29 & STAC8/280/23; Roger B. Manning, *Village Revolts: Social Protest and Popular Disturbances in England, 1509–1640* (Clarendon Press: 1988).
15. Hoyle, *The Estates of the English Crown*, 12.
16. Roger Wilbraham, *The Journal of Sir Roger Wilbraham, Solicitor-General in Ireland and Lord of Requests, for the years 1593–1616*, 49–50, available at http://www.archive.org/stream/journalofsirroge00wilbrich. Accessed 28/1/2009.
17. There is a very heated and long-running debate in the Forest over whether there were ever rights to common rather than tolerated privileges. This has recently been resolved in favour of their definition as privileges. During the seventeenth century, however, this was demonstrably a matter of legal debate with many records claiming commoning and mining rights against those who contended that these were only allowed by grace. In this chapter, these uses will be referred to as rights because that properly reflects the language of the groups that form the core focus of this research.
18. TNA, E112/82/300.
19. TNA, SP 14/69 f. 32.
20. N. M. Herbert (ed.), *A History of the County of Gloucester: Volume V. Bledisloe Hundred, St Briavels Hundred, The Forest of Dean* (Oxford University Press: 1996), 363.
21. TNA, SP14/70/49.
22. By his use of the term 'country', I assume that Northampton referred to the local plebeian population.
23. TNA, SP14/70/49.
24. Manning, *Village Revolts*; Cyril Hart, *The Forest of Dean: New History, 1550–1818* (Sutton Publishing: 1995).

25. TNA, E126/1, fol. 270 r.
26. TNA, E112/83/411.
27. Ibid.
28. For the sake of clarity in this chapter, I will refer to the unrest in the Forest of Dean from 1628 to 1631 as the Skimmington riots, but the leader as John Williams, also known as Skymington, in accordance with how he is described in contemporary documents. The ritual itself will be referenced as skimmington or riding skimmington.
29. John Smith, *The Names and Surnames of all the Able and Sufficient Men in Body Fitt for his Ma(ies)ty's Service in the Warss, within the County of Gloucester ... 1608* (London: 1902).
30. Herbert, *VCH, Vol. V.*, 232–3. TNA, MR 179.
31. Thirsk, *Seventeenth-Century Agriculture and Social Change*, 172.
32. TNA, SP16/188/20.
33. Ibid.
34. TNA, SP16/257/94.
35. Ibid.
36. Sidney Lee, 'Mompesson, Sir Giles (1583/4 – 1651 x 63)', rev. Sean Kelsey, *Oxford Dictionary of National Biography* (Oxford University Press: 2004), online edn. Accessed 14/1/2008.
37. TNA, E125/4, fols. 50–54 & E112/179/28.
38. Sharp, *In Contempt of All Authority*, 206. My emphasis.
39. Sharp, *In Contempt of All Authority*, 206.
40. TNA, SP16/188/20.
41. TNA, SP16/215/57.
42. Ibid.
43. Edward P. Thompson 'The moral economy of the English crowd in the eighteenth century', *Past & Present* 50 (1971), 76–136.
44. TNA, SP16/203/36.
45. Ibid.
46. Ibid.
47. Ibid.
48. For further work on the symbolism of early modern popular crowd action, see John Walter, 'Gesturing at authority: deciphering the gestural code of early modern England', in Michael J. Braddick (ed.), *The Politics of Gesture: Historical Perspectives,* Past and Present, Supplement, 4 (Oxford University Press: 2009), 96–127; David Underdown, '"But the shows of their street": Civic pageantry and charivari in a Somerset town, 1607', *Journal of British Studies*, 50.1 (2011), 4–23.
49. Paul DiMaggio, 'Culture and cognition', *Annual Review of Sociology* 23 (1997), 263–87, 277.

50. Roger Friedland and Robert Alford, 'Bringing society back in: symbols, practices, and institutional contradictions', in Walter W. Powell and Paul DiMaggio (eds.), *The New Institutionalism in Organizational Analysis* (University of Chicago Press: 1991), 223–62.
51. Ibid, 223–62.
52. Simon Sandall, *Custom and Popular Memory in the Forest of Dean: 1550–1832* (Scholars Press: 2013); see also Andy Wood, 'Custom and the social organisation of writing in early modern England', *Transactions of the Royal Historical Society*, 6th Series, 9 (1999), 257–69; Adam Fox, 'Custom, memory and the authority of writing', in Paul Griffiths, Adam Fox and Steve Hindle (eds.), *The Experience of Authority in Early Modern England* (Palgrave Macmillan: 1999), 89–116, 110.
53. Wood, 'Custom and the social organisation of writing'.
54. TNA, E134/22Jas1/East8.
55. Henry S. Maine, *Ancient Law: Its Connection With Early Ideas Of Society, And Its Relation To Modern Ideas* (Henry Holt & Company: 1870), 21.
56. Jack Goody, *The Logic of Writing and the Organisation of Society* (Cambridge University Press: 1986), 138.
57. Gloucestershire Record Office [hereafter GRO], D23/X1.
58. GRO, D5947.
59. Herbert, *VCH Vol. V*, 329.
60. Herbert, *VCH Vol. V*, 329.
61. GRO, D5947.
62. GRO, D5947.
63. GRO, D5947.
64. GRO, D5947.
65. GRO, D5947.
66. Chris Fisher explains that 'In the Forest of Dean, when the relatively large pits began to work in the 1820s, the master introduced the "Little butty" method of work organisation. In this scheme the miners worked in gangs led by skilled adult hewers. The hewer and his partner, the butties, worked on contract rates and employed the other members of the gang on day rates. The little butty was an entrepreneur and an employer in his own right, as interested in the condition of the product market and its fluctuations as the master with whom he bargained for the contract... thus the dispossession of the free miners and the new organisation of the mining industry did not create an homogenous, solidary mass of wage labourers who brooded on their loss. The new generation of miners grew into the altered order, accepted its essential characteristics and struggled to define a place for themselves in it' (Fisher, *Custom, Work and Market Capitalism*, xiii).
67. GRO, D23/X1.

68. GRO, D5947.
69. GRO, D5947.
70. GRO, Q/50/4; Q/FAc1 & D5947/10/1.
71. GRO, D5947.
72. GRO, D2026/F/18.

Remembering Protest in the Late-Georgian Working-Class Home

Ruth Mather

[I]n our domestic capacity, with the suckling at the breast, and the stripling at the hand, the air they inhale shall be filled with the principles of reform.[1]

These were the words of Halifax's Female Reformers, read aloud at a public meeting on Skircoat Moor held less than two months after the Peterloo Massacre. The resolutions marked the occasion when, on 16 August 1819, a large-scale demonstration in Manchester to call for political reform was violently dispersed by military force, resulting in the deaths of 18 people and injuries to several hundred more.[2] The event's main speaker, the radical Henry 'Orator' Hunt, was arrested along with the other speakers on the hustings, and in the weeks that followed a number of prominent radicals were also imprisoned, accused of conspiring to overturn the government. Almost immediately following the Massacre, the magistrates who had ordered the meeting's dispersal took control of the narrative of events, claiming that they had taken the necessary steps to control a revolutionary mob.[3] Following public praise from both the Cabinet and the Prince Regent for so doing, the 'official' version of Peterloo was further safeguarded by the passing of the 'Six Acts' in 1820, which included a tightening of the laws on

R. Mather (✉)
University of Exeter, Exeter, UK

sedition and libel and restrictions to the right of public protest. It is in this context that this chapter examines the ways in which radicals memorialised Peterloo, establishing a counter-narrative of a peaceful demonstration brutally interrupted by a vicious militia on the orders of corrupt local officials. The assertion of this alternative version of events was in itself a form of protest, as well as a means of sustaining a beleaguered movement through the most difficult of times.

This chapter explores the ways in which Peterloo was remembered in practices that originated in the homes of working-class radicals in the north of England,[4] and especially the area around Manchester. The domestic lives of radicals have until recently received little scholarly attention in a historiography that has largely analysed such activities as demonstrations, riots and petitioning.[5] These public displays of political feeling can readily be identified as forms of protest, and are recorded in detail in a range of source material. Domestic forms of protest, on the other hand, are less accessible to the historian. Newspaper reports, which offer such useful insights into riots and demonstrations, rarely record domestic activity. Autobiographies written by radical men of the period offer a little more insight, but home life is rarely glimpsed among details of their public deeds, and autobiographical reflections written by women are almost non-existent in this period.[6] However, Katrina Navickas has demonstrated the potential of recently catalogued Home Office papers to discover more about the relationships within radical families,[7] while Murray Pittock's work on the meanings of Jacobite material culture suggests another avenue of inquiry, albeit one hampered by the fragmentary survival and poor documentation of the object record from working-class homes.[8] The chapter draws upon a range of sources, including surviving objects preserved in museum collections, autobiographies written by known radicals, newspaper reports and the Home Office Disturbance Records, thus pulling together the patchy available evidence to demonstrate the potential of exploring the home as a radical space.

By focusing on the home this chapter also offers new perspectives on early nineteenth-century working-class radicalism. The radical weaver, poet and autobiographer Samuel Bamford asserted that 'In England alone is the term home, with all its domestic comforts and associations, properly understood.'[9] Bamford's words suggest the multilayered importance of home, as an intimate space for personal relationships, a place for rest and relaxation, but also as a symbol of national pride and a site for the negotiation of power relationships based in classed, gendered and racialised difference as well as distinctions associated with life stage, marital status and earning capacities.[10] The ability to make a home, protect its boundaries, and to access its 'comforts' were (and are) all enmeshed in these unequal power relationships, particularly because the home remained a place of work for many working-class men and women in the early nineteenth century. The complex meanings and implications of home therefore make it a fascinating site for the study of the formation and expression of a politicised identity. In this chapter, I demonstrate that working-class radicals in northern England were able to use the home in creative ways to memorialise Peterloo. I argue that by studying the home, we can not only uncover the often-forgotten practical roles of women and children in radicalism, but also understand more fully the emotional investment working-class men and women made in radical politics and the ways in which their political identification could shape their daily lives.

The role of domestic imagery in political discourse, and particularly the opportunities that this offered for women to speak on a public platform, have been discussed elsewhere.[11] Therefore, in this chapter I will focus on the practical uses of the home and the ways in which day-to-day routines and objects were employed in the memorialisation of Peterloo in ways which sustained and expressed a radical identity. However, it is worth noting the symbolic importance of the home within British political culture in this period, as well as its broader relevance as a highly emotive site. Home was envisioned as a mirror of the state, with the patriarchal power of the father over his wife and children reflecting that of the King over his subjects. This hierarchical structure was influenced further by Christian belief. According to a 1794 pamphlet warning British radicals against emulating the Revolutionary French, the anonymous author wrote that 'In the composition and government of families the Supreme Creator hath given a clear intimation of his will concerning the rights of the different ranks of men in any nation'.[12] Religion is also relevant to the practical uses of the home as discussed here. Leora Auslander has pointed to the influence of Protestant culture in the attempted 'cultural revolutions' of the seventeenth and eighteenth centuries. The stress within Protestantism on an individual relationship with God, practiced on a daily basis, was clearly mirrored in the importance of everyday practices and rituals in revolutionary movements.[13] This emphasis on actively living one's politics will also be clearly evident in the following discussion of the ways that radicals remembered Peterloo through domestic practices. Some of these practices drew directly on religious ritual, such as the baptism of children into a community of radicalism, and the use of 'relics' within gatherings to remember the Massacre.

This chapter explores three themes within radical memorialisation of Peterloo which originated in the home – the politicised education of children, the role of commemorative objects, and adherence to a boycott of excisable goods. These seemingly distinct practices have in common the desire to physically manifest the memory of Peterloo in both objects and embodied rituals related to domestic activity, in ways which both negotiated the trauma of the Massacre and defied attempts to close down protest. I argue that the use of these home-based practices of remembrance were both creative and subversive, undermining the symbolic role of home as a model for the established social order at the same time as enabling the radical movement to survive a period of persecution and fragmentation. Furthermore, the domestic nature of these forms of protest enabled the participation of women, whose practical contribution to the radical politics of this period has frequently been underappreciated. In asserting the importance of domestic, everyday forms of remembrance *as* a form of protest, this chapter calls for a wider understanding of politics which encompasses these quotidian forms of resistance and recognises the contribution of those who practiced them.

The Peterloo Massacre and the Six Acts

The events of the Peterloo Massacre and its aftermath bear brief repetition here to convey the extent to which it affected the radical movement in and around Manchester. The meeting was advertised in advance, following the cancellation of a previously-scheduled meeting on 9 August due to concerns over its legality. Its purpose was to 'consider the PROPRIETY of adopting the most LEGAL and effectual means of obtaining a reform'.[14] It was to be addressed by Henry Hunt, a figurehead of the radical movement and an impressive public speaker often referred to as 'Orator' Hunt. Around 60,000 men, women and children from towns across the north-west assembled at St. Peter's Fields, some travelling as far as thirty miles on foot to attend. These marches to the field were carefully co-ordinated, having been practised in advance on local moorland. Many wore their finest Sunday clothing. Samuel Bamford, leader of the Middleton contingent of radicals, impressed the importance of making a respectable appearance, and 'hoped their conduct would be marked by a steadiness and seriousness… as would cast shame upon their enemies, who had always represented the reformers as a mob-like rabble'.[15]

The crowd had assembled and Henry Hunt had taken to the hustings when Special Constables were sent in to arrest him with the assistance of the Manchester and Salford Yeomanry Cavalry. The magistrates, watching events from a house at the side of St Peter's Fields, claimed to have read the Riot Act calling for dispersal before the Yeomanry took to the field, but few, if any of the radicals had heard this. Stuck in the crowd, the Yeomanry began to lash out with their sabres, while the panicked attendees of the meeting desperately tried to escape the crush of people. The 15th Hussars and Cheshire Yeomanry joined the fray in an attempt to assist the Manchester troops. Women and men alike were injured, though women seem to have been disproportionately targeted, and one of the first victims was a two-year-old boy, William Fildes. The wounds of the victims, recorded by the committee for relief of the victims, suggest the degree of the military's brutality, with many seemingly deliberately cut across the face, breasts, arms and legs, or beaten around the head.[16]

The local magistrates claimed that the dispersal was necessary, that due process had been followed in the reading of the Riot Act, that the meeting had aimed to strike terror into the hearts of Manchester's citizens and that the radicals themselves had been armed and had assaulted the military. Furthermore, it was claimed that the military-style drilling that had taken place on the moors was practice, not for walking in respectable order, but for armed rebellion. Though the government had warned against any hasty intervention in the meeting, they vocally supported the actions of the magistrates and the military. They also very quickly put into place legislation aimed at preventing further mass meetings. The so-called 'Six Acts', passed at the end of December 1819, banned both public meetings of more than fifty individuals without the prior permission of a magistrate, and also the display of flags and banners at public meetings, and any military-style drilling. Meeting places faced tighter regulation, including the need for a licence if entrance fees or contributions were taken, and penalties were increased for the publication of seditious or blasphemous material. Justices of the Peace were also empowered to issue warrants for constables to search private homes for arms, entering by force if necessary.[17]

This was a potentially catastrophic moment for the radical movement. After the fear and anger of the initial reaction to Peterloo, radicals found their opportunities for expression of their now-expanded grievances restricted by the new legislation. Hundreds had suffered serious injuries at the hands of the military, and radical leaders were imprisoned, placing huge financial and emotional burdens on the families involved. The loss of a wage could spell disaster for families whose situation was already financially precarious. The government's persistent use of spies and informers further hampered the movement by generating an atmosphere of suspicion, compounded by internal ego-battles amongst leaders. William Chippendale, one of the Home Office's correspondents in Oldham, informed Lord Sidmouth in July 1820 that the 'Six Acts' had 'effectively restrained [the radicals'] active measures' and that 'Jelausy [sic] and Mistrust... prevails amongst the leaders... there is not one amongst them that would trust his own Brother to divide a sixpenny loaf for him.'[18] This was a period when the radical movement could easily have collapsed, had it not been able to find an outlet for the righteous anger of its members.

Remembering Peterloo Through Radical Child-Rearing

As Navickas has noted, one unintended consequence of the Acts was to encourage radicals to find new and creative forms of activism, at the same time as the highly emotional narratives around Peterloo offered scope for reinforced unity.[19] This could include the politicisation of domestic practices and rituals, giving them the significance of religious observance. The deliberate incorporation of radical politics into family identity is a striking example. At an event to commemorate the second anniversary of Peterloo in 1821, no less than eight children were baptised with the first name 'Henry Hunt' by the radical Reverend James Scholefield. Mary Fildes, who appeared on the hustings at St Peter's Field, already had a son named after Hunt: her child was baptised for the veteran radical John Cartwright at the same event, while another family – not to be left out simply because their child was female – named their daughter Henrietta Hunt.[20] Whilst this was not common naming practice, it cannot strictly be said to be uncommon. A search of birth and baptism records on the website Findmypast.com reveals no less than 136 people with the first name 'Henry Hunt', 28 of whom were from Lancashire. Parents in Ashton-under-Lyne, Bury and Manchester seem to have been particularly keen to recognise the radical leader when naming their children. While Hunt appears to have been the most popular figure to be memorialised in this way, other heroes such as Thomas Paine were also honoured, and William Fitton of Royton, near Oldham, went so far as to baptise his five-year-old son Napoleon the month after Peterloo.[21] The use of naming as a means of radical expression drew on the Protestant tradition of naming children for biblical figures or for the virtues parents hoped they might embody, as well as the earlier London Corresponding Society practice of addressing one another as 'Citizen' and thus enacting the levelling of status their politics sought to extend to the nation.[22] The use of a radical name was presumably intended to influence the behaviour of the child, suggesting the values they should emulate were those thought to be personified by the namesake.

Of course, the numbers of parents who chose to name their children for radical heroes was never numerically great, but the practice itself deserves attention because of the level of commitment it suggests to the radical cause.[23] To endow a child with a name so strongly associated with radicalism was a statement of intent, and one that could well have caused raised eyebrows with less politically sympathetic churchmen than James Scholefield, as well as in wider society.[24] Just as baptism brought a child into the church, so baptising children for radical heroes at a Peterloo memorial event declared their incorporation into the radical movement. This was not, however, the only means by which children were included in practices of remembering Peterloo. As suggested by the words of the Halifax Female Reformers which opened this essay, mothers in particular took responsibility for educating their children about their political ideals. This was seen even before the Massacre, when the Female Reformers of Blackburn gave an address, in which they determined to instil 'into the minds of their offspring a deep-rooted abhorrence of tyranny'.[25] The aim was to sustain the radical movement into the next generation, and indeed in this radicals seem to have had a degree of success, with a number of children of known northern radicals going on to be active in Chartism.[26]

At least one resource was specifically designed to assist parents in providing this radical education, and testifies to the importance of establishing an alternative Peterloo narrative that would stand the test of time and inspire future radicalism. The *Manchester Observer* advertised an annotated map of St Peter's Field describing it as:

> an excellent lesson for children. Let their parents instruct them in this important Political Catechism – "Here (No.1) stood the intrepid Champion of his country's liberties;" and "Here (No.3) were placed a cordon of bludgeon'd myrmidons, who were there for the purpose of prevent the people's escape from the sabres of the dastardly Yeomanry Cavalry." "Here, (No.4) were assembled in a secret divan, the hellish confederacy who were to order the commencement of the horr[ible] massacre;" and "Here, (No.5) were mustered the armed associates by which that massacre was to be accomplished;" &c. &c. By this method, the minds of our rising generation might be fully impressed with the awful importance of making a stand for their political privileges.[27]

It is worth noting the language of the *Manchester Observer* here: the use of the term 'Catechism' again deliberately evokes religious practice, in which the key tenets of faith are memorialised to aid in the practice of the faith. The proposed educational exercise also offered the learner a visual aid, enabling them to imagine themselves in the centre of events, and thus promoting identification with the victims of the Massacre. Again, we can also see explicitly outlined the connection between remembrance and ongoing activism. Learning about Peterloo was intended to encourage those who were not there to carry forward the aims of the radicals who were and thus to sustain the movement into the next generation.

The production of a map to be used as teaching aid suggests another theme common to the memorialisation of Peterloo, that of physically materialising reminders of the events of the day. In effect, even the naming of children follows this theme of giving physical form to the memory, given that the children were to embody the characteristics of their namesakes. Some children in the Manchester area also wore the physical markers of their radicalism, attending Sunday Schools in the white hats associated with Henry Hunt or wearing green ribbons, thus marking themselves out as radicals. Responding to the Sunday School Committee's decision to refuse admittance to these children, a correspondent of the *Manchester Observer* reflected that 'their consciences must accuse them, when such a simple thing as a white hat can put them in remembrance of their foul and unnatural proceedings on the 16th'.[28] We can see again how children were incorporated into the remembrance of Peterloo, their wearing of the symbols of radicalism connecting political ideology to family identity, as well as drawing upon cultural ideals of the innocence of children and in turn reflecting the innocence of the victims of the Massacre.

Peterloo in Commemorative Material Culture

A special significance was attached to those objects which had been physically present at the meeting on 16 August. Those radicals charged with carrying a banner were urged to protect it with their lives, and the display in a shop window of the Manchester Female Reformer's banner, taken on the hustings by the troops from Mary Fildes, almost provoked a riot.[29] Nancy Clayton adapted the petticoat she wore to the meeting to create a black flag reading 'Murder on the 16th of August 1819, at Peterloo', which she displayed at the annual dinners she held with her husband to mark the anniversary of the Massacre. Again, the power of this symbol of resistance was recognised by the local constabulary, who attempted to confiscate it even in 1839, some twenty years after its appearance on the field of Peterloo.[30] Items so closely, tangibly connected to this traumatic event were regarded almost as relics, to be carefully preserved as a testament to the shared experience of those radicals who had witnessed Peterloo. This almost sacred significance was recognised not only by radicals, but by also their opponents who were well aware of the emotional impact of the confiscation or destruction of carefully preserved memorial objects.

Canny manufacturers seem to have recognised this desire among radicals to have some form of physical reminder of Peterloo. There was a flourishing market for cheap commemorative goods by the early years of the nineteenth century, the production of Peterloo-related items in particular represented recognition not only of the importance of such objects to their owners but also of the growing consumer power of the working classes. By the late eighteenth century improvements in production techniques and more efficient transportation systems brought cheap prints and ceramics within reach of the artisans and factory workers who were so prominent in the radical movement. In their turn, the working classes seem to have offered an enthusiastic market for cheap decorative objects. Items such as prints, ceramics, textiles and even clocks added homeliness to what could otherwise be sparse interiors. Samuel Bamford described with pride the interior of his weaving cottage in Middleton:

> A humble but cleanly bed, screened by a dark old fashioned curtain, stands on our left. At the foot of the bed is a window closed from the looks of all street passers. Next are some chairs, and a round table of mahogany; then another chair, and next to it a long table, scoured very white. Above that is a looking glass with a picture on each side, of the resurrection and ascension on glass, 'copied from Rubens'. A well-stocked shelf of crockery ware is the next object, and in a nook near it are a black oak carved chair or two, with a curious desk, or box, to match; and lastly, above the fire-place, are hung a rusty basket hilted sword, and an old fuse, and a leathern cap. Such are the appearance and furniture of that humble abode.[31]

Though stressing that none of the goods in the home were particularly fancy, they clearly added character to a room small enough to be described by its owner as a 'cell', a large part of which was given over to the looms on which Samuel and his wife Jemima worked.[32] That Bamford offered such a lengthy description of his 'humble abode' in a memoir of his political life also indicates the importance of domestic material culture in establishing the kind of image of himself Bamford wished to present. Bamford's autobiography, being intended for public consumption, offered a carefully constructed version of himself designed to emphasise aspects of his personality which would be read in a positive light by an audience who might not share his experiences as a working-class radical. His care over the home environment, and the implication that he must have saved in order to obtain such small luxuries, were evidence of his respectability and good management – traits crucial in a man who sought the responsibility of the franchise for himself and men of his class.

Though Bamford, in writing a memoir and gaining widespread readership, had an unusual opportunity to present his domestic interior to the judgement of others, we should beware of assuming that the majority of working-class homes were private spaces. Aside from the friends and family that would be invited within, or the radical meetings sometimes held in the home, the homes of working-class people in general and radicals in particular were subject to less welcome visitations. These might come from Poor Law Commissioners, assessing whether or not the family were deserving of relief, or from social observers conducting earnest studies of working-class life.[33] As mentioned above, the Seizure of Arms Act (one of the 'Six Acts' of 1819) allowed for searches of domestic property for arms and thus rendered radical homes vulnerable to hostile invasion by local authorities. We should, therefore, be wary that objects displayed within the home were safe from prosecution. Domestic objects related to the popular radicalism of this period must therefore be interpreted differently to the explicitly Jacobite objects which Murray Pittock has suggested could be safely kept in the private rooms of elite homes.[34] Yet because of their visual, rather than textual nature, it is possible that Peterloo commemorative objects retained a degree of ambiguity that put them beyond the remit of prosecution. Regardless of the strengthened laws against treason and sedition, the government were wary of inviting ridicule by prosecuting producers of graphic satire. To prove that any satirical words or images had seditious intent required scrutiny of the items in question by a jury, and the government must surely have been aware that attempts to tie such charges to simple household items risked appearing alarmist.[35] Unfortunately, however, the fact that commemorative items received little scrutiny at the time has provided us with minimal written evidence that might aid the historical interpretation of surviving objects.

Ceramic homewares are probably the most commonly occurring items amongst the surviving objects commemorating Peterloo, other than graphic prints and perhaps tokens and medals. Earthenware jugs or mugs of varying quality were decorated with transfer prints which often drew on or copied existing graphic representations of Peterloo. The most common image I have encountered on Peterloo ceramics – and in general in representations of the Massacre – is that of the cavalry trampling protestors, usually women.[36] This is the image on a very simple glazed earthenware plaque that is currently held by the British Museum, probably produced cheaply and *en masse,* so that the transfer is smudged (Fig. 1). Only one Peterloo commemorative I have located features anything that could easily be interpreted as an incitement to actually avenge the violence inflicted by the Yeomanry. This jug, in the collections of the Touchstones Centre in Rochdale, is transfer-printed with the word 'Murder' above an image of the Yeomanry cutting and trampling people, followed by a poem that reads 'The scripture crys out life for life and God ordain'd it so. We'll not forget to repay the debt incurred at PETERLOO' (Fig. 2). The majority of commemorative objects, however, refrain from such explicit calls for revenge. As noted above, most portrayed the radical crowd in a relatively passive role, emphasising the narrative of innocent victimhood and the inhuman brutality of the military. The leaders of the movement, however, were singled out in more celebratory poses, immortalising them as heroes.

Fig. 1 Peterloo Plaque, c.1819. (Printed, painted, and glazed earthenware. British Museum, London)

Fig. 2 Peterloo jug, c.1819. (Printed earthenware and lustre. Touchstones, Rochdale)

Henry Hunt, for example, features prominently and very frequently in the prints on commemorative homewares, further cementing his status as a figurehead for radicals in north-west England.

It is difficult for the historian to judge exactly how and why the majority of commemorative goods were made, bought and used. Unlike the prestige items commissioned by the upper classes, these were for the most part produced cheaply and for a mass market. They thus leave little trace on the written record, since their making was not exceptional nor was their purchase usually recorded by the customer. We can only speculate from the fragments of evidence available. The British Museum plaque, discussed above, is rare in offering an obvious clue to its use, in the form of a hole above the transfer print for hanging on the wall. Other surviving ceramic homewares – mostly jugs or cups – bear little sign of wear, suggesting that they were rarely, if ever used to hold drinks. This could perhaps suggest their use in toasting rituals at radical gatherings, such as those offered at the Peterloo memorial dinners held by long-time radicals John and Nancy Clayton in the 1830s, at which commemorative and symbolic items were prominent within the room.[37] Alternatively, they may simply have sat on a shelf or mantelpiece, quietly communicating the owner's interest in Peterloo to anyone who might enter the room.

Some scholars have speculated that commemorative objects were used both in propaganda campaigns and to raise funds for imprisoned radicals and those who had been injured at St Peter's Fields. This argument has referred in particular to the silk handkerchiefs printed with John Slack's portrayal of the massacre, a number of which survive in the People's History Museum in Manchester, the Working Class Movement Library in Salford, and in other museums and private collections.[38] Malcolm Chase, exploring the febrile atmosphere of potential revolution in the year after Peterloo, found reports of 'English Pedlars' displaying these handkerchiefs across rural Ireland, trying to stir up dissent in communities that already contained considerable discontent.[39] Of course, there may have been a degree of alarmism in the report, and the pedlars in question may simply have been selling their wares. In any case, ceramics were both bulkier and more fragile, and thus less suited to such mobile propaganda missions, but could well have served similar purposes on a more local level, and could certainly have been sold to raise money for the radical cause.

It is important to remember, however, that not only radicals or those sympathetic to their cause who bought, collected or displayed these Peterloo commemoratives. John Crossley, a magistrate who had been present at Peterloo and contributed to the evidence against the radicals, was a known collector of Peterloo memorabilia, with a collection ranging from parts of banners and the truncheon of a special constable through to a stone supposedly thrown by the radicals.[40] Local loyalists marked the anniversary of Peterloo as regularly as radicals, but celebrated it as a great victory over potential revolution rather than the tragedy marked by their political opponents.[41] Indeed, the memory of Peterloo was deployed by loyalists as a threat of the consequences of protest. In November 1820, as radicals celebrated the failure of George IV's Bill of Pains and Penalties against his estranged wife, the loyalist *Courier* remined its readers that '[the radicals] have not yet forgotten the 16th of August; and nothing created a greater dread among them that day than the mouth of a cannon'.[42] For both sides – and indeed for disinterested observers – there was a rapid recognition that Peterloo was a landmark moment of history, and thus commemoratives could simply represent a desire to mark this, rather than to express a political position. The politics of preservation further complicate our interpretation of Peterloo commemoratives. The items that now exist in museum collections are those that have survived and been deemed worthy of their place in that repository, rather than necessarily the objects that meant most to those living at the time.

Boycotting as a Form of Peterloo Remembrance

Given that the evidence for all of these forms of home-based political activism is patchy, one might question the worth of paying such attention to the use of the home in political expression. As suggested above, however, the home was a symbolically significant site in both political and emotional terms. It represented *both* the place where intimate relationships were maintained, *and* the order and hierarchy of the state. To bring politics into the home suggested a depth of feeling and a desire to live one's politics as a key element of one's identity, which could be shared with close friends and family and thus strengthen both political and familial bonds. Yet expressing radical politics at home – to pledge allegiance through objects and practices to ideas felt by many to be dangerous to the established order – was to subvert the role of home as the physical, everyday embodiment of this order.

I have suggested above that working-class radicals used domestic objects to actively remember Peterloo, attempting to ensure the dominance of their own narrative of the events of that day. Likewise, the naming of children for radical heroes was a means to keep their version of the story at the forefront of their own and other's minds. The final form of remembrance I wish to discuss here was that most obviously used as a form of protest, actively designed to seek justice for the violence inflicted on the attendees at the St Peter's Fields meeting. Again, radicals drew on their relatively newly-established consumer power by seeking to enact amongst their supporters a boycott of taxable goods which would weaken the government by reducing the finances available to them. As with commercially-produced commemorative items, the process of boycotting demonstrated a vital link between domestic and public life, that between the home and the market. Decisions taken at family level about whether to consume items associated with domestic comfort, such as tea, coffee and sugar, were related explicitly to a vision for the national economy.[43] Thus, the *Manchester Observer* printed a rallying cry less than two weeks after Peterloo, calling for:

> modes of resistance which an army, however immense, cannot render ineffectual... the resistance of peace: -an abstinence from those articles, your consumption of which, though they are not necessaries, furnishes your oppressors with a revenue that is their security, and the means they employ to oppress you.

> Spirits, beer, tea, coffee, tobacco, snuff: these are articles immensely taxed... if you will relinquish the use of their taxed luxuries (and all the articles I argued against are luxuries,) you will soon behold the blessed effects of your virtue, in the distress, and absolute ruin, of your oppressors.[44]

The boycott was a strategy that had the additional benefit of conveying respectability, in that abstinence from these 'luxury' items reflected self-control, and its advocates stressed that by avoiding unnecessary spending, radicals would benefit both financially and physically. The chairman of a meeting at Huddersfield, for example, told the assembled crowd that 'he himself, by such an abstinence, saved 6s a week in his family, and found himself much better in health'.[45] Thus, boycotting excisable goods offered a form of remembrance for Peterloo, a creative form of protest, and an opportunity for working-class men to demonstrate their fitness for the franchise.

Others were more militant, calling not just for a boycott of taxable goods, but also of the businesses of known opponents of political reform. In strong terms, a correspondent to the *Manchester Observer* argued that radicals should:

> let that man be considered a traitor to the cause of Reform, who expends a penny with one who is either directly opposed to reform, or who pretends to be neuter to your sufferings; and as soon as trade will justify the measure, let every individual be scouted from your society, and branded with the name of Traitor to his Country, who takes a reed (we are more particularly addressing the Weavers) from a Manufacturer, who did not actively, both by his name and his money, support your just claims.[46]

It is unlikely, as indeed the author recognised, that the majority of workers could afford to refuse work on the basis of their employer's politics. Indeed, many must have feared an unsympathetic employer discovering their own political views. Certainly, plenty of men publicly pledged abstinence from taxable goods in lists published by the *Manchester Observer* in the weeks after the initial call for a boycott, but it is difficult to assess how far the boycotts of either taxable goods or opponents of radicalism were actually carried out in practice.[47] Henry Hunt not only adopted the boycott, but also shrewdly began marketing an alternative to coffee and tea made from roasted corn. Others wrote in to the *Manchester Observer* to suggest other replacements for boycotted goods.[48] There is evidence that a boycott *was* successful in one case directly related to the Massacre. James Murray, a Manchester confectioner, was accused of spying at a radical meeting held at White Moss just before the St Peter's Field's meeting, and he suffered a beating at the hands of some of those present. The treatment meted out to Murray was key to the authorities' construction of the meeting as a violent mob, and for his own part Murray declared that he would be 'pleased to go home in a boat over the blood of Reformers'.[49] In the aftermath of Peterloo, Murray, taunted by radicals as 'White Moss Humbug', found his business suffering and was forced to reduce his staff's hours.[50]

Thus, the act of enacting justice for Peterloo through the boycott could have a real impact when carried out effectively. However, John Saxton, the agent for Hunt's Breakfast Powders in the north-west:

> candidly declared that he would not attempt to carry into effect Mr Hunt's rule of temperance… a resolution for a personal reform in the matter of a little cordial, he neither could nor would entertain.[51]

Not all radicals were willing to give up the home comforts available to them, even in the presence of Hunt himself, as was the case with John Saxton. Nor did any of those with Saxton on this occasion seem to regard him as a traitor to the cause, which suggests that the uncompromising rhetoric of the newspaper campaign obscured a more pragmatic reality. Ultimately, the boycott was never adopted widely enough to inflict significant damage on the government's finances, as its advocates had hoped. Nonetheless, for our purposes, it is significant that radicals sought another way to physically embody their politics in response to Peterloo, adapting domestic habits as a form of active memorial. Furthermore, the strategy was clearly powerful enough in the popular imagination to justify its resurrection by the Chartists in the late 1830s, with Chartist women at the forefront of a campaign for 'exclusive dealing', offering their custom only to those 'friendly to the cause of the people'.[52]

The Gendered Nature of Peterloo Remembrance

At the beginning of this chapter, I discussed the dual role of home as at once a space for the nurturing of intimate relationships and as an analogy for state. Feminist scholars have for some time challenged the distinction between 'public' and 'private' worlds, asserting that fluidity between the two is crucial to understanding the political roles of women.[53] The majority of this scholarship has focused on the more readily accessible domestic lives of professional and upper-class men and women, who left letters, diaries and accounts that offer glimpses into the activities of home. This chapter contributes to the field of women's history by suggesting that working-class women likewise were able to proactively adapt domestic practices to express their political views. Along with others, I have argued elsewhere that women drew on their association with the home to assert their right to a political platform, incorporating the domestic experience into radical rhetoric.[54] As noted, women also became particularly symbolic of the brutality of the military at Peterloo, with much of the imagery of the Massacre drawing on the attacks on defenceless women and children. What this chapter suggests is that the presence of women was more than merely symbolic, and in the practice of remembering Peterloo they were able to take an active role.

Men dominated the public face of the radical movement, and in some ways the memorialising processes discussed above seem to have reinforced that dominance. It was Henry Hunt whose name was given most often to children, and his face that appeared so frequently on commemorative items, and where women were represented it was in a passive role. It was men who signed pledges to boycott taxable goods. On a day-to-day basis, however, it seems likely that women were heavily involved in radical practice. We have already seen that women proudly proclaimed their educative role, and were determined to raise children to share their political values. The Halifax Female Reformers also declared that:

> It is our intention to abstain, as much as is possible, from all exciseable articles, and strictly to take care that our earnings do not circulate through the pockets of our enemies[.][55]

It was women who were usually expected to take control of household provisioning, even if they also worked for wages. This may not always have been the case in practice, but there was certainly a cultural assumption that it was women who shopped for and fed the family, and thus it was upon women that the bulk of the work associated with maintaining a boycott is likely to have fallen.[56]

Likewise, women were probably most involved in the cleaning and care of commemorative objects, practices that have much to do with their survival in good condition to the present day. This – like much of the labour expended by women in the radical cause – went largely unrecognised by the male chroniclers of the movement. Those who recorded the activities of radicals, whether in autobiography, news reports, or even in panicked letters to the Home Office, did not discuss the mundane day-to-day activities through which women supported a household. Instead, we are left to glimpse their contribution on the rare occasions where female reformers spoke of their own activity, and by reading between the lines of these accounts, as I have done here. Particularly in a period like that just after Peterloo, when uncertainty and suspicion plagued the radical movement, this kind of everyday work that maintained bonds of unity and solidarity through strengthening a shared narrative was crucial and is deserving of as much attention as the more spectacular episodes of protest and rebellion. As Professor Steve Poole has suggested, we should widen our definition of protest to include more everyday activities that could nonetheless be relevant to political subjectivities. Poole has questioned whether, 'If we spend too much time looking for 'protesters' and studying their 'protests', are we in danger of limiting our own interest in popular agency and popular culture?'[57] Broadening our understanding of what constitutes protest enables us to explore more thoroughly the ways in which ordinary people engaged with politics, and the ways in which political repertoires were tied into wider networks of power and influence.

Conclusions

Recognising the significance of domestic protest practices challenges the historical neglect of the meanings of working-class homes for those who lived in them. For too long, a reliance on the accounts of social investigators, usually from outside the communities they wrote about, has created a popular image of the destitute slum dwelling which denies the agency of working-class people in making and maintaining home as a space for personal expression. It is only recently that historical archaeologists, in particular, have begun to explore the material culture of working-class homes, demonstrating the care and attention that might be paid both to the physical space of home and to the affective relationships enacted within.[58] This chapter has shown the importance of this emergent literature in understanding popular politics, particularly at a time when other forms of protest were subject to severe repression, but has also sought to establish the importance of home more generally in working-class culture. In a period for which written records from the perspective of the working classes were still relatively rare, we must take seriously the relationship of working-class people to non-textual objects if we are to gain a deeper understanding of working-class culture, in spite of the clear methodological problems discussed above.

This is not to suggest that memorialising practices were simply co-opted as a form of protest. Peterloo was a traumatic event: many people in the area around Manchester would have known someone who was there, and for those who attended the violence and attendant fear must have been difficult to forget, even if they or those known to them were not themselves injured. In all of the strategies of remembrance discussed above, we can see how giving form to the memory – whether through rituals of naming, through the use of objects, or through an embodied practice – made tangible the connection to Peterloo, to the aims of the meeting and the meaning of its violent dispersal. Such a process may well have been a means of externalising emotion in order to negotiate the trauma of the event, and the use of memory as a form of protest offered a way to make meaning from tragedy. Though such analyses may seem anachronistic, the use of material and visual forms have long been used across different cultures as a means of dealing with loss and grief,[59] and by closely considering the ways in which memorialisation took place in a space associated with intimacy we may be able to glimpse some of the complexity of historical emotions. Such an analysis moves us towards a more nuanced understanding of political affiliation that recognises the interrelationships of socio-economic structure and emotion.

Notes

1. 'Peaceful Meeting at Halifax', *Morning Chronicle*, 7 October 1819.
2. The exact numbers of those killed and injured at Peterloo is still subject to some debate, though the most authoritative account to date is that in Michael Bush, *The Casualties of Peterloo* (Carnegie: 2005). Bush counted a total of 18 Peterloo-related deaths, though some of these occurred in violent clashes after the actual meeting had been dispersed, and not all were deliberate. See pp. 44–46.
3. Robert Poole, '"By the law or by the sword": Peterloo revisited', *History*, 91 (2006), 255–6.
4. The term 'working class' is used loosely here to denote those dependent for their living on their own labour or that of a family member. There has been much debate over whether the artisans, labourers and small-scale tradespeople who comprised much of the radical movement can be defined as a 'class', and these arguments are too lengthy and complex for rehearsal here. The terminology as used here is meant to encompass a group who

shared similar social networks and outlooks as well as the experience of economic precarity, rather than a relationship to the means of production. I discuss the use of class terminology in more detail in my thesis: Ruth Mather, 'The home making of the English working class: radical politics and domestic life in late Georgian England, c.1790–1820' (unpublished PhD thesis, Queen Mary, University of London, 2017), 13–14. http://qmro.qmul.ac.uk/xmlui/handle/123456789/24708

5. Exceptions include Anna Clark's *The Struggle for the Breeches: Gender and the Making of the English Working Class* (University of California Press: 1995), which takes a somewhat pessimistic view of the working-class domestic life, and Katrina Navickas's '"A reformer's wife ought to be a heroine": gender, family, and English radicals imprisoned under the suspension of Habeus Corpus Act of 1817', *History,* 101 (2016), 246–64.

6. David Vincent's study of working-class autobiography, *Bread, Knowledge and Freedom: A Study of Nineteenth-Century Working Class Autobiography* (Methuen: 1981), found only six female authors for the period 1790–1850, compared to 142 male authors. See also Emma Griffin, *Liberty's Dawn: A People's History of the Industrial Revolution* (Yale University Press: 2013), page 7 & chapter 4; Kelly J. Mays, 'Domestic spaces, readerly acts: reading, gender, and class in working-class autobiography', *Nineteenth-Century Contexts* 30 (2008), 343–68.

7. Navickas, '"A reformer's wife ought to be a heroine"'.

8. Murray Pittock, 'Treacherous objects: towards a theory of Jacobite material culture', *Journal for Eighteenth Century Studies* 34 (2011), 39–63.

9. Samuel Bamford, *Passages in the Life of a Radical and Early Days in Two Volumes,* edited with an introduction by Henry Dunckley, volume II (Unwin: 1905/1850), 260.

10. See Alison Blunt and Robyn Dowling, *Home* (Routledge: 2006) for a discussion of the complex and multi-layered meanings of 'home' (as distinct from 'house').

11. For example, Helen Rogers, *Women and the People: Authority, Authorship and the Radical Tradition in Nineteenth-Century England* (Ashgate: 2000), ch. 1; Linda Colley, *Britons: Forging the Nation, 1707–1837* (Pimlico edition, 1992/1994), ch. 6; Ruth Mather, '"These Lancashire women are witches in politics": female reform societies and radical theatricality in the north-west of England, c.1819–20', *Manchester Region History Review* 23 (2012), 49–64.

12. Anon., *Brissot's Ghost! Or, Intelligence from the Other World; Communicated to a Meeting of Those Who Call Themselves Friends of the People* (J. and J. Fairbairn: 1794), 14–15.

13. Leora Auslander, *Cultural Revolutions: The Politics of Everyday Life in Britain, North America, and France* (Berg: 2009), 51–55.

14. TNA, HO79/3 part 3, fo. 447, Hobhouse to Hay, 23 July 1819, quoted in R. Poole, 'What don't we know about Peterloo', *Manchester Region History Review* 23 (2012), 10.
15. Bamford, *Passages,* 150.
16. For detailed analysis of the injuries inflicted by the military, see Bush, *The Casualties of Peterloo,* esp. 3, 32, and 34, on which Bush concludes that 'the damage inflicted at Peterloo… sprang from premeditation, design and determination'.
17. For full details of the 'Six Acts', see Arthur Aspinall and Ernest A. Smith, 'The "Six Acts", 1819', in *English Historical Documents Online*, volume VIII, 1783–1832 (Routledge: 1959).
18. TNA, HO40/14 fo.62, Chippendale to Sidmouth, 22 July 1820.
19. Katrina Navickas, *Protest and the Politics of Space and Place* (Manchester University Press: 2015), 105.
20. Paul Pickering, *Chartism and the Chartists in Manchester and Salford* (Macmillan: 1995), 41; John T. Saxton, 'Address to Henry Hunt Esq. from the Radical Reformers, Male and Female, of Manchester, August 16th 1821', extract from the New Manchester Observer, included within Henry Hunt, *To The Radical Reformers, Male and Female, of England, Ireland, and Scotland* (T. Dolby: 1820).
21. Napoleon Fitton Chadwick, the son of William Fitton and Hannah Chadwick, was baptised on 26 September 1819. See baptismal record on findmypast.com.
22. See Sophie Coulombeau, '"The knot that ties them fast together": personal proper name change and identity formation in English literature, 1779–1800' (unpublished PhD thesis, University of York, 2014), 74–75 and 238–45.
23. Malcolm Chase has made this point with regard to Chartist naming patterns, as well as raising the valid point that a focus on naming obscures the agency of the children themselves. However, it is a practice of interest here in demonstrating one of the ways in which radicals continued to express their commitment to the radical cause in creative ways and to evoke the memory of Peterloo in spite of repression. See *The Chartists: Perspectives and Legacies* (Merlin: 2015), 185.
24. For more on Scholefield's extraordinary career, see Paul Pickering and Alex Tyrell, '"In the thickest of the fight": the Reverend James Scholefield (1790–1855) and the Bible Christians of Manchester and Salford', *Albion: A Quarterly Journal Concerned with British Studies* 26 (1994), 461–82.
25. *Black Dwarf,* 14 July 1819, quoted in Ruth Frow and Edmund Frow, *Political Women, 1800–1850* (Pluto Press: 1989), 22.
26. See Pickering, *Chartism and the Chartists,* 40–4.
27. *Manchester Observer,* 23 October 1819.

28. *Manchester Observer*, 9 October 1819.
29. Michael Bush, 'The women at Peterloo: the impact of female reform on the Manchester meeting of 16 August 1819', *History* 89 (2004), 222.
30. James Epstein, *Radical Expression: Political Language, Ritual and Symbol in England, 1790–1850*. (Oxford University Press: 1994), 163–4.
31. Bamford, *Passages*, 68–9.
32. Ibid., 68.
33. Some Poor Law authorities published the names and/or addresses of those in receipt of relief and encouraged ratepayers to ensure that the recipients were genuinely in need: see Sheffield City Archives, JC1605: Resolution regarding personal visits to poor people's homes, 1795 and JC1507: A List of the Casual and Regular Out-Paupers of Sheffield… Taken Sept. 30, 1808; London Metropolitan Archives, P71/TMS/588–590: Lists of the Poor. For the politics of social observation, see Sandra Sherman, *Imagining Poverty: Quantification and the Decline of Paternalism* (Ohio State University Press: 2001).
34. Pittock, *Treacherous Objects*, 52.
35. Diana Donald, *The Age of Caricature: Satirical Prints in the Reign of George III* (Yale University Press: 1996), 15.
36. Alison Morgan has explored the way that the mother and child were depicted in Peterloo imagery across a range of genres; see 'Starving mothers and murdered children in cultural representations of Peterloo', *Manchester Region History Review* 23 (2012), 65–78.
37. Epstein, *Radical Expression*, 147–48.
38. C. Burgess, 'The objects of Peterloo', *Manchester Region History Review* 23 (2012), 156
39. Malcolm Chase, *1820: Disorder and Stability in the United Kingdom* (Manchester University Press: 2013), 54.
40. Terry Wyke, 'Remembering the Peterloo Massacre', *Manchester Region History Review* 23 (2012), 111–113.
41. *Ibid.*, 113.
42. Reprinted in *Manchester Observer*, 25 November 1820.
43. See Frank Trentmann, 'The politics of everyday life' in Frank Trentmann (ed.), *The Oxford Handbook of the History of Consumption* (Oxford University Press: 2012), 521–47, esp. 540–6 for a discussion of the interrelationships between home and family and wider society evident in consumption practices.
44. *Manchester Observer*, 28 August 1819.
45. *Manchester Observer*, 13 November 1819.
46. *Manchester Observer*, 28 August 1819.
47. *Manchester Observer*, 4 and 18 September 1819.
48. Kevin Gilmartin, *Print Politics: The Press and Radical Opposition in Early Nineteenth-Century England* (Cambridge University Press: 1996), 108.

49. Anon., *The Trial of Mr. Hunt [and Others] ... for an alleged conspiracy to alter the Law by force and threats; and for convening and attending an illegal, riotous and tumultuous Meeting at Manchester on Monday the 16th of August, 1819* (T. J Evans: 1820), 162.
50. Anon., *The Trial of Mr. Hunt*, 39; Anon., *In the King's Bench, Between Thomas Redford, Plaintiff, and Hugh Hornby Birley, Alexander Oliver, Richard Withington, and Edward Meagher, Defendants, for an Assault on the 16th August ... Report of the Proceedings ... Taken from the Short-Hand Notes of Mr. Farquharson* (C. Wheeler & Son: undated [1822]), 308.
51. Bamford, *Passages*, 182.
52. Dorothy Thompson, *The Chartists* (Maurice Temple Smith: 1984), 135–7.
53. For example, Elaine Chalus, 'Elite women, social politics, and the political world of late-eighteenth century England', *Historical Journal*, 43 (2000), 669–97; Kathryn Gleadle, '"The age of physiological reformers": rethinking gender and domesticity in the age of reform', in Arthur Burns and Joanna Innes (eds), *Rethinking the Age of Reform: Britain 1780–1850* (Cambridge University Press: 2003), 200–219; Kathryn Gleadle, *Borderline Citizens: Women, Gender, and Political Culture in Britain, 1815–1867* (Oxford University Press: 2009); Amanda Vickery, *Behind Closed Doors: At Home in Georgian England* (Yale University Press: 2009); Sarah Richardson, *The Political Worlds of Women: Gender and Politics in Nineteenth Century Britain* (Routledge: 2013).
54. See note 11.
55. 'Peaceful Meeting at Halifax', *Morning Chronicle*, 7 October 1819.
56. John Bohstedt has warned against the assumption that women, especially those employed in economically productive labour, were always the shoppers for their families; see John Bohstedt, 'Gender, household and community politics: women in English Riots, 1790–1810', *Past and Present* 120 (1988), 47. Contemporary texts, however, suggest that this was the expectation if not always the practice in radical households; for example see Francis Place, *The Autobiography of Francis Place, 1771–1854*, edited by Mary Thrale (Cambridge University Press: 1972), 227; Benjamin Shaw, *The Family Records of Benjamin Shaw Mechanic of Dent, Dolphinholme and Preston, 1772–1841*, edited by A.G. Crosby (The Record Society of Lancashire and Cheshire: 1991), 76–7; Esther Copley, *Cottage Comforts, with Hints for Promoting Them, Gleaned from Experience: Enlivened with Authentic Anecdotes* (Simpkin and Marshall: 1825), 24.
57. See Steve Poole, 'Ideas for discussion questions', message 7, 10 June 2010. Online forum post. *Protest History Forum*, accessed 17 February 2017. http://protesthistory.proboards.com/post/22/thread
58. See, for example, John Styles, 'Lodging at the Old Bailey: lodgings and their furnishing in eighteenth-century London', in John Styles and Amanda

Vickery (eds), *Gender, Taste & Material Culture in Britain & North America 1700–1830* (Yale University Press: 2006), 61–80; Alastair Owens, Nigel Jeffries, Karen Wehner, & Rupert Featherby, 'Fragments of the modern city: material culture and the rhythms of everyday life in Victorian London', *Journal of Victorian Culture* 15 (2010), 212–25; Adrian Green, 'Heartless and unhomely? Dwellings of the poor in East Anglia and northeast England', in Pamela Sharpe and Joanne McEwan (eds), *Accommodating Poverty: The Housing and Living Arrangements of the English Poor, c. 1600–1850* (Palgrave Macmillan: 2011), 69–101.

59. Elizabeth Hallam and Jenny Hockey, *Death, Memory, and Material Culture* (Berg: 2001), 5.

Prosecution, Precedence and Official Memory: Judicial Responses and Perceptions of Swing in Norfolk

Rose Wallis

This chapter offers a different perspective on the themes of the politics of memory and contested meanings of protest. It considers the perceptions and responses of the authorities to social unrest, and their role in shaping subsequent understandings of protest. Much of the historiography on social protest has rightly been focused on its perpetrators; but addressing the actions and attitudes of the authorities affords a more nuanced understanding of protest, and the social and political relationships that underpinned it.[1] Concentrating on the Swing disturbances of 1830, this chapter draws on Norfolk as a case study, a county that has received comparatively little attention in this context. The experience of repeated unrest in Norfolk between 1816 and 1830 is significant: it formed a vital part of the complex of causes and contexts that informed the perceptions of the local authorities. By focusing on their perspective, we gain valuable insights into the scope of Swing as a movement.

Swing's historians can now perhaps agree that it did constitute a movement, one that was not nationally coordinated, but in its shared tactics and

R. Wallis (✉)
University of the West of England, Bristol, UK

patterns of diffusion, a popular rising that embodied a mutual awareness amongst its participants.[2] But there has been very little discussion of the perspective of the authorities. Their role in shaping the diffusion of protest has been acknowledged, but whether they saw Swing as systemic, or as an outpouring of local grievances, has not been drawn out. The authorities' conception of Swing is an important consideration in understanding their responses to it. From the evidence presented here, the county magistracy saw Swing as locally contingent, national and international, all at once.

This analysis also pursues the prosecution of Swing offenders and the role of the courts in shaping understandings of protest in its aftermath, in the ways in which the authorities deliberately sought to shape subsequent popular memories of the protests. As such, this chapter offers a more nuanced account of the role of prosecutions in what, until recently, has been framed exclusively as 'repression', as simply putting down rebellion.[3] Work by Carl Griffin and others has sought to move beyond such a narrow reading, emphasising the proactive role the local judiciary played in the shaping of prosecutions at the Special Commissions and at the county courts both in terms of creating examples, but also in the broader context of restoring 'order'.[4] The courts were, as Peter King has argued, 'a vital arena in which social tensions were expressed and social relations reconfigured'.[5] These prosecutions should, therefore, be considered as acts of local and national government.

Past prosecutions of protest must likewise be considered as part of this context of judicial decision-making. They provided an important point of reference in local memory against which subsequent proceedings were understood. Griffin has shown how the experience of protest and its suppression across communities and over the longer-term informed the development and response to rural trade unionism at Tolpuddle in 1834.[6] Certainly, in studies of East Anglia, Swing cannot be divorced from the phases of unrest that preceded it. It has been cast as another battle in a 'protracted rural war'.[7] A. J. Peacock, Paul Muskett and John Archer, in particular, have drawn attention to the most dramatic and open manifestations of agricultural labourers' discontent in 1816 and 1822. These discussions have emphasised the longevity and evolution of popular resistance to changes in the rural economy and society.[8] While the protests of these years have served as an explanation for the occurrence and form of Swing in Norfolk, they must also be considered as part of the context that informed the actions of the magistracy in 1830–1831. The memory of popular protest was, in short, central in shaping both the resort to protest in the present and the responses of the authorities.

To borrow from Andy Wood, this chapter contends that the prosecution of Swing was part of a process of simplifying or condensing the 'messy historical realties' of protest, to establish an official narrative or memory of social upheaval.[9] The process of selection, the prosecution of cases, their punishment, and the rhetoric employed by the courts, reduced the complex of causes to inclusive and exclusive narratives that buoyed particular social relationships. Motives and modes of protest were disaggregated, recharacterising the (more) acceptable and unacceptable faces of Swing. This process of simplification also reveals the ways in which older official memories of protest were mobilised to create new ones. Considering the frequency of open collective protest in Norfolk in this period, the county provides a unique opportunity to consider the formation, and impact, of popular and judicial memories of rebellion.

Swing: Another Battle in the Rural War

Norfolk boasted one of the most advanced agricultural economies in England, and was reputed for pioneering improvements in farming techniques. Such successes in reclaiming land and revolutionising method pushed up land value, and the expense of making and managing improvements, further added to the burdens of tenant farmers. Threshing machines, first introduced to counter labour shortages during the Napoleonic Wars, grew in popularity amongst the yeomanry in peacetime, as they allowed the farmers to cut labour costs and accelerate production. With the majority of the county's population engaged in agricultural labour, an increasing population and demobilisation after 1815, intensified competition for employment.[10]

By 1816, the effects of depression were marked in the county. Reports to the Board of Agriculture outlined the plight of the farmer: land values had increased; without wartime profits and with decreasing prices for produce, he struggled to pay his rents and tithes. Consequently, smaller occupiers were giving up their tenancies, and those who persisted could not afford to employ labour, or pay adequate wages.[11] Thus, increasingly, the poor applied to the parish for relief, further pushing up the rents and the rates. The burden of the depression appeared to affect every stratum of society: many landowners were forced to abate rents and retrench. The majority of respondents to the board testified to the increasing distress of the poor, and approximately half of them indicated an increase in the poor rates, lamenting the pernicious practice of relieving able, but under-employed, labourers. These problems foreshadowed many of the issues and social divisions underlying the disturbances of 1830. Indeed, one respondent from Norfolk had some doubt as to 'how the poor are to be kept peaceable'.[12]

They were not. In the spring of 1816, a series of collective protests broke out: attacks on farm machinery in Suffolk bookended food and wage riots in Norfolk and the Fenlands of Cambridgeshire.[13] The most violent, and arguably most problematic, disturbances took place at Downham (Norfolk), Littleport and Ely (Cambridgeshire). On 20 May, magistrates and overseers meeting at the Crown Inn at Downham received a deputation from a crowd comprised of villagers from the surrounding area and local townspeople. Fronted by Justice John Dering, an offer of 2 s. a day wages and increased allowances for larger families was made. Wishing for the allowances to extend to all (as it had at Brandon in Suffolk), the crowd refused to disperse and the magistrates were forced to flee and hide themselves. Bread was redistributed, and goods and money were demanded of the town's shopkeepers and publicans. The arrival of the cavalry allowed the authorities to regain control, albeit temporarily, dispersing the crowd and taking prisoners. However, the people reassembled the next day and succeeded in securing the release of their comrades from Dering.[14] Allegedly spurred by the successes at Downham, the labourers of Littleport demanded the same concessions on 22 May, and proceeded to Ely with the same end on the 23rd. In both places, riotous crowds demanded money from local tradespeople and beer from the publicans. Finally, on 24 May, Sir Henry Bate Dudley arrived at Ely with the Royston Volunteer Cavalry, and violently dispersed the people still assembled at Littleport.[15]

More than one provincial newspaper reported with incredulity that the labourers were to 'have an advance of wages, and that the persons already taken should be allowed to return to their homes!'[16] To counter the level of concessions made, thirty people were capitally convicted at the Special Commission convened at Ely and at the Norfolk Summer Assizes. Five men were executed at Ely and two of the Downham rioters were hanged at Norwich.[17]

In 1822, threshing machines – concentrated in the southern division of the county –were the avowed targets of the labourers' protests. Multiple petitions to parliament in 1820, 1821 and 1822 testified to the persistence of agricultural distress in the southern and central hundreds of Norfolk.[18] The burden on the rates was felt from Holt on the North coast to Diss in the South.[19] Twenty machines were broken in Norfolk, at Diss, and in the surrounding area – a figure comparable to the number broken in 1830.[20] Threatening letters and fires attended the most concentrated outbreak of unrest in February. The labourers' actions were not marked with the same level of riot or violence exhibited in 1816, but the authorities acted with alacrity, calling on the cavalry and the dragoons to support the apprehension of machine breakers.[21] Although the immediate response may have been more robust, the sentencing of those convicted for their part in the disturbances was certainly more lenient than those of 1816. Two incendiaries were executed, but the majority of those involved in the disturbances in Norfolk in 1822 received terms of imprisonment.[22]

Writing to the Home Office during the disturbances of 1830, Justice John Wright reflected on his experiences of the protests of preceding decades. It had been 'six weeks before I could restore perfect tranquillity' in the spring of 1816, but he considered the machine breaking of 1822 had been put down far more effectively 'by the most prompt and determined measures of the magistrates aided by a troop of yeomanry cavalry'.[23] In both of these years Wright had also formed part of the bench at the Norwich sessions, which handled incidents of misdemeanour riot connected with the more serious outbreaks, and he sat on the Grand Jury at the Spring Assizes in 1822.[24] He clearly felt qualified to make recommendations to the Home Secretary: 'From my experience in these matters I can assure your Lordship that the most effectual way of suppressing the evil spirit which is now unfortunately so prevalent would be to place small parties of dragoons… who would then at very short notice be upon the spot to assist the magistrates.' Wright did not comment on the use of more conciliatory measures, but he hinted at the excessive sensibilities of some of his colleagues: 'One troop', he maintained, 'would be sufficient to beat any mob which Norwich can produce if their local magistrates should not be afraid of sacrificing their popularity.'[25] As we shall see, his critique was not entirely misplaced.

Wright's recollections highlight the legacy of past protest in framing judicial responses. It also appeared to inform the popular resort to unrest in 1830. For the most part, those areas disturbed in 1816 and 1822 appear to have remained quiet. The geographical distribution of unrest in 1830 was focused in the previously undisturbed areas in the north, north-east and centre of the county. Certainly, the ultimate sanction handed down by the Special Commission at Ely and the Assizes at Norfolk in 1816 remained in popular memory, and thus may be considered to have had the desired effect in the west of the county.[26] Archer has attributed the lack of disturbance in south Norfolk to the absence of threshing machines, removed in 1822 and not subsequently restored.[27] The first instances of open protest in 1830 occurred in mid-November in North Walsham and Holt, and concerned attacks on threshing machines.[28] At least 18 incidents of machine breaking were recorded that November and December, and 17 crowd actions. Here, popular grievances extended beyond the issue of machinery, including demands for increased wages and reductions in tithes.[29] Perhaps what distinguished the disturbances of 1830 was the activity of farmers as well as labourers. In the main, the yeomanry had been amongst the targets of the crowd in 1816 and 1822; in 1830, however, the authorities, as Archer has stated, were confronted by an alliance that amounted 'to a case of conspiracy'.[30]

Relations between the gentry and their tenants had deteriorated since the end of the French Wars. Tithes were a persistent issue and had been at the heart of the Norfolk farmers' dispute in 1823. Six thousand had assembled at Norwich that year to hear the radical agitator William Cobbett; when, according to Archer, 'the meeting ended in spectacular fashion when the normally deferential tenantry voted in favour of Cobbett's resolution and petition'. Consequently, landowners and rectors reduced rents and tithes. Having dealt with the labourers' protests the previous year, they could not 'withstand the verbal attacks of their natural allies'.[31] But tensions were made public again by the spring of 1830, when the gentry in their capacity as the county bench, raised the issue of 'proper wages' with the yeomanry on the grand jury. Lord Suffield, chairman of the Quarter Sessions, imputed the farmers had no 'regret for the degraded and miserable condition of the poor, or the slightest manifestation of a desire to improve that condition'. In an open letter, the grand jury reproached Suffield for his 'asperity' and pointed out that a 'want of sympathy for [the] privations' of the poor, 'and want of power to alleviate them, are totally distinct'. They were convinced 'that the distresses of the agricultural poor are mainly to be attributed to the deplorable condition of the farmer, and can effectually be relieved only by a reduction in their burdens'.[32] Allied with the labourers' grievances in the winter of 1830, the farmers pressed their point with far greater force.

The only place to see machine breaking in both 1822 and 1830 was Attleborough. In the Select Committee report of 1821, it had been highlighted as an area where the distress of *farmers* was greatest.[33] In 1830, it was the site of what was perceived to be one of the most serious incidents of riot. On 4 December, a group of labourers, having attacked the workhouse at Attleborough, proceeded to Rev. Franklin's property. The labourers threatened to destroy the chaff-cutting machine and held the aged clergymen for over three hours until he capitulated to their demands for a reduction in his tithes in order that they could be paid better wages.[34] According to Rev. Temple Frere, a justice of Diss, the Rector had faced the 'rough justice' of being dragged through the pond by the crowd. When he appealed to the farmers present to assist, they 'attempted to persuade me that they had been brought there by force. I saw no appearance of force, but on the contrary observed that there was an understanding between the Farmers and the Labourers'.[35]

But Swing as it was manifest in Norfolk was not entirely confined to the 'rural war' in the minds of the authorities. The proximity of disturbances to the county capital made the prospect of disorder spreading to urban areas a terrifying possibility. Writing from Norwich at the end of November 1830, the Lord Lieutenant, John Wodehouse, informed Lord Melbourne that he 'tremble[d] for this town. The Mob are trying to force in to Norwich and to unite in great force'.[36] Wodehouse was particularly concerned for the extension of machine-breaking amongst the city's depressed textile manufactories. Weavers had been implicated in the food riot in Norwich in 1816, and, as Charlesworth has demonstrated, protesters across the county came from a range of occupational groups.[37] Although it was almost exclusively agricultural workers who perpetrated the machine breaking of 1822, the mayor of Norwich expressed concern for the 'feverish temper in the lower classes of the inhabitants of this city'.[38] In 1830, concerns for an alliance between urban and rural workers were heightened, resulting in military forces in the county being concentrated on the protection of the capital.[39]

Some insisted on distinguishing elements of unrest from the problems associated with agricultural society, particularly the occurrence of arson in previously undisturbed areas. Fires at Irmingland and Lingwood were unequivocally attributed to the 'work of some diabolical incendiary', but the labourers stood 'exonerated from all manner of suspicion'. This proved somewhat ironic in the case of the Lingwood fire, as the labourers who had assisted in putting it out, got drunk on the beer they had been given in reward, and proceeded to the neighbouring farm and demolished the threshing machine there. But in the press, the two incidents remained separate: the disorderly actions of the labourers did not detract from their praiseworthy conduct in putting out the fire.[40] Elsewhere in the county, xenophobic paranoia triggered the arrest of European and Irish migrants;

correspondents were convinced of the malignant influence of 'weavers and mechanics', whilst others blamed the example of Continental revolution.[41]

At one level, the disturbances in 1830 were another explosive manifestation of the rural war in Norfolk; a continuation of the problems experienced since at least 1816. But the social relations or dislocations that underscored unrest were increasingly complex. As Archer has suggested, this was more than class antagonism.[42] The magistracy had to contend with the grievances of the farmers as well as the poor labourers, most problematically expressed in concert in 1830. This complex extended beyond the rural: both agricultural and urban-industrial communities shared in the effects of depression, and the authorities had to consider a further alliance of grievances across occupational groups. National and international contexts also impacted on the perception of protest. Swing in Norfolk was not wholly divorced from the disturbances elsewhere. Fear of foreign elements fomenting rebellion, whether from the south-east or the Continent, contributed to the context of unrest.[43]

Faced with such a complex of causes and contexts, the Norfolk magistracy had limited resources with which to respond. The Yeomanry Cavalry, which had proved vital to the restoration of order in 1816 and 1822, had been disbanded without the prospect of revival in 1827.[44] Considering the animosity that existed between the Norfolk gentry and the lower orders of rural society, it is unsurprising to find that many farmers and labourers were unwilling to enrol as Special Constables to support the local authorities.[45] Writing to the Home Secretary, Wodehouse admitted that attempts to augment the civil power in this way had 'been productive of Mischief by affording the Farmers in a Body an opportunity of expressing their discontent at the Landlords and the Clergy'.[46] In the absence of any professional force, the magistracy had to rely on failing social bonds, creating the space for labourers and farmers to extract concessions.

Hobsbawm and Rudé described the public concessions made in Norfolk as a 'remarkable' display of 'indulgence' on the part of the magistrates.[47] After the first incident of machine breaking in November, the North Walsham bench had recommended the disuse of threshing machines, and an increase in wages. The magistrates at Gallow and Diss made similar concessions.[48] In a letter to Wodehouse, the Home Secretary responded to these measures with telling brevity: 'I trust that your expectation that the simple Concession with respect to the Thrashing Machines, will be attended with the desired Effect'.[49] It was not. In addition to the example of concessions from various districts across the county, Lord Suffield suggested that Wodehouse had unwittingly agreed to 2 s. a day being a just wage when remonstrating with a crowd, stimulating further demands for increases in wages.[50] No doubt the shadow of 1816 loomed large as the poor demanded the same concessions across the county.

But Wodehouse went further. By the beginning of December it appeared that peace was returning to Norfolk. Consequently, the committee of magistrates at Norwich recommended a 'general disuse of THRESHING MACHINES' as a 'friendly concession on the part of Proprietors to public opinion, and as proof of their anxiety to remove as far as possible every pretext for the violation of Laws'.[51] This step was more significant than the localised concessions already granted; it was almost unprecedented in the context of Swing as it was a *countywide* measure delivered from the Bench.

The strongest censure came from central government in a circular issued by Melbourne on 8 December. The Home Secretary 'observed, with great Regret' those Justices of the Peace that had approved a 'uniform Rate of wages' or recommended the discontinuance of threshing machines, and instructed them to 'oppose a firm Resistance to all Demands' for wages and against agricultural machinery.[52] Wodehouse was not so agreeable in his response where he stoically defended the conduct of the Norfolk magistracy. The circular had 'been the cause of great uneasiness to many of our Magistrates... I have indeed heard with deep regret that some who were the most active in the late trying occasions, have determined to act no longer.' He claimed the priority of every magistrate had been the apprehension of offenders and their commitment to trial. But, in the particular context of economic hardship, 'we could not forbear to admit, that wages had been generally too low, and that we thought that, under the actual difficulty of finding employment for the Labouring Poor, which has too long existed, Threshing Machines ought to be discontinued'. Wodehouse finally declared 'that, under a perplexing choice of difficulties we have so acted as to check the spirit of insubordination in a much shorter time than has been the case in other counties, and that we have in no instance acted under the influence of threats and intimidation'.[53]

Wodehouse's defence epitomised the problems faced by the magistracy in keeping the peace. The suppression of disorder was of paramount concern, however, as leaders of their communities they also had to address the underlying causes of discontent. Despite the criticisms of Wright, or, more significantly, the Home Secretary, faced with the complex of causes and deeply entrenched social tensions the Norfolk magistrates saw conciliatory measures as a legitimate, indeed necessary part of the limited repertoire of actions available to them.

What was undeniably problematic was the very public nature of the concessions. They had clearly emanated from the Bench, rather than from the private charity of the justices in their capacity as landowners, gentlemen and clerics. This endowed the labourers' protests with the legitimacy of the law. It was widely reported that the rioters at East Tuddenham brandished a paper claiming they 'had got an authority from the magistrates to break threshing machines'. Lord Suffield had even received reports that machines had been broken in the presence of magistrates.[54] He recommended private agreements and had quietly dictated a rate of wages to his tenants.[55] This mode of concession was used to side-step criticisms that the authorities had responded to intimidation, and potential accusations of illegality in setting wages, whilst still ensuring the poor remained beholden to their social superiors.

The concessions granted by the Norfolk magistracy in 1830 betrayed the extent of distress in the county, and the authorities' understanding of it. As had been the case in 1816, the way in which they were granted proved highly problematic, both locally and from the perspective of central government. Official and social authority had been undermined by the apparent capitulation of the gentry in the face of the public. The prosecution of the perpetrators of unrest was an important opportunity for the magistracy to check further disorder and restore their authority. The courts provided the forum in which social boundaries could be redrawn.

Modes of Prosecution and Narratives of Protest

Hobsbawm and Rudé highlighted Norfolk as one of those counties where a Swing offender had a better than average chance of acquittal. The apparently merciful sentencing in the Norfolk courts was cast as a continuation of placative judicial attitudes.[56] But this is an oversimplification. Elsewhere I have drawn attention to the proactivity of the local magistracy in the careful construction of prosecutions at every level, from the county quarter sessions to the Special Commissions.[57] Whilst judicial attitudes were shaped by local contexts, in the winter of 1830–1831, local and central government shared the same concern in the aftermath of such widespread unrest. As the Attorney General stated in defence of the Special Commissions, 'one of the leading principles of the prosecutions [was] the protection of the local authorities'.[58]

This imperative was shared across the Swing counties, but the mode of prosecution was markedly different in Norfolk. The majority of offenders were tried at the county quarter sessions, and very few faced the maximum penalties for either machine breaking or riot.[59] But these choices were calculated according to the immediate needs of the county and in relation to the broader context of unrest past and present. Addressing the court, Sergeant John Frere, chairman of the Norfolk Sessions in January 1831, carefully positioned the county's Swing trials. He noted that the disturbances of 1830 lacked those 'flagrant acts of violence' that had accompanied incidents of protest in other parts of the country; occasions, he continued, that 'imperiously call for much more severe examples than I am happy to say is requisite here'. The 'punishment', he continued, 'inflicted on those who now about 15 years ago were prosecuted at the Isle of Ely… had I doubt not operated as a warning'. In making this contrast, Frere indicated the court did not intend to levy the maximum against many of the perpetrators, but he reminded the public, that 'the dominion of the law must be maintained'.[60] These comparisons were functional: they were used to characterise and rationalise the prosecution of Swing in Norfolk within the popularly understood context of long-term unrest.

Frere's reference to the disturbances of 1816 was significant. That year, as well as in 1830–1831, the county judiciary had to nullify the effects of the very public concessions made by the Bench, which had undermined their authority. But the contrast in the mode of prosecution was stark. The rioters from Downham, Littleport and Ely were tried at the Norfolk Assizes and at a swiftly convened Special Commission held at Ely in June 1816. Signalling their concern for the conduct of the prosecutions, central government sent the Treasury Solicitor, Henry Hobhouse, to oversee the prosecutions. This intervention was not without the support of the local judiciary. Some had called for government assistance; others contributed to the construction of the Crown prosecution case; and many of them made a public show of their endorsement by sitting alongside the Chief Justices at the opening of the Commission.[61] However, the Home Secretary, Lord Sidmouth, evidently entertained some doubt as to the ability of parts of the magistracy, as Hobhouse and some local correspondents were quietly charged with investigating the conduct of the Downham justices.[62]

The purpose of the Special Commission was made clear from the outset. Before any cases had been heard, Justice Abbott stated their purpose in his charge to the Grand Jury: to convince the public 'by the awful lesson which may here be taught, that… the law is too strong for its assailants'.[63] Finding capital charges was not difficult. The admittedly aggressive 'levy of Contributions', as Hobhouse described it, was recast under the law as robbery and other species of theft. Eighty-two men and women were brought before the court facing more than one hundred capital charges.[64] Some of these charges had been pursued with dogged determination. The first case heard before the court had failed on a fault in the indictment. Refusing to let those acquitted go free, a second indictment was drawn up, and Hobhouse was pleased to report that those who had not already been convicted on other charges had at last been found guilty, bringing 'the Session to a most satisfactory Conclusion'.[65]

By the end of the court sitting, 24 people had been capitally convicted. The requisite examples being made, the remaining prisoners were discharged on their own recognisances, with both the Crown counsel and Justice Abbott making much of the mercy afforded them.[66] Of those facing the death penalty, five were left for execution. The men were buried in St Mary's churchyard, Ely, with an epitaph inscribed on the parish church: 'May their awful fate be a warning to others'.[67] The examples made at Ely were reinforced by the prosecution of the Downham rioters. At the Norfolk Assizes in August, 16 were capitally convicted and two, Thomas Thody and Daniel Harwood, were executed at Castle Hill (Norwich) in front on an immense concourse of spectators.[68]

By prosecuting the majority of cases at the county quarter sessions in 1831, the magistrates of Norfolk kept the framing of the trials firmly within their jurisdiction, allowing them to prioritise local interests. It also afforded the opportunity to emphasise the competency and control of the local authorities. Indeed, Sergeant Frere felt that the prosecutions in all counties were better administered by men with local connection and should not be subject to the pressures of public opinion: 'How is it possible that they can better know what is necessary to be done… than those who are aware of the whole nature of the case.'[69]

Yet the organisation of the county trials was not without thought to their public impact: all bar one of the prosecutions made in January 1831 were tried at Norwich. In the regular circuit of sessions, cases would also be tried by adjournment at Kings Lynn and Little Walsingham, facilitating more convenient gaol delivery from Swaffham and Walsingham bridewells. No cases associated with the disturbances were tried at the meeting at Lynn on 25 January, and all the prisoners from Swaffham and Walsingham were delivered to the county capital to face an unusually full bench of magistrates.[70]

Despite this show of social strength from the Norfolk elite, the sessions were presided over by Sergeant John Frere. Notwithstanding the importance Frere placed on local men administering local matters, he cast himself as an impartial arbiter – a non-resident (although a close cousin from Cambridgeshire) and 'not engaged in any of these prosecutions in preference to any of my able colleagues who might, from fatal necessity, have been in some degree concerned in proceedings'.[71] While his presence was used to remove the Norfolk justices from any accusations of partiality or abuse of their power, the Sergeant drew attention to 'the great care and discretion used by the committing magistrates' celebrating the fact that 'not one bill connected with the late unhappy outrages was thrown out by the Grand Jury'.[72]

There was less scope for fatal examples to be made than there had been in 1816. The majority of cases heard at the Norfolk quarter sessions concerned machine breaking, which carried a maximum penalty of seven years' transportation.[73] Significantly, the judiciary exhibited little appetite for more violent sanctions. As Wodehouse's defence to Melbourne had made clear, the magistracy could not ignore the state of deprivation of the county's labouring poor. The perpetrators, Wodehouse considered, were 'Persons here probably heretofore borne of good Characters … were compelled either by open violence or threats to commit the felonies with which they stand charged.' Examples would still be made: the magistrates wished to review all cases 'and only send those to trial, who were seen and known to be Ringleaders and Active Agents in perpetrating the Outrages' which 'might fully answer the ends of justice'.[74] With equal, if not greater calculation than the prosecutions made at the Special Commission in 1816, and those convened at Winchester and Salisbury in 1830 and 1831, Wodehouse sought specific exemplars. This process of selection was pursued in both the county courts, and at the largely overlooked Special Commission organised at Wodehouse's behest for March 1831.

Only nine of the 65 prisoners charged with breaking threshing machines in 1830 received the maximum sentence of seven years' transportation.[75] The majority, as had been the case in 1822, received terms of imprisonment. Archer noted the light sentencing in 1822, suggesting that the otherwise good characters of the perpetrators inclined the courts to clemency.[76] There are also indications that the judiciary were ambivalent towards the use of machines. At the Lent Assizes 1822, the judge reproached the grand jury (comprised of gentleman and magistrates) as 'sufficient attention does not appear to have been paid' to such offences committed in the county. Public recommendations for their disuse had been made, but these had not come with the authority of the Bench.[77]

Those who received the most stringent sentence of transportation in 1831 were a particularly necessary example. Having made a countywide recommendation for the disuse of threshing machines during the disturbances, the magistrates had been subjected to government criticism, which placed the blame for ongoing disturbances with their overconciliatory attitude. More than one testimony referred to the prisoners' claims that they were acting with the permission of the authorities.[78] This popular notion of legality was most evident in the round of machine breaking focused upon the settlements of Cawston, Heydon, Dalling and Reepham.

Henry Parnell, prosecuted for his involvement in two incidents of machine breaking around Field Dalling, had been heard to declare that Justice Sir Jacob Astley had given 'him leave to break all the machines he could find'.[79] Parnell's claim referred to the public notice from the justices of Melton Constable recommending the disuse of threshing machines that had been signed by Astley and several others.[80] At Whinburgh, and then at East Tuddenham, crowds intent on destroying threshing machines made similar assertions and actually 'had a paper in their hand, and offered to show it'.[81] In passing the maximum penalty for machine breaking, seven years' transportation, on men such as William Catchpole and James Gunton – prominent figures in the round of destruction, and the men who produced the paper at East Tuddenham – the magistracy checked suggestions that they had tacitly sanctioned criminal behaviour. Parnell was acquitted on one count of machine breaking, but failed to escape the full rigour of the law: he was charged and prosecuted on a second count of machine breaking, and sentenced to 12 months in prison.[82]

Attacks on figures of authority were likewise treated with greater severity. At Docking, Haddiscoe and Attleborough, the labourers sought redress from clergymen or magistrates and in all cases a confrontation ensued. The case made against the Docking rioters was presented as an overt attack on authority. Sergeant Frere stated, 'If ever a tumultuous and riotous assembly approached the crime of high treason, it was this.'[83] The rioters were accused of an assault on Justice John Davey and one of his special constables. Davey had gone to remonstrate with the assembled crowd, but his attempts to point out their illegality proved futile. His horse was knocked down, at which point he read the Riot Act, and he continued to try to address them. One of the constables was knocked to the ground and struck at whilst prostrate. Davey attempted to assist the felled man and was pelted with stones, one 'rendering him insensible; a surgeon's attendance was necessary, and his life was actually placed in jeopardy'.[84] Seven men were convicted for their involvement in the riot, receiving prison sentences of between four months and two years.[85] Their actions were described by the court 'as a general attack on the Magistracy, an attack upon the government, a defiance of the law and levying war; and had the prisoners been sent to answer for the treason, their lives would have been justly forfeited'.[86]

In his discussion of the prosecutions in 1822, Muskett rightly highlighted the dual purpose of the trials as both 'judicial and political'; that 'if a particular offence could be interpreted as part of a wider conspiracy, or as indicative of a spirit of insurrection, examples had to be made'.[87] But this process of interpretation served a further purpose: in elevating these incidents to the status of political acts, the genuine grievances of the labourers were marginalised, and any legitimacy their impoverished condition bestowed on their protests was nullified.

Recasting the actions of the rioters as insurrectionary in 1816 was a fundamental tactic of the prosecution, used to detract from the capitulation of Dering and his fellow justices. A general narrative was drawn up in advance of the trials, used to underpin all of the prosecution briefs. The account given presented the disturbances as the product of 'an organised system of Riot and Plunder'. The rioters had 'armed themselves with the most dangerous and offensive Weapons':

> Thus prepared and in some degree disciplined by a few unprincipled Men who had lately been discharged from the Militias they assumed a bold and menacing attitude and disguised their intention under the mask of seeking a remedy from distress which they pretended to suffer from the want of employment the low price of labour and the high price of Flour.

The depredations of the 'Norfolk banditti' were made all the more dreadful by repeated reference to the age and infirmity of their victims, 'helpless and inoffensive' farmers, terrified and robbed in their own homes.[88]

The five men executed in the wake of the Special Commission were considered the 'worst offenders', each of the men had been convicted on multiple charges. William Beamiss and John Dennis were singled out as men 'whose condition in life' removed them from any claim to distress; Beamiss was a shoemaker and Dennis a victualler. Neither, it was claimed, could be motivated by the same grievances as the agricultural classes. Isaac Harley was likewise singled out for being amongst the first to attack Rev. Justice Vachell.[89]

Although very few cases were sent to the higher courts in 1830, the Special Commission requested by Wodehouse was, as the courts at Ely had been, orchestrated for maximum effect. The Assizes were usually held at Thetford, but the Special Commission sat at Norwich to hear the cases of what the Assize judges described – in private correspondence – as a 'particular class of prisoner'.[90] Of the eight on trial for arson, Richard Nockolds was the only person executed for a Swing offence in Norfolk.[91]

The opening of the Special Assize at Norwich was described as 'an epocha in the history of Norfolk'.[92] It was the first Lent assize to have been held in the city. Much was made of the fact that the presiding Judge, Sir Edward Alderson, was a 'native' of the county (he had also sat at the Swing Special Commissions in December 1830 and January 1831).[93] Indeed, the proceedings were represented, in the press at least, to emphasise the power and identity of the county. Noting the charges before the court, Nockolds and his accomplices for arson, and several poachers for murder, Alderson considered them to be 'offences of the deepest dye'.[94]

Authority viewed arson with particular abhorrence: incendiaries worked in secrecy, with no other motive than injuring their victim through the destruction of property.[95] Such devastating offences, as we have seen, were repeatedly blamed on a foreign element. As Norfolk's landowners publicly exclaimed, 'It is for the honour of our country, it is for our credit as men, that we must find out and punish these cowardly miscreants. Englishmen were never assassins! Englishmen were never incendiaries…'.[96]

Nockolds was not a foreigner, but aspects of this xenophobic attitude permeated his case. In the words of Judge Alderson, he was 'not an agricultural labourer… driven to extremities" but a weaver residing in Norwich. He had given up 'the restraints of religion' and been corrupted by Cobbett and Carlisle; the Sunday reading-room he had established was seen as a nursery of dissent. All legitimacy that could be derived from the plight of the labourers was denied Nockolds. The judge concluded: 'you therefore committed this act for the purpose of exciting general confusion and alarm throughout the country'.[97]

Similar distinctions were made in the execution of Noah Peake and George Fortis in 1822. Both men were convicted for firing haystacks, and had admitted to writing threatening letters to, 'by a flash and a scare' as Peake put it, 'alarm the farmers and induce them to make a more ample allowance to the poor'.[98] Whilst the magistracy had connected their actions with machine breaking in private correspondence, no reference was made in the course of proceedings to connect arson with more overt protest.

But Fortis and Peake were both ex-servicemen, a fact that was used to present their actions in a more sinister light, as the potential instigators of rebellion.[99]

Nockolds' case provided a more potent example: his trial and execution were conducted in Norwich, his home and the county capital, to ensure maximum exposure. He was hanged in front of his family and a considerable crowd who watched in silence. Dispatching him in this way reinforced the line that the authorities had drawn between the agricultural and urban labourers, separating communities united by shared grievances.

In those cases where the conspiracy between labourers and farmers had been most apparent, the labourers fared far worse than their allies. Dealing with the disloyalty of the farmers was problematic for the magistracy. Their betrayal of class loyalties, in siding with the labourers, made them worthy of punishment, but they could not be so easily divorced from the agricultural community. In attempting prosecutions, the attitude of the magistracy appears ambivalent. But they were reminded of the potential hazard of forcing the issue when the jury, drawn from the yeoman class, frustrated attempts to incriminate fellow farmers.

The disturbances at Attleborough and Haddiscoe were marked by the challenges they posed to the Establishment; but of more concern, by the complicity of farmers in the labourers' actions. The aged Rev. Franklin was held captive for several hours. Some 200 labourers and 20 farmers were reported to be present, but no more than one or two of the farmers gave any assistance to Franklin. The labourers had attempted to force an increase in wages and consequently a reduction in tithes to achieve that end. Echoing the report of Temple Frere, the court was certain that 'some pre-meditated understanding, some unfair and unhandsome communication' existed between the labourers and their employers.[100]

In the prosecution, everything possible was done to highlight the criminality of the labourers involved in the disturbances. The crowd assembled at Franklin's property were also accused of attacking the Attleborough workhouse. Their abuses were greater still because they took place in the early hours of a Sunday morning. Sergeant Frere went to pains to highlight the immorality of this breach of the Sabbath. Most sinister were the insurrectionary undertones of some of the statements the rioters were alleged to have made. Samuel Smith had been heard boasting, 'that the devil was dead; they were the strongest party, and always should be; that this was only the beginning; that they were at the feet but should go up to the head'.[101] Seven men were sentenced for their involvement. The perceived ringleaders, labourers Robert Smith, Samuel Smith and John Stacey, were imprisoned for two and a half years, two years, and 18 months, respectively.[102] The severity of their sentencing was acknowledged in the petition for their release made by Franklin himself.[103]

In answering queries regarding the absence of farmers in the convictions, Frere stated that if other men 'no matter in what situation they might be' had been detected and apprehended, they 'would most assuredly have been dealt with equal if not greater severity than any of the prisoners at the bar'.[104] There is no evidence to suggest that any of the farmers present were ever brought before the court.

The intervention of farmers proved critical to the prosecution of a riot at Burgh St Peter. The incumbent of the parish, Rev. William Boycott, had agreed to meet representatives from the labourers to discuss the issue of wages. He alleged that the assembled crowd abused him and attempted to extort money. Initially, the clergyman refused to give any sort of concession. However, he explained that 'nearly all the farmers were present', and when one publicly declared he would give everything he was refunded to the labourers, Boycott felt compelled to consent to a refund.[105] The jury were apparently satisfied with the arguments made in defence of the labourers: that the crowd had not posed any genuine threat, and that the criticisms levelled at Rev. Boycott – that he had neglected his duties as a clergyman by failing to visit the sick or relieve the poor – were legitimate. All the defendants were acquitted.[106]

In his summation, Frere struggled to rationalise the jury's verdict. He noted Boycott's youth and inexperience in his office, and that he could not escape some of the blame as 'the assembly was in some measure, convened by the Reverend Gentleman himself'. Consequently, Boycott's case was held up as proof 'that concession only produces further violence'. With regard to the jurors themselves, Frere could not fathom 'whatever notion they could have had in their minds' but presented their behaviour as a reflection of the fairness enshrined in the institution of the jury trial: 'such a verdict makes me reflect on and join in the sentiment with the poet when he said, "England with all thy faults, I love thee still."'[107]

Frere continued to maintain that any farmers proved to have been complicit in the disturbances would be punished. However, little effort appeared to be made on this front by the courts. The only farmer tried at the sessions in January 1831 was Lee Amis of Roughton, who was charged with instigating a riot. It was alleged that he had encouraged a group of labourers who had accosted Stephen Sutton, a fellow farmer. The labourers considered Sutton 'the person who oppressed the poor'.[108]

Amis was a small farmer, occupying eight to ten acres of his own. He and Sutton had disagreed at local vestry meetings, where Amis had advocated paying 'good wages' rather than supplementing them from the rates. How far the meagre circumstances of the defendant, or his previous disputes with the victim, led the jury to acquit Amis is uncertain. They may have also considered the incident to be the product of drunkenness, the crowd having been given beer by many others – a fact that was drawn attention to in the proceedings.[109] Clearly, while parochial politics had informed the disturbance at Roughton, the jury did not seek to make an example of Amis as a troublesome farmer. Indeed, the attitude of the jury in this case, and in their generosity to the rioters at Burgh St Peter may have been influenced by their sympathy with men of a similar standing: yeomen who shared the burden of tithes and poor rates. Certainly, this class had used the Norfolk courts before as a forum in which their disputes with the gentry might be aired.

Aside from Amis, charges were brought against two other farmers, John Carmen and David Roll, at the county sessions in April 1831. Carman was acquitted owing to a fault in the indictment, and the chief witness for the prosecution against Roll, Mr. E. Wodehouse (a member of the Commission of the Peace), wished to 'withdraw all further prosecution, with a view to putting an end to these cases, and in the hope the defendant would see the impropriety of his conduct and desist from such a course of proceeding in the future'.[110] Similar attempts had been made in 1816 to prosecute Henry Benson, a farmer of considerable means, charged with inciting riot. Having struggled to secure evidence against Benson, Hobhouse allowed the indictment to be traversed. It was then agreed that the case would be dropped if Benson admitted his error and entered into sureties for good behaviour; finally, the charge was respited.[111] In 1816, and in 1830, despite Frere's statements to the contrary, the Bench did not wish to antagonise their 'natural allies' or risk an embarrassing acquittal.

Quietly dispensing with the farmers in this way still served the court's purpose in creating a particular narrative of Swing, absolving their tenants of responsibility and ending their alliance with the labourers who bore the brunt of punishment. Whilst many of Frere's statements bordered on the hyperbolic, the rhetoric employed and the patterns of prosecution worked towards the creation of a particular understanding of Swing in its aftermath.

Using 1816 as a precedent, popular memories of protest and punishment were evoked to rationalise the prosecution of unrest in 1830. From the public forum of the courts, the authorities sought to perpetuate a new narrative of events, an official memory disseminated in an attempt to inform subsequent popular memories of Swing.

Conclusion

The prosecution of protest by the county magistracy has been presented here as a calculated act of local government. The precise nature of repression was framed by local social and political contexts, and the local memory of past protests, as much as by statute law and the demands of central government. In Norfolk, the Swing disturbances of 1830, as Archer has suggested, must be considered in relation to the protests of the preceding 15 years. The riots of 1816 and 1822 informed the form and distribution of unrest in 1830, but also the perception and prosecution of protest by the authorities. The failing social relations that underscored the 'rural war' had deteriorated further by 1830. The antagonism between the gentry and their tenants added another dimension to popular unrest. Following King's argument, the interactions of the middling classes influenced the context of unrest.[112] In Norfolk in 1830, the farmers capitalised on the space created by the labourers' protests, bargaining their loyalty in return for concessions.

But Swing must be understood in a broader context, beyond any tripartite organisation of rural society. The magistracy were affected by the disturbances in neighbouring counties and radical agitation at home and abroad; they also had to consider the experience of poverty in other occupational communities, notably the depressed weavers of Norwich. From the perspective of authority, Swing crossed local, national and international bounds. Faced with this complex set of relations, the magistracy had limited resources with which to suppress unrest. In the absence of the volunteer troops in 1830, the local benches of Norfolk opted to make concessions to protesters, establishing patterns of response that, while locally relevant, jarred with countywide recommendations and created issues of parity in neighbouring districts. In persisting with public conciliatory measures, despite criticism from colleagues and central government in 1816 and 1830, the magistracy revealed their recognition of the very real problems that existed in their communities since at least the end of the French Wars. It likewise indicates their sense of responsibility, but also their determination to maintain paternal social relationships that bound the poor to the propertied.

The role of the courts, perhaps the last weapon in the judicial arsenal with which authority could be secured, is significant. As Douglas Hay has argued, the courts were the site of very public contests regarding the probity of concessionary measures. It was a forum in which policy lines could be drawn.[113] By trying the majority of cases at the county quarter sessions, the Norfolk justices had greater control over proceedings, allowing them to shape the prosecutions according to local needs. It also provided a platform to emphasise the competency of local government. The public comparison made with the prosecutions in 1816 was likewise a calculated move. By positioning the prosecution of Swing in relation to the brutal examples made at Ely, the magistracy could justify their continued lenity in the charges brought in 1831, highlight their beneficence to the county at large, and reduce the impact of Swing. Despite its scale, Swing in Norfolk was presented as less alarming than the unrest experienced in 1816.

However, the Norfolk bench still shared in the task of all parts of government in the aftermath of Swing: the restoration of authority. Consequently pointed examples were made. The Special Commission convened at Norwich in March 1831, whilst very different to those held in the southern Swing counties, was nonetheless a show trial; an opportunity to make a very pointed example of Richard Nockolds.

The narratives presented by the courts at every level were intended to redefine a particular understanding or memory of unrest: the transportation of those who would appropriate the authority of the law, the penalties levied against non-agricultural workers, and the characterisation of the most violent acts as 'un-English', allowed the judiciary to make potent examples which were distinguished from the genuine distress of rural workers. The xenophobic sentiments that permeated some of the trials further sought to divide the rural and urban.

Keith Snell has highlighted the role of 'local xenophobia' in checking the development of class-consciousness. Particularly in the depressed conditions following the Napoleonic Wars, concerns for limited resources and employment opportunities strengthened prejudice and fear of 'foreign' interlopers. Swing, however, revealed the possibility of collective action across parish, occupational and even county boundaries.[114] In the processes of selection and mode of prosecution, the courts created the acceptable and unacceptable faces of Swing. They redrew social bounds to include even those modes of protest or grievances that ensured the poor were beholden to authority, and excluded those that challenged the status quo. Even the light handling of the farmers appears as a calculated measure to end inter-class collaboration between the middle and lower orders, particularly when there was some resistance to the bench manifest in the petty jury. In this way, the magistracy attempted to fracture the potential of Swing as a broader social movement. Divested of any political agency or semblance of burgeoning class-consciousness, chided like children for attacking their 'best friends', the protests of the agricultural labourers were presented as a failure. The very public dissemination of this narrative via the courts and the press must be considered an attempt to shape subsequent popular memories of Swing: endeavouring to deny any meaningful precedent beyond a reminder of the operation of law, confining Swing to the 'last labourers' revolt' – an impression that endured.

The judicial understanding of Swing, and the sorts of narratives created by the courts were not confined to Norfolk. Even in counties that experienced few acts of overt protest, the perceived threat of unrest from without, altered social relationships, pressing the authorities to react and creating political space in which grievances could be aired by all sectors of society. Somerset provides a case in point, where, in the absence of riot, the authorities were forced to concede to farmers and labourers. They likewise felt the distresses of industrial and urban communities, testifying to the more pervasive scope of Swing. In the regional courts and the Special Commissions the same careful shaping of prosecution can be discerned: the most potent examples being made of those outside agricultural society, and those who made the most overt challenges to authority.[115] By addressing protest from the perspective of the authorities, a more complex picture of causes is revealed. The operation of the courts, and in particular, the official memory of unrest they sought to create in the process of prosecution, under scrutiny, betrays the scope of Swing as a much broader social movement.

NOTES

1. Harvey J Kaye, 'E. P. Thompson, the British Marxist historical tradition and the contemporary crisis' in Harvey K. Kaye and Keith McClelland (eds), *E. P. Thompson: Critical Perspectives* (Polity Press: 1990), 259–260; Adrian Randall, 'Captain Swing: a retrospect', *International Review of Social History* 54 (2009), 427.
2. Steve Poole, 'Forty years of rural history from below: Captain Swing and the historians', *Southern History*, 32 (2010), 12–19; Carl. J. Griffin, *The*

Rural War: Captain Swing and the Politics of Protest (Manchester University Press: 2012), 321–2.
3. Eric J. Hobsbawm and George Rudé, *Captain Swing* (London: Phoenix Press, 2001/1969), 258–63.
4. Griffin, *The Rural War*, 248–59; Carl J. Griffin, '"Policy on the hoof": Sir Robert Peel, Sir Edward Knatchbull and the trial of the Elham machine breakers, 1830', *Rural History,* 15 (2004), 130; Rose Wallis, '"We do not come here… to enquire into grievances we come here to decide law": prosecuting Swing in Norfolk and Somerset', *Southern History,* 32 (2010): 159–75; Rose Wallis, 'The relationship between magistrates and their communities in the age of crisis: social protest c. 1790–1834' (PhD thesis, University of the West of England, 2016).
5. Peter King, 'Edward Thompson's contribution to eighteenth-century studies. The patrician: plebeian model re-examined', *Social History* 2 (1996), 222; Peter King, 'The summary courts and social relations in eighteenth-century England', *Past and Present* 183 (2004), 127.
6. Carl J. Griffin, 'The culture of combination: solidarities and collective action before Tolpuddle', *Historical Journal* 58 (2015), 443–80.
7. John Archer, *By a Flash and a Scare: Arson, Animal Maiming, and Poaching in East Anglia 1815–1870* (Breviary: 2010/1990), 49; Carl J. Griffin, *Protest, Politics and Work in Rural England, 1700–1850* (Palgrave Macmillan: 2014), 138.
8. Alfred J. Peacock, *Bread or Blood* (Victor Gollancz: 1965); Paul Muskett, 'The East Anglian riots 1822', *Agricultural History Review* 32 (1984), 2; Archer, *By a Flash and a Scare*.
9. Andy Wood, 'Deference, paternalism and popular memory in early modern England', in Steve Hindle (ed.), *Social Relations and Social Change in Early Modern England* (Boydell and Brewer: 2013), 234 and 246.
10. Archer, *By a Flash and a Scare,* 26–8.
11. Board of Agriculture, *Agricultural State of the Kingdom* (Board of Agriculture: 1816), esp.185–227.
12. Ibid., 190, 199, 205 and 219.
13. Andrew Charlesworth, *An Atlas of Rural Protest 1548–1900* (Croom Helm: 1983), 146.
14. The National Archives, HO 42/151, fos. 3–6, Suffield to the Home Office, 11 June 1816; Peacock, *Bread or Blood,* 86–92.
15. Cambridgeshire Archives [hereafter CA], K 283/L/1/22 Narrative of the riotous transactions at Littleport, Ely and Downham 22–24 May 1816; Peacock, *Bread or Blood,* 95–111.
16. *The Star,* 26 May 1816, also cited in Peacock, *Bread or Blood,* 92–3.
17. Peacock, *Bread or Blood,* 93.

18. Parliamentary Papers [hereafter PP], 1822 (236) Agricultural distress. A list of all petitions, which have been presented to the House of Commons in the years 1820, 1821, and 1822; complaining of agricultural distress.
19. PP, 1825 (299) Labourers' wages. Abstract of returns prepared by order of the Select Committee of last session, appointed to inquire into the practice which prevails in some parts of the country, of paying the wages of labour out of the poor rates.
20. Muskett, 'The East Anglican riots', 5.
21. TNA, HO 40/17, fos. 133a, 135, 3, 4 and 78, various letters, 27 February–8 March 1822; Charlesworth, *An Atlas of Rural Protest*, 148–51.
22. *Norfolk Chronicle*, 16, 23 and 30 March, 20 April, 22 July, and 29 October; Norfolk Record Office [hereafter NRO], C/S 1/21 Quarter Sessions book, MF 658; Muskett, 'The East Anglian Riots', 5–9.
23. TNA, HO 52/9, fos. 101–2 Author obscured, Kilverston, to Melbourne, 2 December 1830.
24. NRO, C/S 1/21, Quarter Sessions book, MF 658; *Norfolk Chronicle*, 30 March 1822.
25. TNA, HO 52/9, fos. 101–2.
26. See below.
27. Archer, *By a Flash and A Scare*, 59–60.
28. TNA, HO 52/9, esp. fos. 174, 187, 193; *Norwich Mercury* and *Norfolk Chronicle*, 4 December 1830 to 22 January 1831; Archer, *By a Flash and A Scare*, 59–60.
29. TNA, HO 52/9, various fos.; NRO: C/S 1/ Quarter Sessions Minute Books 1830–31; MF/RO 36/1 Calendars of Prisoners for Assize; *Norwich Mercury* and *Norfolk Chronicle*, 1830–1831. For tabulations, see Wallis, 'The relationship between magistrates and their communities'.
30. Archer, *By a Flash and a Scare*, 63.
31. Ibid., 56.
32. *Norwich Mercury*, 3, 20 and 27 March 1830.
33. PP, Report from the Select Committee, to whom the several petitions complaining of the depressed state of the agriculture of the United Kingdom, were referred, 1821 (668), 189.
34. *Norfolk Chronicle*, 15 and 22 January 1831.
35. TNA. HO 52/9 fos. 75–77, Temple Frere to Melbourne, 3 December 1830, and fo. 65–67, 6 December 1830.
36. TNA, HO 52/9 fos. 165, Wodehouse to Melbourne 29 November and fos. 144–7, 30 November 1830.
37. Charlesworth, *An Atlas of Rural Protest*, 146.
38. *Norfolk Chronicle*, 18 May 1816; TNA, HO 40/17, fo. 10, Rackham to Sidmouth, 6 March 1822.
39. TNA, HO 52/9, fos. 165 and 144–7, Wodehouse to Melbourne 29 and 30 November 1830.

40. *Norwich Mercury*, 4 and 11 December 1830.
41. TNA, HO 52/9 fos. 90–1 and 176–82, Berney to Melbourne, 2 December, and Anon. near Aylsham to Peel, 25 November 1830; NRO, WLS XLIX/54 Letter, 11 December 1830 Grigson to Wodehouse.
42. John Archer, *Social Unrest and Popular Protest in England 1780–1840* (Cambridge University Press: 2000), 18.
43. TNA, HO 52/9, fos. 90–91, Berney to Melbourne, 2 December 1830; see also above.
44. John R. Harvey (ed.), *Records of the Norfolk Yeomanry Cavalry* (Jarrold and Sons: 1908), 236–8.
45. TNA, HO 52/9, fos. 16–17, 72–3 and 79, W. Withers to Melbourne, Holt, 2 December, Wodehouse to Melbourne, Norwich, 4 December, and, letter to the Rev. Slapp from Attleborough Hall, 30 November 1830.
46. TNA, HO 52/9, fos. 72–3, Wodehouse to Melbourne, Norwich, 4 December 1830.
47. Hobsbawm and Rudé, *Captain Swing*, 154–5.
48. *Norwich Mercury*, 11 December 1830.
49. NRO, Kim 6/38, Melbourne to Wodehouse, 26 November 1830.
50. TNA, HO 52/9, fos. 151–3, Suffield, Gunton Park to Melbourne, 30 November 1830; NRO, WLS XLIX/54, 426X9, Kimberly correspondence.
51. TNA, HO 52/9, fo. 19, An address to the Inhabitants of the County of Norfolk, 3 December 1830.
52. NRO, GTN 5/9/40 printed circular, 8 December 1830.
53. TNA, HO 52/9, fos. 14–15, Wodehouse to Melbourne, 16 December 1830.
54. *Norwich Mercury*, 15 January 1831; TNA, HO 52/9, fo. 151, Suffield to Melbourne, 30 November 1830.
55. TNA, HO 52/9, fos. 151–3, Suffield to Melbourne, 30 November 1830.
56. Hobsbawm and Rudé, *Captain Swing*, 257–62.
57. Wallis, '"We do not come here…"', 159–75; Wallis, 'The relationship between magistrates and their communities', 208–52; see also Griffin, *The Rural War*, 248–59.
58. John H. Barrow (ed.), *The Mirror of Parliament*, vol. 1 (Longman: 1831), 95.
59. NRO, C/S 1/24, Quarter Sessions Book MF 660; *Norfolk Chronicle*, 22 January 1831.
60. *Norwich Mercury*, 15 January 1831.
61. TNA, HO 42/151, fos. 30–1, Suffield to Sidmouth, 10 June 1816; CA, K283/L49/18–20, Dering to Ely magistrates, 8–11 June 1816, and Isle of Ely Assize minute book, 1801–1820.
62. TNA, HO 42/151, fos. 30–31 and 316–17, Suffield to Sidmouth, 10 June, and Hobhouse to Beckett, 19 June 1816.

63. Phillip Warren (ed.), *Report of the Trials for Rioting at Ely and Littleport 1816* (Wilburton: 1997/1816), 5.
64. CA, K283/L49/7 Hobhouse to Evans, 3 June 1816, and K283/L14, Indictments; TNA, HO 42/151, fos. 348–57, Calendar of Prisoners, 17 June 1816.
65. TNA, HO 42/151, fos. 137–8 and 335, Hobhouse to Sidmouth, 19 June, and Hobhouse to Beckett, 21 June 1816.
66. TNA, HO 42/151, fos. 353–54, Bolland to Sidmouth, 21 June 1816; *Norfolk Chronicle*, 29 June 1816.
67. Charles Johnson, *An Account of the Ely and Littleport Riots in 1816* (George T. Watson: 1948/1893), 66, 77.
68. *Norfolk Chronicle*, 24 August 1816; Peacock, *Bread or Blood*, 93–4.
69. *Norwich Mercury*, 22 January 1831.
70. NRO, C/S 1/24 Quarter Sessions books, MF 660 (January 1831); *Norwich Mercury*, 8 January 1831.
71. *Norwich Mercury*, 8 January 1831.
72. *Norfolk Chronicle*, 22 January 1831.
73. Ibid.; NRO, C/S 1/24, Quarter Sessions books, MF 660.
74. TNA, HO 52/9, fos. 49–50, Wodehouse to Melbourne, 10 December 1830.
75. *Norwich Mercury*, 15 January 1831.
76. NRO, C/S 1/21, Quarter Sessions book, MF 658; Archer, *By a Flash and a Scare*, 55.
77. *Norfolk Chronicle*, 30 March, 22 May, 19 October 1822.
78. *Norwich Mercury*, 8 and 15 January 1831.
79. *Norwich Mercury*, 8 January 1831.
80. TNA, HO 52/9, fo. 149, Notice to farmers from the Magistrates of Melton Constable, 26 November 1830.
81. *Norwich Mercury*, 8 and 15 January 1831.
82. NRO, C/S124, Quarter Sessions books, January 1831, MF 660/4 (see fos. 45–6); *Norwich Mercury*, 15 January 1831.
83. *Norwich Mercury*, 22 January 1831.
84. *Norfolk Chronicle*, 22 January 1831.
85. NRO, C/S 1/24, Quarter Sessions books, January 1831 MF 660 (see fos. 48–9); *Norfolk Chronicle*, 22 January 1831.
86. *Norwich Mercury*, 8 and 22 January 1831.
87. Muskett, 'The East Anglican riots', 9.
88. CA, K283/L49/7, Hobhouse to Evans, 3 June 1816; and, K 283/L/1/22, Narrative of the riotous transactions, May 1816.
89. TNA, HO 42/151, fos. 353–54, Bolland to Sidmouth, 21 June 1816; *Norfolk Chronicle*, 29 June 1816; Peacock, *Bread or Blood*, 174–6.
90. *Norwich Mercury*, 12 March 1831; TNA, HO 44/52, Judges of the Norfolk circuit to Home Office, 4 and 8 March 1831.

91. Stella Evans, 'The life and death of Richard Nockolds hand loom weaver of Norwich', in Michael Holland (ed.), *Swing Unmasked: The Agricultural Riots of 1830 to 1832 and their Wider Implications* (FACHRS: 2005), 170–84.
92. *Norfolk Chronicle*, 26 March 1831.
93. Hobsbawm and Rudé, *Captain Swing*, 259.
94. *Norfolk Chronicle*, 26 March 1831.
95. Steve Poole, '"A lasting and salutary warning": incendiarism, rural order and England's last scene of crime execution', *Rural History* 19 (2008), 4–5.
96. Richard M. Bacon, *A Memoir of the Life of Edward Third Baron Suffield* (Privately printed, Norwich: 1838), 324; Archer, *By a Flash and a Scare*, 60.
97. *Norwich Mercury*, 2 and 16 April 1831.
98. *Norfolk Chronicle*, 6 and 22 April 1822.
99. TNA, HO 40/27, fo. 30, Justices of Norwich to Sidmouth, 2 March 1822; Archer, *By a Flash and a Scare*, 57–8.
100. *Norwich Mercury*, 15 January 1831; *Norfolk Chronicle*, 22 January 1831.
101. Ibid.
102. NRO, C/S 1/24, Quarter Sessions books, MF 660; *Norfolk Chronicle*, 22 January 1831.
103. NRO, C/Saa 1/15, Franklin to the Visiting Justices of the County Gaol, 25 July and 22 September 1831.
104. *Norfolk Chronicle*, 22 January 1831.
105. *Norwich Mercury*, 15 January 1831.
106. Ibid.
107. *Norwich Mercury* and *Norfolk Chronicle*, both 22 January 1831.
108. *Norwich Mercury*, 8 January; *Morning Chronicle*, 3 January 1831.
109. Ibid.
110. *Norwich Mercury*, 19 April 1831.
111. CA, K283/L49, various, June 1816 and January–February 1817; TNA, HO 42/151, fos. 357, Calendar of Prisoners Isle of Ely Special Assizes, 17 June 1816.
112. King, 'Edward Thompson's Contribution to Eighteenth-Century Studies', 226.
113. Douglas Hay, 'The state and the market in 1800: Lord Kenyon and Mr. Waddington', *Past and Present* 103 (1999), 156–7.
114. Keith D.M. Snell, 'The culture of local xenophobia', *Social History* 28 (2003), 23–9.
115. Wallis, 'The relationship between magistrates and their communities', part II.

The Politics of 'Protest Heritage', 1790–1850

Steve Poole

In contemporary Britain, 'heritage' has been actively promoted by a succession of governments, partly as a driver for the post-industrial leisure economy, and partly as a signifier of cohesion in an increasingly fractured world, yet the public commemoration of politically sensitive sites and events continues to inspire controversy. Consequently, an important factor in the rise of 'heritage studies' since the 1990s has been the recognition of issues concerning subaltern or 'dissonant' forms of commemoration and belonging; understandings of the past that do not necessarily reflect 'official' models of heritage interpretation.[1] Dissonance, originally framed as a concept by John Tunbridge and Gregory Ashworth to define sites of memory where meaning and interpretation may be contested or non-consensual, has been applied more broadly in recent years to encompass any public readings and uses of the past which seem at odds with what Laurajane Smith has termed the 'authorised heritage discourse'. This discourse, she argues, has not only dominated understandings of what heritage is, but is also inherently conservative. Effectively, it has shaped a consensual national narrative that 'explicitly promotes the experience and values of elite social classes', which works 'to exclude the historical, social and cultural

S. Poole (✉)
University of the West of England, Bristol, UK

experiences of a range of groups,' and acts 'to constrain and limit their critique'.[2] This discourse should not be considered all-encompassing, however, as the later work of scholars like Paul Shackel and of Smith herself on aspects of working-class and industrial heritage has forcefully argued. Indeed, by its very nature, any heritage may be regarded as dissonant to some degree since 'authorisation' is fluid and never a fixed category in and of itself. For David Lowenthal, heritage was always 'a marvellously malleable creation', for Raphael Samuel it is 'a hybrid, reflecting or taking part in style wars, and registering changes in public taste', and moreover, as Rodney Harrison has put it, 'The authority to control the stories told about the past makes it a conflicted resource'.[3]

The realisation that conflicts over the ways in which 'difficult', tragic or divisive episodes in history were as pressing for men and women in the past as they are today has not been without impact on the conceptualisation of new histories from below, and in the proposition of a 'heritage from below'.[4] It has proved far easier for local administrations and heritage professionals to memorialise the armed Chartist rising of 1839 at Newport, South Wales, for instance, than to reach agreement on the erection of a monument to the unarmed casualties of the Peterloo massacre in Manchester twenty years earlier. Despite the association with 'physical' rather than 'moral' force Chartism, the former mining and steel-making valleys of South Wales have seized upon Newport's failed insurrection as a signifier of the region's proud and gritty industrial heritage, a process which began with the naming of John Frost Square and a series of centenary celebrations in 1939. Since then the city and its surrounding area have seen a proliferation of public sculptures, Chartist trails, an annual 'Convention' and a series of angry protests over the city council's decision to destroy a thirty-year-old commemorative mural to make way for a new shopping centre in 2013. Elsewhere, historic acts of protest and resistance are now publicly marked with annual festivals; at Tolpuddle, Dorset, where every July the TUC and a crowd of thousands celebrate the legacy of six agricultural labourers transported to the colonies in 1834 for forming a trades union; at Burford, Oxfordshire, where the execution of three leaders of the Leveller movement in the civil war is commemorated; and at Burston, Norfolk, where a gathering every September remembers an early twentieth-century strike at the village school after two Christian socialist teachers were unjustly sacked. As Hilda Kean has pointed out, if one common theme in all these acts of commemoration is the experience of defeat, another is the celebration of righteous struggle against the odds, where 'fortitude is praised as success'.[5]

Clearly, in the public commemoration of protest and the struggle for democracy, the control and appropriation of authorised memory today is of concern to grass-roots communities and civic authorities alike. Within the academy, histories of radicalism in Britain have complemented many of these concerns, suggesting that for protest participants in the past, the politics of memory were no less pressing than they are today. A growing body of work on the place of memory in the development of radical working-class culture in England has explored the early nineteenth-century use of symbolic dining, singing and toasting, either to celebrate the birthdays of legendary radical figures like Paine and Hunt, or to mark the injustices done to past 'martyrs', principally the seventeenth-century heroes Hampden and Sydney, the 'Scottish patriots' of 1793, Gerrald, Muir, Skirving, Margarot and Palmer, and the victims of Peterloo in 1819.[6] This work has drawn welcome attention to the importance placed by later generations of reformers on the historical legacies of the 1790s and the post-war mass platform, but has had rather less to say about the creation of commemorative practice by the Jacobins themselves in the 1790s. Secondly, while David Karr and others have acknowledged that nineteenth-century radical culture was 'not monolithic', and that 'insurrectionist heroes' like Robert Emmet were as frequently celebrated as peaceful campaigners, it has been agreed that commemorative practices tended to represent the movement as 'unproblematically constitutionalist'.[7] In addressing the first of these observations, this essay assesses ideas about the nature and methodology of radical memory and its public expression in the 1790s through the practice of London Corresponding Society (LCS) lecturer, John Thelwall. The interpretation of History is a recurrent theme in Thelwall's thought, but his interest went beyond the urge, common amongst later radicals like Thomas Cooper, to simply rebalance dominant conservative histories of the national narrative.

In the second, it problematizes the idea of a constitutionalist consensus in the later period, partly on the grounds that fluid definitions of radical 'constitutionalism' make it a less than helpful category of explanation. No clear theoretical division between insurrection and constitutionalism existed for contemporary radicals, since the latter was often cited in justification of the former. Moreover, radical approval for physical force martyrs like Emmet depended greatly upon a Romantic recognition of the United Irishmen as an army of resistance fighting a legitimate war against

British imperialism. Emmet's popularity was never reflected in any complementary commemoration of English Spencean revolutionaries, or of Colonel Despard who met the same fate as Emmet on the scaffold seven months earlier, but in London rather than Dublin. As Ian McCalman has put it, despite a consistent and principled adherence to Paine's republicanism, this 'ragged band of London ultra-radicals remain unmemorialised to this day'.[8] Their neglect may have been as much to do with the nuances of Spencean belief as their insurrectionary impatience, however, for it will be argued here that English radicals, of whatever stamp, were not always in agreement about who or what constituted a fit subject for commemoration, or the means by which it should be achieved. Their own authorised heritage discourse was by no means settled.

Signifying the Landscape: John Thelwall and Robert Southey

Making his way on foot around the rural peripheries of London in 1792, the young reformer John Thelwall paused beside a memorial obelisk to the fifteenth-century Battle of Barnet and reflected upon the location and function of commemorative markers. Inscriptions on stones like these may seem a 'mere statement of fact and chronology', he wrote, but as signifiers of those past events considered worthy of commemoration by men with the means to erect them, memorial stones must inevitably influence the historical understanding of anyone who encountered them. And the particular memories they were designed to shape, Thelwall realised, tended to reinforce political orthodoxies whilst simultaneously erasing alternative or dissonant forms of memory. The Barnet marker offered no overt interpretation, but some value lay in its simple recording of events and date. 'Chronology is so very important for the right understanding of History', he reflected, 'and names and dates are so difficult of retention, that I must own that it would give me considerable satisfaction if, on every spot throughout the kingdom where any memorable transaction had taken place, a little square pillar like the present, were erected, with some such brief and simple narrative, for the information of the traveller.'[9]

The narratives layered onto chronology by Thelwall as he traversed the capital, jotting his impressions in a series of 'politico-sentimental journals', were rarely either brief or simple however; on the contrary, they served frequently as counterpoints to conservative Whig and Tory interpretations offered by standard geographies and travel guides. Thelwall's poetic reflection on the Battle of Barnet therefore, was subtitled 'The Horrors of Royal Ambition' when it appeared in his own radical periodical, *The Tribune*. And Dartford Common, conventionally memorialised, like Hadley Green, as a site of medieval conflict between rival aristocratic houses, was realigned in Thelwall's verse to evoke the more improving memory of the Peasants' Revolt, or 'Wat Tyler's insurrection'. This was an event Thelwall was anxious to rescue from the hostile and dominant histories of chroniclers like Hume since, 'every part of this kingdom presents so many memorials of the horrible massacres by which the Rights of Kings have been maintained'.[10] But Thelwall's radicalism here was not straightforwardly or didactically counter-hegemonic and his proposed marker stones were not intended merely as corrective truths. As Judith Thompson has shown, Thelwall frequently subverted the conventions of travel literature to reimagine the English countryside less as a repository of fixed historical memory and more as 'an expansive open air forum for the Socratic exchange of ideas'.[11] Thelwall's Socratic ideas were of an advanced kind, moreover, for Socrates was 'the first democratical lecturer mentioned in history, and the founder of the unsophisticated, and unrestricted system of *sans-culotte* philosophy'.[12] For Thelwall, the landscape of ideas was a landscape of democratic sociability, embedded with signifiers of radical memory and mediated by conversation and reflection.[13]

Thelwall was not the first enlightenment thinker to express sentiments like these; indeed, his own observations were grounded in a practice already well explored in mid-century poetics. The logic of Mark Akenside's short poem for a proposed monument at Runnymede (1758) for example, was similarly driven by locative mechanics: 'This is the place / Where England's ancient barons, clad in arms / And stern with conquest, from their tyrant king / Then rendered tame, did challenge and secure / The charter of thy freedom'. Having once established a context, reflection is framed and prompted: 'Pass not on / Till thou have bless'd their memory'.[14] Whilst Akenside's emphasis on baronial muscle exposes his politics as Tory rather than populist, the recognition of the national landscape as a site of contest in the 1790s prompted other writers to make commemorative or epitaphic 'inscription poems' to jolt the memory of passing travellers. Some, like those produced by Wordsworth and Coleridge, were not explicitly political, but the same cannot be said of Robert Southey or of the early feminist and friend of Thomas Muir, Anna Barbauld, whose 'Inscription for an Ice House' (1795) connected prosaic domestic economy with thoughts about the 'rights of nature'.[15] Southey's inscription poems were imagined for public installation at sites that included Smithfield for the Peasants' Revolt, and Chepstow Castle for the imprisoned seventeenth-century regicide Henry Marten.[16] Unsurprisingly, none were actually so placed, but they were frequently re-circulated in later years in the columns of radical newspapers where their didactic purpose distinguished them from the Thelwall's more dialogical proposals. A poem of 1797, intended for 'a monument in the New Forest' for example, and aiming to divert the neutral picturesque gaze to the tyrannical reign of William Rufus, who famously fell to his death there, reappeared in Thomas Wooler's *British Gazette* in 1822. Another, intended for a column at Newbury, urged spatial association with the Civil War's most famous parliamentarian: 'Art thou a Patriot Traveller? on this field / Did FALKLAND fall the blameless and the brave / Beneath a Tyrant's banners: dost thou boast/Of loyal ardor? HAMBDEN perish'd here, / The rebel HAMBDEN, at whose glorious name / The heart of every honest Englishman / Beats high with conscious pride'.[17]

The peculiar interest taken by the Jacobins of the 1790s in the consolidation and representation of progressive public memory played an important part in shaping the ground upon which the battle of ideas would later be fought. Thelwall's rented London lecture rooms in Beaufort Buildings, off the Strand, were emblematically decorated with improving radical physiognomies, the contemplation of which, he believed, would remind his audience of their virtuous lineage and inspire them to future action. Although these probably included long dead exemplars like Hampden and Sydney, they were not to subsist in an historical vacuum but as links in an unbroken chain binding the past to the future. So, when Thelwall went down to the Portsmouth hulks to visit the Scottish martyr Joseph Gerrald, then awaiting transportation for his part in the Edinburgh Convention, he resolved to get a likeness made. 'I wished that some memorial of that great man should be left behind him, for the instruction of his country. I wished to procure the means of decorating these walls with the bust of that revered patriot that, fixing my eye frequently upon the image of his countenance, I might be inspired with similar virtues'. Another of the convicts, Thomas Muir, was also immortalised as he lay in the hulks. Thomas Hardy 'saw Mr Banks, an eminent statuary, take a cast from Muir's face, from which he afterwards made a bust', and 28 years later, Hardy was still sending engravings of Muir, taken from Thomas Banks's cast, to his friends and supporters.[18]

Jacobin heritage, however monumental in its practice, was rooted in intangible tradition. The London silversmith John Baxter, who wrote a comprehensive *New and Impartial History of England* for the LCS in 1795, was at pains to record some of the ways in which popular understandings of the past had influenced the course of subsequent events. Many in the LCS will have shared Thelwall's view of Magna Carta, for example, that it was little more in practice than 'a barrier between two great parties in the nation; one of which was sometimes prevalent and sometimes the other… sovereigns and nobles', but, for Baxter at least, the historical forces that brought it about had a wider significance. Even among the Norman barons, he wrote, 'the memory of a more equal government under the Saxon princes, which remained with the English, served to diffuse the spirit of liberty and made the barons both desirous of more independence to themselves and willing to indulge the people'.[19] English Jacobins like Thelwall and Baxter may not have been quite ready to join Paine in dismissing historical precedent as a basis for the rights of man, but neither did they celebrate Magna Carta with the fervour of the constitutionalist Whigs. In this they followed John Cartwright's dictum, 'That "Magna Charta is the great foundation of the English constitution" I must positively deny. It is indeed a glorious member of the superstructure, but of itself would never have existed, had not the constitution already had a basis and a firm one too.'[20] Moreover, the terms of reference and the organisational structure adopted by the corresponding societies in the 1790s would help to define a plebeian public sphere in which arguments for democratic reform might be rehearsed nationally, locally, and without property qualification. But neither democratic inscription poems nor Thelwallian marker stones were ever installed in physical form.[21] If they had been, Samuel Bamford's journey on foot from Middleton to London in 1820 might have been recorded somewhat differently.

Bamford walked to the Court of Kings Bench to receive sentence following his conviction for unlawful assembly at Peterloo in 1819, yet radical reinterpretation rarely came to him as he journeyed south to the capital. It is true that he visited the grave of the executed leader of the abortive Pentrich rising, Jeremiah Brandreth, on his way through Derby and experienced an involuntary outpouring of 'heartfelt emotion' as he stood beside it, but otherwise his historical reflections were conventional. He noted, without comment, the graves of Knights Templar at Rothley, 'the chamber in which Richard the Third slept on the night previous to the battle of Bosworth', and at Northampton, 'with feelings of veneration', one of the monuments erected by Edward I to mark the resting places of Queen Eleanor's coffin. He had hoped to enjoy the liberties of 'our

English yeomen of old' in Needwood Forest, but a local man informed him that 'the forest lands were nearly all enclosed', and when he finally stood where Thelwall had stood beside the memorial to the Battle of Barnet on Hadley Green, he noted only that it marked 'where the famous battle was fought in the wars of the roses'. So much for Thelwall's ambition, although Bamford's success in locating Brandreth's grave was remarkable in itself since it is usually presumed to have been as unmarked then, three years after the executions, as it is today.[22] What Bamford, Baxter, Southey and Thelwall all shared, however, was a broad understanding of the importance of memory as an ideological field of conflict, a principle that applied not only to the past but also to the present. In 1820, Bamford knew only too well that the wealthy and partisan Grand Jurors who had overseen his conviction would inspire the sympathetic remembrance of their class after death, but he was unwilling to allow their role as suppressors of liberty to go unnoticed: 'Posterity must know these things, in order that when they point to the tombs of these noblemen, they may not confound them with those of their family, who had not any such words or deeds to answer for.'[23]

Contestable Heroes

If the triggering of historical memory through material signs in the landscape was one area of commemoration that invited contest, the establishment of a radical calendar of anniversaries, and the interpretation of the pantheon of heroes whose narratives underpinned it, was another. Annual celebratory dinners, often to mark the birthdays of such relatively uncontroversial heroes as Tom Paine and Henry Hunt, were one means through which a radical commemorative calendar was established in the post-war period, particularly through the revitalised Hampden Clubs. These gatherings punctuated the ritual year of British Jacobinism and ensured cultural continuity in periods of decline and suppression, but they did not immediately attract wide notice. Richard Carlile recalled his first attendance at a dinner to celebrate Paine's birthday in 1818, 'at an obscure tavern where the matter was known only to a few that could be trusted, and private as we were, there were some apprehensions that the suspension of the Habeas Corpus Act might detain us all in gaol'. Clearly, Tom Paine dinners would not be established as heritage cornerstones overnight, and as an acquaintance of Carlile advised him, '"You will not dine numerously at that tavern for the first year; many will doubt its practicability, but if you go on to dine annually for two or three years at such a tavern, you will accumulate a very large company'". Sure enough, in 1824 Carlile sat down to dinner very publicly with 75 fellow democrats at the City of London Tavern, 'the first tavern of the metropolis'.[24]

But radical dinners were sites of conflict as well as unity. Appropriate ways of affirming Paine's 'immortal memory' were contestable and prone to disruption by dissenting voices from Spencean and ultra-radical participants. At least one unnamed malcontent was a regular critic, although the moderate majority learned to ignore him so that, 'even the Spencean did not disturb the harmony of the company. He was borne with and smiled at but not reproached'. Veteran radical fundamentalists like John Gale Jones, who had stood second only to Thelwall as an orator in the LCS, watched hawkishly for any expressions of compromise over divisive issues like Paine's republicanism. In 1826, Jones shattered the 'harmony of the company' by taking issue with loose interpretations of republicanism that associated it too strongly with patriotism. A toast was proposed by the chair to 'General Mina and the patriots of Spain', but Jones objected to his 'attaching patriotism to a party', and in any case, Paine should be remembered as a republican but never as a patriot:

> He wished to direct their attention to the character and conduct of the persons who were called 'patriots'. He must repeat, by the way, that he wanted the word 'patriot' expunged at least from their vocabulary. It argued narrow principles and limited objects. It seemed to say that their exertions were and ought to be limited to the soil that gave them birth, and he therefore wished that the word 'patriot' should be expunged and that of 'Republican' substituted… 'Patriots' had been the cause of wars and bloodshed.

He finished with a lengthy history of 'Republican' struggle, 'the cause for which Wallace bled, Riego suffered and Washington fought and conquered', and 'the cause which armed the Republicans against Charles and led them to decapitate an infamous tyrant'.[25]

Republicanism, in other words, was not to be considered merely as a more accountable form of government, but rather as a universal principle of virtue. Paine's legacy was clear while men like Jones watched over it, but Cobbett's remained somewhat insecure. Radicals who had been led either by pragmatism or self-doubt to waver in their commitment to a universal franchise did not recommend themselves to public commemoration and Cobbett would never attract the recognition of Paine or Henry Hunt because his radicalism was far too nuanced. 'He is gone', declared the *Poor Man's Guardian* on Cobbett's death in 1835. 'His influence died away before him. It almost seems as if his memory were to follow…' That he passed away without much comment was ascribed by some to his 'not having been linked to any of our great parties,' but the *Guardian* thought it was because his name was not 'linked with any great principle'. On the contrary, it argued, his politics were inconsistent, he chose not to align himself with the Hampden Club mass platform, and he would be remembered with affection only for his *Twopenny Trash*. 'Let the title be inscribed on his monument', it suggested, perhaps in preference to his name.[26] Memorialising inconsistency or the promoters of partial measures might serve some purpose in itself, however, for it was important to the early Chartists to distance themselves from 'the Russell reform delusion' and the negative impact it had had on the movement for universal suffrage in Hunt's day. The working class, it was asserted, were resolved never to be fooled again by Whig trickery or by Whig monuments to false dawns.[27]

As we shall see, the Huntite radicals of the post-war years secured their own place in the radical pantheon by passing an undiluted universal suffragist ideology to the Chartists. The Spenceans, meanwhile, have been sidelined by Chartists and historians of radicalism alike, if not for their understanding that armed struggle was inevitable, then certainly for their diversionary agrarianism and their ambivalence towards parliamentary reform in a world of economic inequality.[28] This neglect was not for want of ambition among the Spenceans themselves, who were more than ready to create small acts of commemoration to their own insurrectionary martyrs. Arthur Thistlewood used a public dinner 'to celebrate the memory of Thomas Spence' in 1817 to toast the 20th anniversary of the death of 'the brave Parker at the mutiny at the Nore who failed because nothing was acted upon'. Another Spencean dinner honoured Colonel Despard and Lord Edward Fitzgerald and, if an informer from Leicester is to be believed, a December gathering was called 'to celebrate by supper' the death of Princess Charlotte.[29] Low black comedy of this kind clearly distinguished Spenceans from orthodox followers of Hunt. Watson, Thistlewood, Preston and another shoemaker, John Hooper, had themselves been acquitted of high treason earlier in 1817 for their part in the Spencean-inspired Spa Fields rising and Hooper, whose health never recovered from his imprisonment while awaiting trial, died at the end of the year. Efforts were made to organise a hero's funeral for him, his body left 'to lie in state' in a room on the Blackfriars Road, decked out with black crepe and candles, and visited by 'an almost incredible number' of sympathisers. It was decided to bury Hooper at St Dunstan's, Stepney, next to John Cashman, the sailor hanged for breaking into a gunsmiths' shop during the 1816 rising. The 'friends of freedom… placarded the streets with invitations to the populace', and the authorities, mindful of reports from informers that Thistlewood and Preston were hoping for an outbreak of violence on the return journey, lined the streets with constables and sent 'a large body of officers' to the churchyard. Hooper's funeral procession was designed to attract attention, with '52 couples in black cloaks, gloves and crepes', and 'two mutes with crepes and hatbands', leading a large crowd though the streets of the East End to St Dunstan's. The Spenceans, who perhaps harboured hopes of turning this corner of the churchyard into a permanent site of ultra-radical memory, launched a public appeal for 'a stone to commemorate the virtue, integrity and patriotism of that humble and honest shoemaker,' and were roundly mocked for it by the ministerial press. Some chided them for not going far enough, suggesting instead, 'a subscription for a statue to this great man, which might be placed in the centre of Spa Fields'.[30] No evidence of a permanent marker on Hooper's grave exists today and it is probable that, like Brandreth and Despard, he never had one. However, government concerns over the consequences of any renewed call to commemoration after the execution of Thistlewood and his fellow 'Cato Street conspirators' in 1820 may help to explain the denial of formal burial to the condemned men and their anonymous interment under quicklime in Newgate gaol. Material sites of memory for Spencean insurrection were not to be facilitated.

The 'Acquitted Felons' of 1794

The clearest evidence of dissonance in the development of a collective radical memory can be drawn from the surprising exclusion of the London Corresponding Society. Discussing the Chartist movement's adoption of their own heroic forebears since 1770, Matthew Roberts has suggested that their apparent indifference towards the LCS lay in the plebeian character of the 1790s agitation; that Chartist toasts tended to be reserved for radical 'gentlemen'.[31] But it was not quite that simple. One of the most keenly remembered moments in the development of metropolitan radicalism was the triumphant acquittal on charges of High Treason of 12 leading members of the LCS and the Society for Constitutional Information. They included Thelwall, John Horne Tooke, Thomas Spence and Thomas Holcroft, who, while not independent gentlemen, were hardly plebeian.

The public commemoration of these acquittals became the most firmly fixed annual act of remembrance in the Jacobin calendar. Every year from 1795 to 1854, celebratory London gatherings were held on 5 November, the 'acquitted felons' themselves appearing as guests of honour, and as many as 200 people sitting down to dine and toast the sovereignty of English juries. Despite the death of Thelwall, the last surviving defendant, in 1834, these meetings remained, rhetorically at least,

> a rallying point for the veteran reformers of the generation that was passing away, and the rising reformers of the generation that was starting into political life and uniting them in oneness of principle and feeling… There were many to whom that event was a matter of history, who associated it in their minds with events recorded of times gone by, but who were there made to feel the reality of those exciting scenes, the importance of that struggle and the blessed influence of that deliverance.[32]

But however much being 'united in oneness of principle and feeling' may have been the stated aim, the politics of radical commemoration were complex. Toasting the Scottish martyrs, Thomas Hardy, or trial by jury were not in themselves divisive, but interpretative emphasis might be, as John Gale Jones demonstrated once again at a treason trials dinner in 1819. Unless these meetings were used explicitly to maintain a commitment to universal manhood suffrage, he objected, annually honouring the acquitted felons served little purpose. Another LCS stalwart, Alexander Galloway, appealed for unity by offering toasts to trial by jury and to Hardy, 'a man whose name Englishmen should never forget,' but Jones was not to be derailed. He would drink Hardy's health, he announced, but he would not do it with men who had become lukewarm about the suffrage for to do so would be a betrayal of Hardy's memory.[33] Certainly, these annual get-togethers had assumed a moderately liberal character by the 1820s, somewhat at odds with the full-blooded Jacobin ideology on which they were founded. Thelwall's unexpected return to the political stage as a supporter of John Cam Hobhouse, the Whig candidate in the 1819 Westminster election, exposed the breadth of the chasm that had opened up between old supporters of the LCS and post-war metropolitan radicals like Hunt and Cobbett, who dismissed Hobhouse as a Liberal opportunist.[34] Both Hunt and Cobbett remained aloof from the treason trial dinners, along with the rising generation of Spenceans. Gale Jones, whose political career began in the LCS, continued to attend, but inconsistently, and he held Thelwall responsible for conniving to keep 'universal suffrage and annual parliaments... as carefully out of sight and hearing as though they had been entombed in the grave'.[35]

The alienation of Gale Jones is remarkable. He was certainly the most active, consistent and energetic LCS veteran still playing a central role in metropolitan radical politics in the post-war years and he would remain an unwavering advocate of the Jacobin reform programme until his death in 1838. Clearly, however, there was little appetite amongst the radicals associated with either Hunt's Hampden Clubs or the Spencean minority for memorialising figures whose commitment to universal manhood suffrage had become compromised. By 1823, when many of the original 12 had passed away, gentlemanly radicals like Thelwall were comfortable enough offering a toast to 'reform', but no longer prepared to be drawn into public arguments about the specificities of universal suffrage and annual parliaments.[36]

A few years later, the widening gulf between the old guard who identified with the LCS trials and the new blood of Chartism was well demonstrated by the men appointed to chair the treason trial dinners. They included the Whig MP, Charles Buller, in 1837 and the Anti-Corn Law Leaguer, G. H. Heppell, in 1838, both of whom led toasts to 'reform' and trial by jury but not to universal suffrage.[37] In 1844, on the fiftieth anniversary of the trials, the chair was taken by another Anti Corn Law League man, William Coates, who proposed a toast to the felons with the claim that, 'all they wanted was reform – that reform which Earl Grey proposed and King William the fourth granted and which the peers of England assented to'. As an act of memory, of either the trials or the Reform Act, Coates's sentiments were out of line with Chartism, and would have drawn robust protest from men like Gale Jones had they lived long enough to hear them. But even Thelwall, the longest surviving 'acquitted felon,' had been dead for ten years by then, and as toasts to 'liberal government' prevailed in the 1840s, and the traditional toast to the uncompromising major Cartwright was unaccountably dropped, Chartism was never mentioned and Chartists remained conspicuous by their absence.[38] When the London Chartists met in 1845 to commemorate the first French republic of 1792, they did so without reference to the corresponding societies and without toasting the memory of any of its leading figures except the Scottish martyrs and the United Irishmen. It was a telling omission, given the length and political breadth of the toasts they did make; 34 of them in all, from Wat Tyler, William Tell and Koskiusko to the republican heroes of the civil war, radical poets like Milton and Shelley, and Chartists associated with armed struggle, Frost, Williams, Jones and Shell, 'the hero of Newport'. Even Preston and Davenport, two Spenceans, were included.[39] What had become of the 'heroes' of the LCS? In 1848, George Julian Harney summarised his own position:

> I have not forgotten the historical fact of the acquittal of Horne Tooke, Thelwall and others, which acquittal is celebrated every year... by a set of *bourgeois* liberals and political adventurers, who meet to guzzle and glorify each other and toast 'Trial by Jury'. The celebration of 'the glorious triumph of Trial by Jury' is in these times a glorious exhibition of humbug. 'Trial by Jury' like most of 'our excellent institutions' is a very good thing for the rich and the *bourgeoisie* but, as regards the poor, they would not be much worse off if they were subjected to trial by court-martial.[40]

The annual treason trial dinners, appropriated, disarmed and reshaped by a Whig establishment anxious to create an evolutionary foundation myth for their own ascendancy, are an object lesson in the fluidity of commemorative practice in this period, but they were not unique in that. Historians have drawn attention to the ways in which disagreements between household suffrage advocates like Joseph Hume, LCS veterans like Galloway and Chartists like O'Connor and Harney, obstructed the committee charged with erecting a monument to the Scottish martyrs of 1793. While O'Connor was determined to preserve their memory as manhood suffragists, Hume was anxious to reinvent them for middle class approval along milder lines.[41] Liberal Edinburgh certainly appropriated the martyrs as allies in the struggle against aristocratic privilege and delighted in the view to be enjoyed of the new monument by respectable railway passengers. '"Can this be the aristocratic city in which these men were unjustly condemned"? the traveller will naturally enquire. "Yes", let him be answered, "the city is the same but the times are changed. The memory of Thomas Muir and his high-souled associates is fondly cherished where they were treated as felons, while their persecutors, who were then high in place and honour, are now remembered only to be execrated"'.[42] But the Liberal adoption of former Jacobin reformers did not necessarily mean that all reformers now celebrated a common heritage.

Statues, Memorials and Dissonant Memory

Unsurprisingly, English radicals reacted critically to the early nineteenth-century growth of statue and monument building in honour of the nation's political elite. Some hoped only that these acts of state-sponsored commemoration would do their memory work in reverse and become sites of derision. Cobbett hoped for a fate of this kind for Pitt's statue in London's Guildhall in 1817, that parents would 'take their children to it as they grow up, recount to them all his deeds, from his dawn to his extinguishment, and tell them to shun that as they would the curses of their forefathers'.[43] Once again however, democratic radicals were susceptible to division, not only over who or what was to be commemorated, but over the form any such commemoration might take. The difficult relationships nurtured with statues, memorials and busts suggest that it was often easier to criticise the loyalist appropriation of public space and the erection of monuments to the unworthy than it was to agree on an alternative. 'This is the justice to be obtained from the hereditary spoilers and slayers of mankind', complained the *Poor Man's Guardian* in 1833, 'They will build statues to Wellington and the Duke of York but they will build none to William Tell or Robespierre'.[44] Two years later, Henry Hunt too was dead and a monument was raised to him at Ancoats, Manchester, fittingly enough by the northern Chartists. Unlike Cobbett, or Thelwall who died largely unmourned in 1834, Hunt's adherence to an uncomplicated and uncompromising programme of universal manhood suffrage and annual parliaments ensured universal approval amongst the parliamentary reformers that followed him; indeed Feargus O'Connor modelled his own self-image as the symbol of Chartist consistency in the 1840s on Hunt's example. The unbroken line was captured graphically on the banner of the Wigan Chartists in 1838, with 'a full length portrait of Feargus O'Connor… Hunt's monument in the distance. Motto on a scarlet scroll, gold letters – O'Connor, Hunt's Successor', and again at a Chartist march in Manchester in 1841 where one banner displayed 'a splendid oil painting of Feargus O'Connor with Henry Hunt pointing from the clouds and giving him the following charge – "welcome Feargus, thou hast been found faithful; now lead my people on to Victory!"'[45]

Calls for a commemorative marker to Hunt were heard almost immediately, frequently accompanied by renewed criticism of State sponsored statues to false 'greatness'. The memorial committee of 1835 hoped to build a permanent riposte to the Establishment for, as William Nuttal put it, 'a monument to Mr Hunt would be the bitterest pill to the aristocracy that ever was compounded.' George Hadfield rehearsed the familiar complaint about the reactionary nature of orthodox memorials; 'In all ages, ancient and modern, monuments had been erected only to the memory of individuals renowned for tyranny or eminent for the wholesale murders they have committed on their fellow men in support of despotism', but now, 'he earnestly besought the working classes of this country to set an example to the world and for once to erect a monument to the memory of a man whose whole life had been devoted to their interests'.[46] But, despite Chartist support, it took seven years to raise sufficient money to get the work underway. At a mass rally to lay the foundations in 1842, a number of 'sacred' objects were interred first in a lead-lined cavity, including a copy of Hunt's *Memoirs* and 'tokens of that bloody day, 16 August 1819'. The memorial would stand in regular dialogue with the present, it was hoped, with a vault beneath, 'in which those who prove faithful in death to the people's case may be interred,' ensuring 'their names and character would be respected after their departure'. This never happened; indeed, the obelisk was still unfinished a year later. O'Connor had to remind the Chartists that completing it 'ought to be an object with everyone connected to the Democratic Movement'. The *Northern Star* agreed. 'The government had erected monuments to their Nelsons, their Wellingtons and Pitts but none to such men as Hunt. Let the people then see to the completion of Hunt's monument for he had done more… for the public good'. Even when completed, a classically robed representation of the orator, planned for the pinnacle, proved elusive.[47] Although the ambition to use the monument as a site for subsequent radical burials was never realised, the hope of creating a permanent site of radical memory, on a grander scale either than the Spencean initiative at Stepney, or of the more traditional dissenters' burial ground at Bunhill Fields, had been clearly stated.[48]

But radical objections to state memorials were not confined to their conservative selectivity; a more general critique of hubris also played a role. Approval for Emmet for example, was strengthened by his own plea from the dock that no memorial should be raised to him until Ireland won its independence; a valedictory speech so powerful that it was sometimes dramatically performed at radical meetings.[49] And when Thomas Hardy died in 1832, Thelwall delivered a graveside oration insisting that this was 'not a grave to demand a pompous monument or colossal effigies', for Hardy's 'monument' should be memory itself.[50] And it was just as well perhaps, because Hardy's memorial stone was 'going to decay' by 1851.[51]

Radical anxiety about opulent and boastful monuments to the virtuous found clear expression in William Godwin's *Essay on Sepulchres* (1809) which proposed any number of memorials to long overlooked 'reformers, instructors and improvers', but only of the simplest wooden crosses. The purpose of memorialisation, insisted Godwin, was not veneration but continuing dialogue, a means by which moral heroes might live on in the imagination and inspire the living with their thoughts. 'Let them live as my friends, my philosophers, my instructors and my guides,' he wrote.[52] Godwin's proposal then, harmonised closely with his former friend Thelwall's putative landscape marker scheme in that its radicalism lay not in pompous counter-eulogy but in dialogical provocation. In the *Chartist Circular's* opinion, virtuous radicals like Tell, Hampden, Washington and Wallace lived on in the 'vivid imagination' of the people and 'no monument need they to preserve their names and perpetuate their glory and renown'. If not marked by a simple Godwinian cross, a 'little green mound or grey cairn' would suffice, since 'the gorgeous obelisks of a Blenheim or a Waterloo can only excite a feeling of painful regret over the wickedness and ambition of man'.[53] Some of Richard Carlile's provincial followers even questioned the need for 'portraits, statues and relics' of past heroes for they read them as signs not of virtue but of idolatry.[54]

However prominent in their day, many radicals died in poverty and their families were in no position to raise expensive monuments to them in any case. Paine, Gale Jones, Margarot, Hardy, Galloway and Preston all died penniless, as did the less celebrated Benjamin Rushton of Ovenden, 'the grand old man' of Yorkshire and Lancashire Chartism. 'He died poor', noted Benjamin Wilson, 'as many other reformers have done', and though his funeral attracted a procession two miles long, his grave was a simple one. While poverty was a practical constraint, it also hinted at simple virtue. 'The foundation stones of liberty are the graves of the just', declared Ernest Jones at Rushton's funeral, 'the lives of the departed are the landmarks of the living; the memories of the past are the beacons of the future'.[55] This is the context in which we must view the fate of Tom Paine's skeleton, exhumed in America in 1819 by Cobbett and William Benbow and brought back to England for reburial beneath a monument that was never built. Consequently, by the time plans to build it were revived a quarter of a century later, Cobbett was dead and the bones were lost.[56]

Ambivalence over the raising of memorials to 'great men' was balanced by alternative proposals for monuments to 'the people' or to important events, expressed most regularly in calls for a monument in Manchester to the fallen at Peterloo. Anniversary commemorations of the massacre with meetings, 'on the spot where the dreadful tragedy was performed', were held almost every year, turning presence itself into embedded memory. In 1838 for instance, the Chartist orator Henry Vincent urged a crowd of 20–30,000 people to return each year to 'this sacred spot' because, 'We declare to the face of England's aristocracy that remembrance of that bloody deed will stimulate us to renewed exertions until their unhallowed power is destroyed'.[57] The difficulty experienced by radical movements in completing memorials either to past heroes or formative events can, of course, be largely explained by their having little control over the use of public space and scant resources with which to build upon it. In 1835, the veteran Spencean Allen Davenport thought the solution lay in the collective purchase of land for the creation of popular gathering places; effectively plebeian parks.

> The governments must have their malls, their parks, and their Champ de Mars, to view and exercise their hordes of state destructives. Why should not the people have their little parks or champ de mars, to assemble in, to exercise their moral and intellectual faculties and to discuss the best means of preserving the fruits of their labour... In the centre, an humble monument might be erected bearing the names of the five hundred victims who have been incarcerated in a hundred different dungeons for nobly resisting the tax on knowledge and rescuing the liberty of the press from the oppressor and the monopolist. Another might be raised to execrate the atrocious massacre of St Peters' Field, Manchester, August 16th 1819, on which might be inscribed the names of those killed and wounded by the yeomanry cavalry... Even the affair of Cold Bath Fields, May 13th 1833, would not be unworthy of a monument if the devices were well arranged. On one side might be represented columns of raw lobsters with bludgeons, cutting down in their drunken rage, men, women and children without mercy. On another side, Lord Melbourne, the now Prime Minister, peeping through the window of the House of Correction to inspire his bloodhounds with courage to go on with the slaughter.

Alongside these monuments, Davenport suggested a series of ornamental trees symbolising 'union', 'liberty', 'knowledge' and 'social life', and finally a smattering of statues to 'the most worthy among the working classes'.[58] Only the most informal plebeian protest movements, harbouring less respectable aspirations than the Chartists or the more moderate Spenceans, ever found practical ways to erect public memorials however.

In 1843, the 'Rebecca' crowds who destroyed turnpikes in South Wales, 'raised three pillars built of stone, 27 feet high, on one of the hilltops about a mile from the road in the neighbourhood of Llangadock, in commemoration of their success. Two of them are together, which they have named "Rebecca and her daughter", the third is at a little distance and is named "Miss Cromwell"'. How long they were permitted to remain in place is unknown.[59]

Unsurprisingly, those few formal radical monuments to alternative heroes that were commissioned and completed with comparatively little fuss in the first half of the nineteenth century were dedicated to broadly uncontroversial figures. Major Cartwright, for example, universally regarded as one of the modern movement's most non-contentious founders, and whose unblemished advocacy of reform went back to the time of the American war, had taken no active part in any of the controversies of post-war radicalism, and his death in 1824 was universally lamented. Burdett, Wooler and LCS stalwarts like Alexander Galloway immediately called for a memorial, 'like a family picture, to be handed from father to son', as the *Black Dwarf* put it.[60] The broad-based committee quickly convened to raise subscriptions included not only men like these, but several gentlemen of independent means, Joseph Hume and at least three more liberal MPs. The 'The non-reformers are a powerful body', warned Galloway, 'and the united energies of all friends to real reform are called for, to effect anything like success. The major may not have done much by effects but he had left an example worthy of eternal admiration, and what brighter or better legacy can be bequeathed than a good and glorious example?'[61] This was not so much a ringing endorsement of Liberalism perhaps as an admission that without co-operation on this matter at least, no monument of any quality would ever be built. When the reform movement revived at the end of the decade, the subscription that had been languishing since Cartwright's death was revived with it, and the expense of a commemorative statue close to his house in Bloomsbury finally met. It was completed in 1831, as demands for the Reform Act gathered momentum, with an inscription on the base boldly reminding Whiggish reformers that Cartwright has been 'the firm, consistent and persevering advocate of UNIVERSAL SUFFRAGE, equal representation, vote by ballot and ANNUAL PARLIAMENTS'.[62] In 1834, a second monument to Cartwright, an obelisk marking his grave in St Mary's Churchyard, Finchley, was completed, and in 1843 a monument to John Hampden was erected at the site of Chalgrove Field, 200 years after his death during the early stages of the Civil War. Hampden was revered by universal suffragist radicals as a representative of republican virtue, and by liberal Whig reformers as an upholder of parliamentary sovereignty. So his bicentennial monument was uncontroversially bankrolled by establishment figures, including Lord Brougham, the Duke of Bedford, and Lord Nugent, who had already distinguished himself by exhuming Hampden's body in an effort to disprove stories propagated by Royalist sympathisers that the patriot's death had been caused not by enemy fire, but by the explosion of his own pistol. These gentlemanly subscribers had their own names engraved on one side of the plinth and Nugent wrote the inscription, noting that Hampden 'died while fighting in defence of the free monarchy and ancient liberties of England' and 'against the measures of an arbitrary court'.[63]

The shared veneration of radicals, Liberals and Chartists for reforming patriots like Cartwright and Hampden played some role in the revisionism of the Cambridge school of historians in the 1980s, and particularly those associated with the ideas expressed in *Currents of Radicalism*. For these historians, radical, Liberal and Chartist lineage was coterminous and fundamentally constitutionalist at its core. But this has oversimplified the Chartist attitude to insurrectionary action, configuring armed risings as immature outbursts of frustration rather than legitimate elements in the assertion of rights. In this sense, Hampden's monument was not so uncontroversial after all, for the enthusiasm of the liberal elite to embrace it provoked radical reflection on the commemoration of armed conflict, particularly amongst the Chartists.[64] Thomas Cooper, for example, a vocal opponent of 'physical force' in the 1840s, was nevertheless struck by the hypocrisy of those who would erect monuments to Hampden while consigning to transportation the Chartists who took part in the ill-fated Newport Rising of 1839. In the notes to his prison poem, *The Purgatory of Suicides* (1845), Cooper compared Hampden's death with that of the 19-year-old cabinet maker from Pontypool, George Shell, who had been shot and killed by the military at Newport. Shell

> loaded and fired his piece three times with the greatest intrepidity, before he fell in the streets of Newport. We do not write history like the glorious old Greeks, or the memory of such a hero would not be lost! –Let me remember that a Nugent – to whom all honour! –   has had the moral courage to exert himself, and successfully, for the erection of a column on Chalgrove Field, at the bi-centenary of Hampden's death. May not a *noble* be found in November 2039, to commemorate Shell's fall at Newport with equal earnestness?

Moreover, Cooper reflected, the objective of the rising had been forcibly to enact the Peoples' Charter, a goal 'equally as noble, although not so imposing, as the triumph-in-arms of the Barons of Runnymede – or the "Glorious Revolution" of 1688'. If Hampden's deeds were to be commemorated, 'why blush to own admiration for the heroism of poor Shell?'[65] Cooper reiterated these nuanced views in public speeches. If Hampden deserved a column at Chalgrove Field, then Frost deserved one at Newport, he declared, because 'Noble as Hampden's struggle was, it was less noble than Frost's…Hampden "drew the sword and threw away the scabbard" to overthrow high tyranny in government and religion, but his mind, large and comprehensive as it was, did not design the enfranchisement of every Englishman arrived at the age of manhood'.[66] The use of physical force, in other words, did not necessarily mitigate against positive commemoration, and to insist upon a distinction between constitutionalism and armed struggle is to misunderstand the gulf in political thought between Chartists – even 'moral force' educationalists like Cooper – and Liberals.[67] For men like Nugent and Hume, physical force was comprehensible only within an evolutionary narrative in which a rational present is born of a primitive past.

Conclusion

The relationship between radical politics, history and memory in late eighteenth- and early nineteenth-century England was a vital one, but it was also complicated. While the Jacobins of the 1790s may have prepared the ground for radicalism's first anniversary calendar by calling for the annual commemoration of the LCS treason trials, the status of these events was altered by apparent changes in their character and meaning between 1795 and 1854. The ease with which the celebration of 'Trial by Jury' was accommodated not only by universal suffragist and republican radicals, but by the mildest reformers amongst the Liberals and Whigs, gradually diluted Jacobin memory and negated the energising power of the anniversary dinners. Rather than find themselves in harmonic concord with middle class liberalism by mid-century, Huntites, Spenceans and Chartists refused to fraternise and, instead, turned their backs. They may have co-operated over the creation of liberal-backed monuments to Cartwright or the Scottish martyrs, but they did not instigate them, remained critical, and they were, in any case, frequently ambivalent about the form and function of monuments to 'great men'. Radical ambivalence towards the setting up of monuments to fallen heroes reminds us too that historical memory is not always best preserved in material remains. Nick Mansfield's regret over the indifference of the modern labour movement towards the preservation of the material structures in which it was developed – the buildings of the working-class movement – should perhaps be considered partly in this light. This was a democratic tradition that understood and appreciated the integrity of what we now call 'intangible heritage' in the West, long before UNESCO codified it for the World Heritage Convention's commitment to cultural diversity.[68] Anniversary gatherings to mark the birthdays of a few men of unimpeachable character – Paine, Hunt and O'Connor – created a virtuous line of succession that mainstream radicals were comfortable with and, unsurprisingly, these anniversaries sometimes became battlegrounds in their own right as self-appointed fundamentalist guardians like John Gale Jones watched hawkishly over the toasting. Ultimately, however, ideological adherence to the demand for universal manhood suffrage shaped mainstream working-class radical commemoration much more emphatically than any methodological or strategic divisions over the shifting sands of 'constitutionalism', or 'physical/moral force'.

These early nineteenth-century debates over memory and identity remain pertinent today for they indicate *longue durée* continuities of flux in the making of protest heritage. As Smith and Campbell remind us, heritage is a discourse offering 'a framework for thinking about and acting on social "problems" associated with the past' and these discourses 'work to make the past meaningful and actively negotiate the meaning of the past for the present'.[69] The radical democrats of the LCS, the Spenceans, the Hampden Clubs and the Chartists did not engage that discourse in a vacuum any more than the commemorators of Tolpuddle, Peterloo or the Newport Rising are able to do today. They were as conscious, indeed, of the importance of controlling or 'authorising' a heritage discourse as the ideologues of the British Communist Party became under the early influence of the British school of Marxist historians on the eve of the Second World War. 'We remind you of the heritage of England's long struggle for freedom', ran the hyperbole urging mass participation in a *March of History* to invoke once again the spirits of Hampden, Sydney, Milton and Cromwell, 'We communists march with the very essence and spirit of the English tradition, we are out to carry forward English history to new achievements. We call on YOU, Londoner of 1936, to join us in the march to a Free and Merry England.'[70] The world war waged upon English democratic traditions that the Communist Party was trying to prevent broke out nevertheless three years later, one hundred years after the Newport Rising and one hundred years before the date projected by Thomas Cooper for a memorial to be raised to the insurrectionary patriotism of George Shell. In fact, Cooper's point was a remarkably modern one; authorised heritage is not a fixed discourse but a fluid one, mediated by the specificities of culture, time and place and always reinterpreted through the agency of the present.

NOTES

1. See Rodney Harrison, *Heritage: Critical Approaches* (Routledge: 2013) for recent discussion about 'official' and 'unofficial heritage', for example. For dissonant heritage, see Gregory Ashworth and John Tunbridge, *Dissonant Heritage: The Management of the Past as a Resource in Conflict* (Wiley: 1996).
2. Tunbridge and Ashworth, *Dissonant Heritage*; Laurajane Smith, *Uses of Heritage* (Routledge: 2011), 30.
3. Laurajane Smith, Paul A. Shackel and Gary Campbell (eds), *Heritage, Labour and the Working Classes* (Routledge: 2011); David Lowenthal, *The Heritage Crusade and the Spoils of History* (Cambridge: University Press: 1998), 226; Raphael Samuel, *Theatres of Memory, Volume 1: Past and Present in Contemporary Culture* (Verso: 1994), 211; Harrison, *Heritage: Critical Approaches*, 193.
4. See Iain J. M. Robertson, 'Heritage from below: class, social protest and resistance', in Brian Graham and Peter Howard (eds), *The Ashgate Research Companion to Heritage and Identity* (Ashgate: 2008), 144–56.
5. Hilda Kean, 'Tolpuddle, Burston and Levellers: the making of radical and national heritages at English labour movement festivals', in Smith, Shackel and Campbell, *Heritage, Labour and the Working Classes*, 273.
6. Particularly, James Epstein, *Radical Expression: Political Language, Ritual and Symbol in England* (Oxford University Press: 1994), pp. 177–201; Robert G. Hall, 'Creating a people's history, political Identity and history in Chartism', and Antony Taylor, 'Commemoration, memorialisation and political memory in post-Chartist radicalism: The 1885 Halifax Chartist reunion in context', in Owen Ashton, Robert Fyson and Stephen Roberts (eds), *The Chartist Legacy* (Merlin: 1999); David S. Karr, 'The embers of expiring sedition': Maurice Margarot, the Scottish martyrs monument and the production of radical memory across the British South Pacific', *Historical Research*, 86 (2013), 638–60; and the essays in Paul A. Pickering and Alex Tyrrell (eds), *Contested Sites: Commemoration, Memorial and Popular Politics in Nineteenth Century Britain* (Routledge: 2004).

7. David S. Karr, '"The embers of expiring sedition"', 239–40.
8. Iain McCalman, 'Preface', in Pickering and Tyrrell (eds), *Contested Sites*, p. xiii.
9. John Thelwall, *The Peripatetic or Sketches of the Heart, of Nature and Society...* Vol. 3 (self-published: 1796), 110.
10. Thelwall, *Peripatetic*, Vol. 2, 37. See also S. Poole, '"Not precedents to be followed but examples to be weighed": John Thelwall and the Jacobin sense of the past', in Steve Poole (ed.), *John Thelwall: Radical Romantic and Acquitted Felon* (Pickering and Chatto: 2009), 161–73.
11. John Thelwall, *The Peripatetic; edited with an introduction by Judith Thompson* (Wayne State University Press: 2001), 45.
12. John Thelwall, *The Rights of Nature Against the Usurpations of Establishments* (H.D. Symonds: 1796), 21.
13. Thelwall, *The Peripatetic* Vol. 3, 110.
14. Mark Akenside, 'Inscription VI, For a Column at Runnymede', *A Collection of Poems in Six Volumes. By Several Hands*, Vol. VI (R, and J. Dodsley: 1758), 34.
15. The point is argued by Lisa Vargo, 'Anna Barbauld and natural rights: the case of "Inscription for an ice-house"', *European Romantic Review* 27 (2016), 331–39.
16. Lynda Pratt, 'Southey in Wales: inscriptions, monuments and romantic posterity', in Damien Walford Davies and Lynda Pratt (eds), *Wales and the Romantic Imagination* (Univeristy of Wales Press: 2007), 86–103; Paul Jarman, 'Feasts and fasts: Robert Southey and the politics of calendar', in Lynda Pratt (ed.), *Robert Southey and the Contexts of English Romanticism* (Ashgate: 2006), 49–69.
17. *Wooler's British Gazette*, 2 February 1822; Lynda Pratt, 'Robert Southey, writing and romanticism', *Romanticism on the Net* 32 (2003); 'Southey's West Country', in Nicholas Roe (ed.), *English Romantic Writers and the West Country* (Palgrave: 2010), 201–18.
18. John Thelwall, 'On prosecutions for pretended treason', *The Tribune*, 1 (1795), 281; Thomas Hardy, 'Memoir of Thomas Hardy', in David Vincent (ed.), *Testaments of Radicalism: Memoirs of Working Class Politicians, 1790–1885* (Europa: 1977), 70.
19. John Thelwall, 'Historical strictures on Whigs and Tories...', *The Tribune* 1 (1795), 171; John Baxter, *A New and Impartial History of England* (H.D. Symonds: 1795), 114.
20. Quoted in Harry T. Dickinson, 'Magna Carta in the Age of Revolution', *Enlightenment and Dissent* 30 (2015), 16.
21. There was, however, a notable growth in the placing of memorials on British battlefield sites during the nineteenth and early twentieth centuries, and these markers have indeed been a locus for contested public interpretation of

the events they record in ways that Thelwall would certainly have recognised. See Ian Atherton and Philip Morgan, 'The Battlefields War Memorial: commemoration and the battlefield site from the Middle Ages to the modern era', *Journal of War and Culture Studies* 4 (2011), 289–304; Dolly MacKinnon, '"Correcting an error in history": battlefield memorials at Marston Moor and Naseby, 1771–1939', *Parergon* 32 (2015), 205–35.

22. Samuel Bamford, *Passages in the Life of a Radical* (Oxford University Press: 1967/1884), 278, 282, 284, 292.
23. Bamford, *Passages*, 272.
24. *The Republican*, 3 February 1826. As James Epstein has argued, Carlile was in any case instrumental in the rehabilitation of Paine as a central figure of inspiration to post-war popular democrats: *Radical Expression*, 127.
25. *The Republican*, 3 February 1826. The most likely candidates are Thomas Preston and Allen Davenport.
26. *Poor Man's Guardian*, 11 July 1835.
27. *Northern Star*, 10 November 1838; 30 August 1845; *Poor Man's Guardian*, 7 February 1835.
28. The development of a Chartist counter-historical narrative, and its marginalisation not only of Spenceans but of black and minority ethnic radicals and of women is traced in Robert G. Hall, 'Creating a people's history: political identity and history in Chartism, 1832–1848', in Ashton, Fyson and Roberts, *The Chartist Legacy*, 232–55.
29. TNA, HO 40/7/1, Precis of Correspondence Relative to Disturbances etc. in London, 1817–18, Part 1, June to September, p. 2, and HO 40/7/2, Part 2, Oct, pp. 48, 54; HO 40/7/8, James Lyon to Lord Sidmouth, 12 December 1817.
30. *Morning Advertiser*, 6 January 1818; *Morning Chronicle*, 12 January 1818; *Kentish Weekly Post*, 13 January 1818; *Chester Chronicle*, 16 January 1818, TNA, HO 40/8, Information dated 9 January 1818; HO 42/171, Testimony of John Smith 15 November 1817; HO 42/173, Edward Marshland to Henry Hobhouse, 11 January 1818. For Hooper's funeral, see also David Worrall, *Radical Culture: Discourse, Resistance ad Surveillance, 1790–1820* (Wayne State University Press: 1992), 124–5.
31. Matthew Roberts, 'Chartism, commemoration and the cult of the radical hero, c.1770–c.1840', *Labour History Review*, 78 (2013), 20–21.
32. *Northern Star*, 9 November 1850.
33. *Morning Advertiser*, 6 November 1819.
34. Ironically, in 1847 Hobhouse would lose his parliamentary seat at Nottingham to Feargus O'Connor.
35. For more on these disputes, see *The Champion*, 17 January, 14 February 1819; *Morning Chronicle*, 18 November 1818, 3 September 1819.
36. *Morning Chronicle*, 6 November 1823.

37. *Morning Advertiser*, 6 November 1837; 6 November 1838.
38. *Morning Advertiser*, 6 November 1844. For the controversy over the toast to Cartwright, see Thomas Cleary's letter of protest in *Morning Chronicle*, 7 November 1842.
39. *Northern Star*, 27 September 1845.
40. *Northern Star*, 23 December 1848.
41. Alex Tyrrell and Michael T. Davis, 'Bearding the Tories: the commemoration of the Scottish political martyrs of 1793–94', in Pickering and Tyrrell, *Contested Sites*, 25–56; Karr, 'The embers of expiring sedition', 653–4.
42. *Northern Star*, 9 August 1845.
43. *Black Dwarf*, 31 December 1817.
44. *Poor Man's Guardian*, 17 August 1833; *Northern Star*, 2 October 1841.
45. John Belchem, *'Orator' Hunt: Henry Hunt and English Working Class Radicalism* (Breviary Stuff: 2012/1985), 211–2.
46. *Poor Man's Guardian*, 26 September 1835.
47. *Northern Star*, 7 April 1842 and 12 August 1843, 24 August 1844; Terry Wyke, 'Remembering the Manchester Massacre', in Robert Poole (ed.), *Return to Peterloo: Manchester Region History Review*, special edition 23 (2012), 116–17. No further memorials on such a scale would be erected to British radicals until the death of Feargus O'Connor a decade later. By 1860, two monuments had been built to Chartism's most notable leader, an obelisk in London's Kensal Green cemetery and a statue in the Nottingham arboretum. The difficulties faced by these two projects are discussed in detail in Paul A. Pickering, 'The Chartist Rites of Passage: Commemorating Feargus O'Connor' in Pickering and Tyrrell, *Contested Sites*, 101–26.
48. Bunhill Fields contains the graves of Hardy and Gale Jones, amongst others. Gale Jones, noted *The Satirist*, was buried 'beside the rest of the Liberal dust; and posterity will no doubt raise a monument over the whole Liberal cemetery': *The Satirist*, 17 March 1838.
49. For Emmet's speech being 'very ably given by S. Walker' at a meeting of Ashton Chartists, see *Northern Star*, 16 November 1844. Emmet crafted this speech as 'a claim on your memory… that my memory and name may serve to animate those who survive me': Kevin Whelan, 'Robert Emmet: between history and memory', *History Ireland* 11, 3 (2003), p. 51.
50. *The Times*, 20 October 1832.
51. *Northern Star*, 8 November 1851
52. Rowland Weston, 'History, memory, and moral knowledge: William Godwin's essay on sepulchres (1809)', *The European Legacy* 14 (2009), 651–65.
53. *Chartist Circular*, 23 September 1839.
54. Epstein, *Radical Expression*, 146.

55. Benjamin Wilson, 'The Struggles of an Old Chartist' (Halifax: 1887), reprinted in Vincent, Testaments of Radicalism, pp. 220–1. For Galloway's death, see *Northern Star*, 18 December 1847, and for Preston's, *Northern Star*, 8 June, 31 August 1850.
56. Paul A. Pickering, 'A "grand ossification": William Cobbett and the commemoration of Tom Paine', in Pickering and Tyrrell, *Contested Sites*, 70–1.
57. Terry Wyke, 'Remembering the Manchester massacre', 113–4; *Northern Star*, 18 August 1838.
58. *Poor Man's Guardian*, 16 May 1835.
59. *Northern Star*, 16 September 1843.
60. *Black Dwarf*, 21 December 1824.
61. Frances D. Cartwright (ed.), *Life and Correspondence of Major Cartwright*, Vol. 2 (H. Colborn: 1826), 290–6.
62. *Poor Man's Guardian*, 23 July 1831.
63. *Northern Star*, 3 June 1843. Nugent was anxious to prove that, on the contrary, Hampden had been shot in the back by two musketeers. The evidence remains inconclusive.
64. Eugenio F. Biagini and Alastair J. Reid (eds), *Currents of Radicalism: Popular Radicalism, Organised Labour and Party Politics in Britain 1850–1914* (Cambridge University Press: 1991). For critical reappraisals of the tendency of these arguments to soften distinctions between 'working-class' Chartism and 'middle-class' Liberalism, and of the ways in which Chartist autobiographers represented their own militant pasts, see Robert G. Hall, 'Chartism remembered: William Aitken, liberalism, and the politics of memory', *Journal of British Studies* 38 (1999), 445–70, and Matthew Roberts, 'Chartism, commemoration', 3–32.
65. Thomas Cooper, *The Purgatory of Suicides. A Prison Rhyme. In Ten Books*, 2nd edition (J. Watson: 1858), 158–9.
66. *Northern Star*, 22 November 1845.
67. Cooper also demonstrated an understanding of physical force as a legitimate constitutional process in his lectures on English history to Chartist audiences. See Hall, 'Creating a people's history', 237–9.
68. Nick Mansfield, *Buildings of the Labour Movement* (English Heritage: 2013), viii.
69. Laurajane Smith and Gary Campbell, 'Don't mourn, organise: heritage, recognition and memory in Castleford, West Yorkshire', in Smith, Shackel and Campbell, *Heritage, Labour and the Working Classes*, 86–7.
70. Cited in Samuel, *Theatres of Memory*, 207. For a critical discussion of the uses of intangible heritage see Rodney Harrison and Deborah Rose, 'Intangible heritage' in Tim Benton (ed.), *Understanding Heritage and Memory* (Manchester University Press: 2010), 238–76.

Memory and the Work of Forgetting: Telling Protest in the English Countryside

Carl J. Griffin

There is a tendency in protest studies to valorise and glorify all acts of social protest. In part, this is a function of protest scholars being so close to their archives, and that their material is a lived presence in their lives, so that it is almost impossible to conceive of their foci as being anything other than heroic, acts of great social good. And, of course, many historical acts of social protest and their attendant practices can be so conceived: few would dispute the innate good writ in the objectives of Chartism, or in the exposure and defeat of deceitful marketing practices in an eighteenth-century food riot. But in many cases the resort to social protest – and here we shall make a distinction between political activism as understood in the twenty-first century as engaging in purposive acts to bring about cultural or political change and the broader concept of protest – was a reaction to a social dysfunction. Indeed, much protest was motivated not by a desire to effect social or economic change but to avoid it, what social movement theorists call defensive or conservative action.[1] As Roger Wells noted in relation to food rioting, the practice was evidence of a breakdown in social relations, that other means of seeking redress – the tools of E. P. Thompson's 'moral economy' – had failed

---

C. J. Griffin (✉)
University of Sussex, Brighton, UK

© The Author(s) 2018
C. J. Griffin, B. McDonagh (eds.), *Remembering Protest in Britain since 1500*, https://doi.org/10.1007/978-3-319-74243-4_9

and that poor consumers now needed to use direct action to right perceived wrongs and improve their lot.[2]

Such a reading has implications for how we conceive the effects of protest. Whether food riot, incendiarism or the sending of a threatening letter, protest was not only evidence of a dramatic dislocation in the community but also invariably a marker that the agrarian equipoise would be disturbed, and that a new lived reality would emerge. But we know remarkably little about how communities responded and made sense of what had happened after the protest. This might take the form of the stirring up of tensions and the testing of solidarities in the investigations that followed the act (and given that under the auspices of the Black Act of 1723 pretty much any act of resistance could be framed in law as criminal). It could also take the form of individuals being placed into custody, and perhaps later sent to gaol, transported or even hanged. As the editors of this volume have explored elsewhere, the event of protest so often has been used, has provided the political logic, to justify new forms of social control and new techniques to discipline dissent.[3]

This chapter addresses this major lacuna in the study of protest history through the particular context *not* of what followed episodes of social protest or how such moments of social dysfunction were remembered per se, but rather in the interplay between remembering and forgetting. Given that, conceptually, forgetting is memory's other, the more-than-passive act of not remembering,[4] in trying to better comprehend the dynamics of forgetting we necessarily also need to understand the relationship between actively remembering and actively (trying) to forget. Both, this chapter contends, exist in practice not as polar opposites but as part of the same spectrum of community actions, co-constituents of the work that communities needed to do in the 'aftermath' to refigure solidarities and to move beyond.

In this, I am not claiming that previous studies have not been attentive to the selective ways in which past protests have been popularly inscribed. As Andy Wood has noted of the 1549 'commotion time', for many individuals rebellion – and by inference other forms of protest – represented a 'personal catastrophe that was best wished away'.[5] For not only was the evidence of social dislocation and the potential further breaking down of social relations that followed damaging, but the impacts of violence and reputational damage might also be best 'forgotten'. It starts from the standpoint central to the recent emergence of critical heritage studies: that memory is not a given, rather it is something created, staged, performed and mediated, something that exists at the intersection between recall and the material. As Robert Hall has noted of one-time Chartist activists forging new political lives in the 1850s and 1860s, 'in the case of certain painful or divisive remembrances, the best approach was simply to try to forget'.[6] Thus the need to forget, that is to say to inscribe past events in ways that were no longer damaging to the community or to the individual, required work.

The work this chapter examines is that done by rural working people, the labouring families, servants, artisans, miners, manufacturers, small peasant farmers and petty traders that made up the plebeian rural community. Any consideration of demotic work is necessarily shaped by the understanding that collective memories are invariably informed and responsive to elite attempts to hijack meanings and frame collective memory in their attempts to deny the agency and validity of protest. What follows examines this idea in the context of the (very) long eighteenth century, drawing upon a range of examples from the passing of the Black Act to the Swing quasi-insurrection of 1830–31. Before this, it is necessary to think through both how we currently understand – in the phrase of Hobsbawm and Rudé – 'aftermaths' and how we conceptualise the use of problematic pasts in understanding the history of protest.

Aftermaths: Protest, Memory, Forgetting

While the relationship between History and memory is necessarily a conceptually awkward one, the need for historians to address social responses to disasters and atrocities has forced a critical engagement. Indeed, much of the shift in our conception of memory (and the work that it does) can be traced to attempts to understand responses to individual, and especially collective, trauma. In studies of the Holocaust and Hiroshima, amongst other atrocities of the modern age, memory has come to be seen not just as a way of connecting with and mentally memorialising the past, but also as a problem, as something that can be cast as traumatic and debilitating. Of course, such memories are not necessarily shared, and differences in claims to the past can become, as played out most vividly in Jewish history, terrains of conflict anew.[7] Similarly, according to Henry Rousso in his study of the effects of the Vichy regime in wartime France, symptoms of guilt and shame – what he labels 'the Vichy Syndrome' – continue to create political, cultural and social divisions.[8] As such, the need to remember tragedy, but at the same time inscribe the past in the collective memory as useful necessitates both recall (as framed through the material and shared repetition) and forgetting.[9] Conversely, as Steve Legg has asserted in his study of the memory of nationalist struggles in colonial Delhi, against attempts to produce official memories of periods of strife, work is also often needed in the fight of the 'refusal to forget' and the production of sites of 'counter-memory'.[10]

As Paul Ricoeur has claimed, in recording the past, all acts of inscription involve mutations in memory, and these mutations have effects. But in the act of inscribing – and here I use the term to include anything from the casting in stone, to the writing down, to oral transmission – a shift occurs from 'I was there…' to the sharing of a 'system of places and dates' as personal memory becomes eliminated in the process of memory becoming historiography.[11] This is, so the analysis goes, an active and dynamic process, something that requires work in translating. Here, then, work is done precisely because individuals and communities *need to forget*. As is well understood in the context of genocide and trauma studies, disasters, social dislocations and individual trauma could be so devastating for the continued existence of the community that such events were not actively recalled, rather their memory was repressed, the past repurposed, reimagined without. Further, as Paul Connerton suggests, while forgetting is memory's other, it is also an important constituent part in the making of memory. But against this need to forget was the continual reminder of all pasts as grooved in the bodies of the people and as written in the symbolism of their material worlds; sites of failure and tragedy never being totally (culturally) erased.[12]

Such critical understandings have the potential to radically transform our understanding of the work that the past does. And it is precisely for these reasons that the study of memory, and its conceptual twin commemoration, has become one of the defining critical intellectual projects of the humanities in the past two decades, including in History and Critical Heritage Studies.[13] At a meta level, the analysis of the work and place of memory has become an intellectual totem of critical studies of modernity, a conceptual device at the centre of poststructuralist attempts to destabilise the grand narratives that defined the modern political-intellectual project.[14] This is critical work in two senses. First, in that studies of popular memory are a vital way in which big stories, which necessarily ride roughshod over difference – whether different experiences or difference over space and time – can be dismantled. Analyses of popular memory allow for more modest, rich and contextually sensitive stories to be told which are truly attentive to difference.[15] Second, through focusing on popular understandings and experiences of the past, memory studies allow for not only alternative stories and narratives to emerge, but also different – and dissenting – voices to be heard. As Iain Robertson's work on 'heritage from below' has shown so powerfully, past conflicts are often told and used in ways which then work for working communities rather than subscribing to hegemonic scripts of the past, thus creating a space in which the potential for remembering protest becomes a tool of liberation in the present.[16]

Here collides the need to think through local context to understand the politics of memory and the poststructuralist emphasis on the need to write 'modest stories', often figured on the spaces of experience.[17] This has found form in protest history through detailed, but subtle and nuanced attempts to both tell episodes of conflict in rich context but also in microhistories of communities in conflict, the work here, again, of Reay on the 'Battle of Bossenden Wood' and Wells on Burwash and more recently Steve Poole and Nick Rogers on Bristol as a centre of social conflict provide rich and suggestive examples.[18] And yet histories of protest in the modern world have tended not to be concerned with what came after the protest. But not only, as the introduction to this chapter asserted, has what comes after acts of protests been subjected to remarkably little in the way of systematic work, the memory work done by individuals and communities in 'forgetting' and selectively invoking certain pasts after protests has not been subjected to critical scrutiny. Indeed, while our understanding of the community contexts that begat protest has deepened immeasurably, we still know remarkably little about the work that communities did to get by after 'commotion times'.

None of this is to say that analyses of 'aftermaths' – that which came after the protest – have not figured at all in studies of protest in the (very) long eighteenth century; rather, they have tended to focus on either on repression, policy responses, or have examined the future resort to protest.[19] The prevalent concept of 'crisis years' – on which see Malcolm Chase's fine recent book devoted to the events of 1820[20] – also necessarily draws upon the understanding that the framing of crisis was in itself a function of what came after the protest as much as that which came before. Thus, in Rudé's study of 'disturbance' on the 'eve' of the First Reform Bill (1831), we see the 'consequences' of the Swing quasi-insurrection, whose 'political effects were [supposedly] virtually nil', other short-lived 'movements' and 'associations' amongst industrial workers, and the 'climax' of the 1831 reform crisis as manifested in urban rioting.[21] Similarly, in Nick Rogers' study of the 'mayhem' of 1748–53, the idea of a crisis in social relations is centre stage, and explored through the lens of 'riots and reprisals'. His work considers, amongst other things, the 'legacy of bitterness' in the 'aftermath' of the Bristol and Somerset turnpike riots which meant that it was difficult to bring prosecutions, and of the situation with regard to smuggling in Kent and Sussex, where the government and local agencies were 'too weak' to break the culture of coastal smuggling.[22] But such studies, however suggestive, do not start from the standpoint of what follows. They do not ask how communities responded in the aftermath of protest. It is telling that arguably the most suggestive and interesting account of the impact upon social relations of episodes of social protest comes in the form of Jim Crace's Booker Prize-shortlisted novel *Harvest*, the plot of which centres on the aftershock of acts of animal maiming and incendiarism protesting a planned enclosure.[23] What follows analyses this interplay between active recall, burying and remaking in relation to past protests.

Aftermaths: Knowing, Telling, 'Forgetting', Revising

I: Rioting and Firing

As the late John Rule put it:

> A [Cornish] miner born in 1750, would have childhood memories of the food riots of 1757, and could have participated in food riots in 1773, 1793, 1795, 1796 and 1801. If he were lucky enough to live to be 62, then he could also have experienced the food riots of 1812. Apart from food rioting, he would have been a youth at the time of the pottery smashing, and [may] have participated in the riots of the 1780s.[24]

Rural workers learnt how to behave, how to protest, not only from watching what went on around them in childhood but also through sharing the experience of past protest with others. In this way, accounts to both continuity and novelty could be made by drawing on the memory of the people. Thus, according to reports of a food riot at Newcastle in June 1740, this was 'the most notorious Riot that ever happened in the Memory of Man'. Corn having been exported from the docks, the surrounding colliers, 'rushing into the town', destroyed the town house and the town records.[25]

Thus, memory was mobilised, but also both, literally, destroyed and remade. As John Bohstedt has argued of the food riots of 1740, the first ever 'national' wave of food rioting, in many rapidly industrialising communities of the north, what to do, how to act in such circumstances was not yet known, meaning that communities improvised and made things up as they went along.[26] But food rioting was not a new phenomenon, even if its forms and rules had changed,[27] and, as Thompson has suggested, its legitimacy at least in part rested in the 'popular memory' of the 1630 Book of Orders – itself 'republished, unofficially, in 1662, and again in 1758'.[28] As such, those who migrated to work in such 'new' communities brought with them their knowledge of how to act collectively in the face of threats to their well-being, successes mobilised, failures written out.[29]

The script might relate to a community, to a specific place, but it was also portable and mutable. Thus, according to John Aubrey in his *Natural History of Wiltshire* (finished in 1691): 'the [community] history [the script] was handed downe from mother to daughter… [the practice for] the maydes to sitt-up late by the fire [to] tell old romantique stories of the old time'. And, as Aubrey suggested of a Katherine Bushell of Ford, near Chippenham, 'being excellent at these old stories… had the history from the conquest downe to Carl. I [King Charles I] in ballad'.[30] In this way the script – that hidden transcript theorised by James Scott in relation to the protests of peasant communities in south-eastern Asia – of what to do, while fundamentally staying true to the story, to the rules of narrative, evolved. The script also evolved in response to changing conditions and circumstances. As Adrian Randall has noted of eighteenth-century food rioters, 'cohesion and collective support in crowds' was forged in earlier confrontations with employers, market dealers and the authorities. So, once a community had rioted successfully they were far more likely to riot again. The 'folk memory and sense of confidence that came from previous actions' was a 'strong mobilising agency'. Andrew Charlesworth has also noted that this culture of food rioting 'grew stronger and was enriched as a cumulative collective memory of previous struggles' as the eighteenth century unfurled.[31]

In all of this success is paramount. The script is a record of success. We know that success could be imported, remodelled, remade, but what of failure? Remembering here could work in different ways. In her account of loyalism and radicalism in Lancashire in the 1790s and early 1800s, Katrina Navickas details the case of the 'Royton Races', a meeting of the local reform club at Royton on 21 April 1794 that was broken up by a reportedly 4,000-strong Loyalist 'Church and King' mob and army recruits from Oldham. Six members of the club were arrested for riotous assembly and assault, though ultimately only one person was convicted. This was a bloody affair and put pay to further such open reform meetings in Royton, but the legacy of the reform struggle lived on, not least in the 'Jacobin library' that was maintained there. Further, Royton remained associated with reform in the region. It hosted peace meetings in 1801, while Tandle Hill in the parish was the location of drilling and marching by radicals in the run-up to the Peterloo Massacre in 1819, a contingent from Royton present on that fateful day at St Peter's Field. Yet the memory of the attack – the failure – at Royton was mobilised and kept alive not in the rhetoric of reformers but of loyalists. Thus, when Royton reformer Lieutenant-Colonel Joseph Hanson stood as independent candidate for Preston in 1807 an election song by his opponents went:

> To Royton he once went to make revolutions,
> For like his friend Bony he hates constitutions;
> But the King's Dragoons, in all that saw no fun,
> And a charge sword in hand, made the jacobins run.

In the continuation of the culture of reform at Royton we see the active remembering of what came before the attack of 1794 and a deliberate performance of defiance, but the 'races' were not remembered publicly.[32] There can be no doubt that the radicals of Royton never forgot the suppression of the 'races'; rather, it was marked in the community body, but it served no good to mobilise and revivify the memory in building new radical futures.

Deeper community memories were critical in relation to incendiarism and the other tools of terror occasionally practiced in the English countryside, tools whose use was always evidence that social relations had broken down. The classic expression of this breakdown is the activities of the Blacks – variably of Waltham Chase, Farnham and Windsor – a gang or set of forest dwelling gangs who were engaged in a long-running battle with forest officers regarding state attempts to exploit the forests in the late 1710s and early 1720s. While this is not the place to go into forensic detail as to their machinations and methods,[33] it is important to note that long after their activities were suppressed and dissipated the folk memory of their activities was so strong and enduring that it had two effects. In areas where the Blacks had operated, public memory was evidently suppressed for the fear of both the terror affected by the Blacks' protests and the effect of the toll of their repression by the British state on local communities. The story of the Blacks lived on *everywhere* in the form of the existence of the Black Act, it being a Public General Act, though, as Peter King has recently shown, the geography of its use was decidedly uneven.[34] But to invoke their actions to justify and vivify future acts of resistance in their areas of operation would do no good and potentially significant harm. This is not to say that the forests of the Hampshire–Surrey–Berkshire borders were absolutely quieted by the trial of the Blacks and the passing of the Black Act, but no reference was made to the Blacks. As Thompson noted, no newspaper published an account of the trial of the Blacks, while only one popular pamphlet was subsequently produced to mythologise their actions. 'No "emergency"', reckoned Thompson, 'can have left less impression in print nor imprinted itself more feebly on the popular memory.'[35]

Yet in areas of the south where they had not operated, the assumed name – Black, Blacks – was invoked for decades after by protestors as a way of instilling terror. This was perhaps best summed up by the wording of a threatening letter sent to Mr. Ridge, the keeper of the Forest of the Isle of Wight in late 1736:

Remember the Walton [sic] Blacks

The letter was sent in the context of attempts to put down deer stealing in the forest. In true Blacks style, it warned that his horse would 'be shot under him', and that his 'Habitation laid low about his Ears'. It was only after the killing of 'several' deer in the forest and what was supposed to be an attempt on Ridge's life – shots being fired into his bed chamber at night – that a pardon was offered for accomplices who came forwards and a £50 reward for information advertised in the *London Gazette*.[36] Thus, the power of the word Black (or Blacks) was kept alive, and its terror magnified, by such acts that undid the community work of forgetting.

Community memories of lone events of terror could run deep too. In November 1757 an 'Old woman' was accused of setting fire to the barns and corn stacks on Frith Farm in Newnham, near Faversham, Kent. Over the next sixty years the parish supposedly remained a model of effective social relations. That is, until 20 September 1823, when the same farm was again targeted by incendiarists. According to the press, the 'oldest inhabitants' – presumably only children or teenagers when the previous fire occurred – were quick to remind the community of what had happened sixty years previously. The inference here is that, individually, the event had not been forgotten but that collectively it had been erased from the script of the community, not having been constantly refracted through storytelling as we might otherwise assume. This, then, was a process of unforgetting, of having to admit that past painful memories had occurred and continued to shape the community.[37]

Sometimes the scars were far fresher, the acts of forgetting in process rather than complete. A fire on Hatchell Farm, Hound near Hamble on the south coast of Hampshire on 4 September 1830 followed a fire two years previously. 'Readers', lamented the *Southampton Mercury*, 'will no doubt remember the premises were destroyed by fire several years ago and the culprit was never caught.' Here we have forgetting evidently in progress, for not even the correct year could be remembered. The 1830 fire, however, reinvigorated the long-since-abandoned efforts to catch the 1828 fire-setter. Indeed, eventually 'the culprit' of the first fire was caught, arrested, tried, found guilty of the fire and hanged. The recent incendiarist remained at large, however, although some believed that he was also the perpetrator of the latter fire.[38]

Of course, the act of not letting people forget, of not allowing the memory of calamity to be written out of the community script, was precisely the point of gibbets – the bodies of those executed 'hung in chains' – and scene of crime executions, both hegemonic attempts to firmly lodge failure in the active community memory. The landscape of the gibbet acted, so Sarah Tarlow and Zoe Dyndor have suggested, as a material mnemonic, a reminder of the triumphalist power of the state and the perfidy of rebels, although in community memory there was often a blurring of the line between 'shaming notoriety and immortal celebrity'. Perhaps it is no surprise that last scene of crime execution in England and Wales was for incendiarism, the Somerset village of Kenn the location in September 1830. Crime scene executions lodged themselves firmly in the collective memory of communities. Even today, Steve Poole notes of Kenn, some farming families 'are able confidently to show visitors the exact spot in Seven Acre field where the gallows were erected in 1830'.[39]

II: *Swing*

Intermittently in the first decade of the twentieth century, the naturalist and author William Hudson made the downland villages of Wiltshire his home. Following his earlier studies of Hampshire and West Cornwall,

Hudson's intention was to study the wildlife of the Wiltshire Downs and to observe the folk of the country. Though better known as a botanist and ethologist, Hudson also proved an able ethnographer, building ready bonds with many families and teasing out the history of the place. Though his account, published as *A Shepherd's Life* in 1910, shifted from reportage to fictionalised tellings, it is possible to discern the fact from the fiction in his accounts of conversations about 'that miserable and memorable year of 1830'. That year had witnessed the largest-ever protest movement in rural England, the so-called Swing Riots. This was the greatest concentrated machine breaking movement in history, the greatest wave of arson in Britain, the largest single number of prosecutions for a protest movement, and was responsible for the biggest single set of criminal transportations to the penal colonies of Australia and Van Diemens Land. There were, he noted, a few aged people of the downland villages whose memories stretched back to the 'doings of the "mobs"'. But beyond the breaking of threshing machines in and around Hindon and the securing of some concessions from farmers and the parishes, the events of 1830 represented 'old unhappy things' to the communities of Hudson's study. 'It was notorious', he noted, 'that numbers of poor fellows were condemned' by 'scoundrels' who, smelling 'blood-money', were 'only too ready to swear away the life of any man'. The executions and transportations of men, mostly young, that followed the rising, cast a pallor onto those left. While wages initially rose, the farmers finding the labourers 'more submissive than they had ever been, the lesson they had received having sunk deep into their minds, they cut off the extra shilling… But there were no more risings.'[40]

Hudson's account shows that the events of 1830, however painful, were never fully forgotten – even eighty years later – by those who were only children at the time. The act of recall by the most elderly residents of the Wiltshire downland villages, the idea of notoriety and unhappiness all attest powerfully the different ways in which Swing remained writ in the body of the community. We need to be careful though. It is quite possible that the 'memory' of Swing was not only charged by forgetting but also refracted by subsequent events, what Michael Rothberg has called multidimensional memory.[41] Indeed, Swing was little talked about nor publicly invoked by rural workers. It was urban radicals who kept the memory alive;[42] in the years immediately beyond 1830 Swing was mobilised as a justification for both the New Poor Law of 1834 and the Rural Constabularies Act of 1839.[43] Rural workers themselves did not refer to Swing.[44] During the protests against the New Poor Law of 1834–6 and in the Revolt of the Field in the 1870s, I have found no mention of Swing – except by the authorities as a warning to rural workers of the dangers of protest. Indeed, a report in the *Standard* bemoaning the New Poor Law and the 'lurid flames of midnight conflagrations' that protested its introduction, made a reference to the 'Swing riots' by way of delineating a recent history of 'misgovernment'.[45] Even during the exceptionally well-documented, but short-lived union organisation at Tolpuddle in late 1833 and the early months of 1834 there was no direct reference to Swing. Indeed, George Loveless, the chief union organiser and instigator, denied he had been involved in Swing – and this despite that one of his brothers had been arrested, and subsequently escaped, for being involved in a Swing mobilisation. Notwithstanding George Loveless' protestation under questioning that he was not 'a rioter', but had instead been part of a parish watch against incendiarists, a Tolpuddle farmer later testified to Frampton that both brothers were involved in the wages rising: George vocal in the crowd; James attempting to convince the men to go and support a parallel rising at nearby Piddletown.[46]

Those who took part in Swing disturbances had good reason to very quickly establish coherent narratives that made sense of and rationalised the rising, and specifically what they and others did not do. Self-assertions that they had been swept along, coerced, bribed beyond resistance, and otherwise unwitting participants made much sense as strategies in attempting to avoid prosecution and punishment. For instance, when cross-examined by counsel Cooper at the Berkshire Special Commission, labourer Luke Middleton, charged with threshing machine breaking in the parish of Wasing, Berkshire, on 19 November 1830, proclaimed that:

> It was after I was taken into custody that I gave this account of the mob. I walked about with the mob with a little walking stick. I only looked on. I did no mischief. I had no particular promise that I should be forgiven if I would come forward against these men. There was nothing against me. Mr. Mount and Mr. Congreve on Saturday morning told me my character was excellent good. I do not recollect that any promise of forgiveness was made me… I cannot recollect whether or not any promise was made me. My memory is excellent good, but I cannot recollect what I never heard, or what I did not understand.

Whatever the actuality of the events of 19 November, Middleton was evidently dissembling, the process of forgetting in process and on display in the courtroom.[47]

This was also a strategy of mercy that was deliberately deployed by those elites who wanted to avoid reprisals and restore community life to how it had been before. Rev. Bramall, the perpetual curate of Elham, the original Swing centre of machine breaking, was pastorally mindful of his Christian duty to his charges and also fearful of being a victim of a vengeful incendiarist. Bramall managed to convince fifty of the machine breakers to come forward and surrender voluntarily. On being told that it would lessen their chances of conviction if they confessed – the vicar not being a clerical magistrate and having no jurisdiction to make such claims – many of the men were quick to help Bramall to help themselves. While some claimed that they were under the impression that it was not against the law to break threshing machines, others – with Bramall's evident support – claimed they had been press-ganged and bribed beyond bodily resistance with beer.[48]

Deliberately forgetting when being questioned by magistrates and the police and in court was a critical way in which community cohesion might be maintained. Swing's archive is replete with depositions from those involved in Swing mobilisations, by family members and other witnesses stating that they could not remember specific points about the protests. One wife of a Swing activist from Bossingham in East Kent related to the local magistrate that she knew that groups of men were going about the surrounding farms breaking threshing machines, but that she did not know what her husband got up to when he went out in the evenings.[49] Phillip Porter, a wheelwright's apprentice, charged with two counts of arson on the West Kent–Surrey–Sussex borders, was acquitted when the evidence against him was discredited. William Boxall, an unemployed labourer, came forward to collect a £100 reward for evidence and claimed that Porter had, just a few days before one of the fires, stated in conversation that: 'There will be a damned good one in the middle of the place.' Boxall, on asking where Porter meant, was told 'up at Mayfield, where all the ploughs and harrows are kept'. In court, however, Boxall admitted that 'I say many things when I am tipsy, which I forget when I become sober'. Porter was duly acquitted.[50]

Memory, recall, was a tool of the prosecution, a word, a concept mobilised against activists rather than by them with the intention of defiantly and indisputably placing defendants. This evidence was necessarily selective and presented in partial ways, something which is illustrated by Heather Falvey's chapter in this volume in relation to the prosecution of early modern protests. Likewise, Peter King's pioneering work on judicial discretion has illuminated the multiple strategies invoked by the judicial authorities to secure a predetermined end.[51] It should hardly be a surprise, therefore, that deponents were equally selective in terms of how they framed their recall of events. This was, of course, self-preservation for those called upon to give evidence, a way of avoiding the gibbet or the hulks. But it was also something that denied agency and publicly drew a line under the protests, something the bitter, government-sponsored, organised and funded prosecutions made imperative. According to Hobsbawm and Rudé, and yet to be systematically challenged, across southern and eastern England 644 rioters were imprisoned, 505 transported to Australia, and 19 executed. Thus, whatever the impact on the adoption of threshing machines – in many places meaningful mechanisation of agricultural tasks was put back to the 1840s – and temporary increases in wages, Swing ultimately represented a failure, a brief joyous moment when the world was turned topsy-turvy.[52]

This judicial response placed a particularly heavy premium on informing, the circulation issued by Lord Melbourne on 23 November 1830 offering £500 – about £50,000 in present-day terms – which acted to further fissure communities. Even as early as late October, following the first trial of Kentish machine breakers, and following an incendiary fire against the parish overseer, a chilling piece of graffiti was scrawled on a nearby wall: 'Down with machines. Death to informers'.[53] Indeed, the offer of the £500 reward was prompted by the fact that the magistrates in Kent were finding it difficult to secure evidence, such were the 'threats of vengeance against Informers'. In cases of incendiarism, securing any evidence beyond the circumstantial was proving almost impossible.[54] The reward, together with the dispatch of London police officers to assist in procuring evidence, all coordinated by the Treasury Solicitor, George Maule, had some impact. Indeed, several fire-setters were brought to trial, though one alleged Kentish incendiarist – Alex Brown – fled to Calais to avoid prosecution.[55]

Such pressures took a heavy toll on plebeian community cohesion. The following case is instructive. Labourer Bartholomew was subjected to a bitter verbal tirade and an even more violent assault at the William IV pub at Bridge, in the Elham Valley, being accused of having 'split against the Party'. His actions were seemingly responsible for Henry Hulkes having been sentenced to seven years' transportation for breaking farmer Friday's threshing machine at neighbouring Bekesbourne. Those guilty of the assault even offered a gallon of beer to anyone would lynch Bartholomew.[56] If forgetting was initially impossible, to move on communities needed to invest in keeping quiet, to publicly perform denial. Indeed, as noted, that so soon after the events of 1830 Swing as a public discourse quickly became something used only covertly, and then something that quickly lost even its potential to terrify, is suggestive of the need to publicly forget. We can see the legacy of Swing in the immediate aftermath in the acts of midnight incendiaries and in taproom conversations about trying to secure the movement's concessions and in protests against those who sought to quickly renege on the promises made. Further, in the refusals of labouring families gathered at incendiary fires to help extinguish the flames we see a tacit, implicit, silent cry about the memory of Swing because it could not be said publicly and explicitly.[57] This is the figuring of the memory of Swing into something else, something that drew on the bitterness of the repression – where it was vituperative and so often *ad hominem* – and turned Swing and rural communities inwards, the memory hidden deeper; the act of forgetting, of becoming archival, actively invested in. This process was manifest in what Keith Snell has called the culture of deferential bitterness, that outwardly deference was shown – to protect jobs, poor relief, community cohesion – but inwardly resentments were held deep, occasionally elliptically expressed through satire and the practice of the tools of rural terror.[58]

Swing was also subject to a series of attempts to mythologise and depoliticise the movement. By the end of January 1831, a plethora of pamphlets, plays and performances and dramatic narrative accounts of Swing were published – and selling well. These ranged from pseudo-biographicals, short stories through to 'serious' attempts to try and understand the movement. Such 'instant histories' were fundamental to framing the still malleable public understanding of the protests. Swing was thus variably cast as one of several things: a decayed small farmer; the son of a tenant farmer; 'the most lawless in the village'. Swing, so this analysis goes, was not an everyman, nor did he represent everyman; he was not the common labourer that actually swelled the movement's ranks.[59] Instantly, re-remembered, Swing assumed a different history that denied protestors' agency as activists and denied the movement coherence. It thereby helped to lay the ideological groundwork for repressive legislation. So repeated, the public 'truth' about Swing soon became set and established. Responding to a wave of incendiary fires in the late autumn and winter of 1831, the press were quick to announce that Swing was at work, but that 'he' was invariably 'violent' and 'evil'. In the words of a report in the *Times* report of an incendiary fire against a tenanted farm of Kent grandee Lord Sondes in the downland parish Throwley: '"Swing" is no respecter of persons, or & noblemen so truly benevolent as Lord Sondes … might indeed, expect some consideration.'[60] To rephrase E. P. Thompson, it was not only posterity that places an enormous condescension onto the heads of lost peoples, but also the processes of mythologisation, especially so when invested in as a hegemonic strategy by elites.[61]

Conclusion

Analysing that which is supposedly hidden, buried and suppressed is necessarily complex and partial. Without being able to ask eighteenth-century food rioters or Swing activists about their attempts to make sense of their – and their communities' – involvement in acts of protest that were suppressed, that in some way failed, we can only ever get at some of the motivations, let alone what are surely often competing and contradictory impulses and actions. What is detailed here, however, suggests that acts of forgetting were many and important in helping to remake social relations and forge new solidarities. Conscious forgettings are, after Ricoeur, an act of 'putting things back in their place'. This was a critical constituent of deciding what to publicly remember, and invoke, of what was added to the script of the community. But as the example of Hudson's early twentieth century researches into Swing and the recall of the Kenn execution site show, nothing is ever truly lost, especially that which is so traumatic. To forget required – requires – developing devices and strategies, an act of placing out of mind but in sight. This might be material mnemonics in the landscape, marks on and in the body, or the occasional, private recollection of that which could not be spoken about in public.[62] Conversely, we see in Hudson's respondents an evident non-linearity to memory. The interplay here is between personal recall, the incorporating of other received narratives, and refracting the memory of the event through subsequent events (Rothberg's multidirectional memory),[63] rather than just an act of recall set in stone. Thus, remembering necessarily involved some act of forgetting.

This dynamic was most obvious in relation to the many immediate needs of individuals and communities to forget. For activists on trial narratives needed to be reworked, remembered differently, to suit individual and collective needs and purposes, while to rebuild solidarities and community relations after protests had been put down and/or repressed necessarily required a shared script that worked for all: 'It wasn't me', 'I cannot remember', 'I don't understand what happened', 'I was forced', 'We were swept along'. And soon after, the protest, that which failed, could be publicly denied altogether through silence. In this, as the foregoing analysis shows, the reworking of the account of the protest – whether of the Blacks, the Royton Races or Swing – happened quickly and the community moved on. The past protest was not forgotten per se, rather variably reworked or buried. Yet this does not absolutely fit neatly with Connerton's model of 'humiliated silence', his seventh and final mode of forgetting. While they fit with his emphasis that such acts of forgetting were 'covert, unmarked and unacknowledged', the responses detailed here related only to collective shame in a performed and ironic way, expressing contrition through gritted teeth (and a box of matches in one hand) if you will.[64]

In this way, we might usefully understand plebeian communities, individual bodies and the landscapes in which they lived as bearing the characteristics inherited of past tragedies, something akin to a cultural form of Lamarckism, the theory in evolutionary biology that an organism can pass on characteristics that it acquired during its lifetime to its offspring (aka 'soft inheritance').[65] It is all there, but it is just that in the shift from the personal to the community narrative, the archive is used selectively, past events become written in the matter of place and in the body of the community, the inheritance there but not necessarily obvious. Through remembering to remember and remembering to forget, the past was constantly folded, remade, reanimated, becoming something always new. Even that set in stone can become quicksilver, fluid.

And here is an important lesson for protest historians. As Ian Dyck noted of William Cobbett's political-intellectual mission, his historical writings were deliberately set in opposition to elite attempts to 'secure control of popular memory' through the publication of penny abridgements 'of the works of the great liberal historians'. Cobbett's alternative accounts were attempts to 'preserve and fortify the independence of the people's historical consciousness'.[66] The process of writing history is never free from attempts to solidify collective memories of the past in selective and partial ways, to forget some aspects of that which has come before to move on. As James Jasper has implored, however, it is imperative that we do not forget the conclusions of past historians, or try to bury them; otherwise, we are doomed to oscillate from one idea to another, to forget the lessons of protest.[67]

Notes

1. Jürgen Habermas, 'New social movements', *Telos* 49 (1981), 33–7; Graham Chesters and Ian Welsh, *Social Movements: the Key Concepts* (Routledge; 2010), 60–1.
2. Roger Wells, *Wretched Faces: Famine in Wartime England, 1793–1803* (Alan Sutton: 1988), 175, 178; Edward Palmer Thompson, 'The moral economy of the English crowd in the eighteenth century', *Past and Present* 50 (1971), 76–136.

3. Briony McDonagh and Carl J. Griffin, 'Occupy! Historical geographies of property, protest and the commons, 1500–1850', *Journal of Historical Geography* 53 (2016): 1–10, 10.
4. Paul Ricoeur, *Memory, History, Forgetting* (University of Chicago Press: 2004).
5. Andy Wood, *The 1549 Rebellions and the Making of Early Modern England* (Cambridge University Press: 2007), 214.
6. Robert Hall, 'Chartism remembered: William Aitken, liberalism, and the politics of memory', *Journal of British Studies* 38 (1999), 445–70.
7. Katharine Hodgkin and Susannah Radstone, *Contested Pasts: The Politics of Memory* (Routledge: 2003); Yosef Hayim Yerushalmi and Harold Bloom, *Jewish History and Jewish Memory* (University of Washington Press,: 1982); Lisa Yoneyama, *Hiroshima Traces: Time, Space, and the Dialectics of Memory* (University of California Press: 1999).
8. Henry Rousso, *The Vichy Syndrome: History and Memory Since 1944*, translated Arthur Goldhammer (Harvard University Press: 1991).
9. For instance, see Andrew Charlesworth's pioneering analysis of reading places of official memory against the grain: 'Contesting places of memory: the case of Auschwitz', *Environment and Planning D: Society and Space* 12 (1994), 579–93.
10. Steve Legg, 'Sites of counter-memory: the refusal to forget and the nationalist struggle in colonial Delhi', *Historical Geography* 33 (2005), 180–201.
11. Ricoeur, *Memory, History, Forgetting*, 147–8.
12. Paul Connerton, *How Modernity Forgets* (Cambridge University Press, 2009).
13. Tom Winter, 'Clarifying the critical in critical heritage studies', *International Journal Of Heritage Studies*, 19 (2013), 535, 541–2.
14. On these dynamics see Jacques Derrida, *Archive Fever: A Freudian Impression* (University of Chicago Press: 1996); Michel Foucault, *Language, Counter-memory, Practice: Selected Essays and Interviews* (Cornell University Press: 1980).
15. For such an example, see Brian Conway, 'Active remembering, selective forgetting, and collective identity: the case of Bloody Sunday', *Identity*, 3 (2003), 305–23.
16. Iain Robertson, 'Heritage from below: class, social protest and resistance', in Brian Graham and Peter Howard (eds), *The Ashgate Research Companion to Heritage and Identity* (Ashgate: 2008), 143–58.
17. Nigel Thrift, *Non-representational Theory: Space, Politics, Affect* (Routledge: 2008); Hayden Lorimer, 'Cultural geography: the busyness of being 'more-than-representational'', *Progress in Human Geography* 29 (2005), 83–94, esp. 91.
18. Barry Reay, *Microhistories: Demography, Society and Culture in Rural England, 1800–1930* (Cambridge University Press: 2002); Roger Wells,

'Crime and protest in a country parish: Burwash, 1790–1850', in John Rule and Roger Wells, *Crime, Protest and Popular Politics in Southern England, 1740–1850* (Hambledon: 1997), 169–235; Steve Poole and Nicholas Rogers, *Bristol from Below: Law, Authority and Protest in a Georgian City* (Woodbridge: 2017).
19. See Wells, *Wretched Faces*, chs 12–16; Katrina Navickas, *Loyalism and Radicalism in Lancashire, 1798–1815* (Oxford University Press: 2009); Katrina Navickas, *Protest and the Politics of Space and Place, 1789–1848* (Manchester University Press: 2015); Eric Hobsbawm and George Rudé, *Captain Swing* (Laurence and Wishart, 1969), ch. 15; Carl Griffin, 'Swing, Swing redivivus, or something after Swing? On the death throes of a protest movement, December 1830–December 1833', *International Review of Social History* 54 (2009), 459–97.
20. Malcolm Chase, *1820: Disorder and Stability in the United Kingdom* (Manchester University Press: 2013).
21. George Rudé, 'English rural and urban disturbances on the eve of the First Reform Bill, 1830–1831', *Past and Present* 37 (1967), 87–102, 91.
22. Nicholas Rogers, *Mayhem: Post-war Crime and Violence in Britain, 1748–53* (Yale University Press: 2012), 211–17, 119, 121.
23. Jim Crace, *Harvest* (Pan Macmillan: 2013).
24. John Rule, 'The labouring miner in Cornwall c.1740–1870: a study in social history' (unpublished PhD thesis, University of Warwick, 1971), 193.
25. *General Evening Post*, 1 July 1740.
26. John Bohstedt, *The Politics of Provisions: Food Riots, Moral Economy, and Market Transition in England, c. 1550–1850* (Ashgate: 2013), ch. 4; John Bohstedt, 'The pragmatic economy, the politics of provisions and the "invention" of the food riot tradition in 1740', in Adrian Randall and Andrew Charlesworth (eds), *Moral Economy and Popular Protest: Crowds, Conflict and Authority* (Basingstoke: 2000), 55–92.
27. Buchanan Sharp, 'The food riots of 1347 and the medieval moral economy', in Randall and Charlesworth (eds), *Moral Economy*, 33–54.
28. Thompson, 'Moral economy', 109.
29. On this see point see: Andrew Charlesworth, 'From the moral economy of Devon to the political economy of Manchester, 1790–1812', *Social History* 18 (1993), 205–17.
30. Adam Fox, 'Remembering the past in early modern England. oral and written tradition', *Transactions of the Royal Historical Society*, 6th series, 9 (1999), 234.
31. Adrian Randall, *Riotous Assemblies: Popular Protest in Hanoverian England*. (Oxford University Press: 2006), 112; Charlesworth, 'From the moral economy of Devon', 210.
32. Navickas, *Loyalism and Radicalism in Lancashire*, 39, 152.

33. The classic account of the passing of the Black Act remains Thompson's magisterial Whigs and Hunters: Edward Palmer Thompson, *Whigs and Hunters: The Origin of the Black Act* (Allen Lane: 1975).
34. On the variable geography of its use, see Peter King and Richard Ward, 'Rethinking the Bloody Code in eighteenth-century Britain: capital punishment at the centre and on the periphery', *Past and Present* 228 (2015), 159–205.
35. Thompson, *Whigs and Hunters*, 223, 24.
36. *London Gazette*, 12 April 1737; Thompson, *Whigs and Hunters*, 229.
37. *The Times*, 8 October 1823; *Kentish Post*, 7 December 1757.
38. *Hampshire Chronicle*, 15 December 1828 and 7 March 1831; *Southampton Mercury*, 11 September 1830.
39. Sarah Tarlow and Zoe Dyndor, 'The landscape of the gibbet,' *Landscape History*, 36 (2015), 86, 72; Steve Poole, '"A lasting and salutary warning": incendiarism, rural order and England's last scene of crime execution', *Rural History* 19 (2008), 173.
40. William H. Hudson, *A Shepherd's Life: Impressions of the South Wiltshire Downs* (Cambridge University Press: 2011/1910), 212–3, 206–7.
41. Michael Rothberg, *Multidirectional Memory: Remembering the Holocaust in the Age of Decolonization* (Stanford University Press: 2009), see esp. ch. 1.
42. For instance, see *Northern Star*, 16 December 1837 and 3 March 1838.
43. Carl Griffin, *The Rural War: Captain Swing and the Politics of Protest* (Manchester University Press: 2012), 336.
44. The last attempts to mobilise the memory of Swing in the countryside came during the reform crisis by politicking urban radicals. For instance, during the autumn of 1832, the Horsham Political Union printed a 'one penny paper' that was hawked about the streets entitled 'Swing Redivious [sic]'. But this was little to do with the demands of most Swing activists, rather the spirit of Swing was reworked to critique the established Church and the local authorities: Ibid., 307–8.
45. *Standard*, 29 October 1835.
46. Roger Wells, 'Tolpuddle in the context of English agrarian labour history, 1780–1850', in John Rule (ed.), *British Trade Unionism: The Formative Years* (London: 1988), 121; George Loveless, *Victims of Whiggery* (London: 1838), 10; James Frampton, Moreton to Lord Melbourne, 2 April 1834, reproduced in Walter Citrine, *The Martyrs of Tolpuddle* (TUC: 1934), 183.
47. *Evening Mail*, 31 December 1830. Also see the report in *Berkshire Chronicle*, 1 January 1831.
48. Kent History and Library Centre [herein KHLC], U951 C177/26, 27, and 13. Rev. Bramall, Elham, to Rev. Price, 6 October, and Rev. Price to Knatchbull, no date (probably 7 October); and List of 37 persons involved

in machine breaking between 25 August and 22 September who voluntarily surrendered and were bound by recognisances to appear at the next Assizes, no date.
49. KHLC, Q/SBe 120/2 and 14, various depositions, September and October 1830.
50. *Kent Herald*, 3 June; TNA, HO 52/8, fos 89–90, 231–3, and 261–2, Joseph Berens, Kevington, Foots Cray, 8 June; Bromley Bench, 9 June; and, Clerk, Whitehall, 3 September, to Robert Peel; *London Gazette*, 11 June; *Maidstone Gazette*, 10 August; TNA, Assi 94/2066, Indictment of Phillip Porter, Kent Summer Assizes 1830.
51. Heather Falvey, 'Relating early modern depositions', in Carl Griffin and Briony McDonagh (eds), *Remembering Protest in Britain since 1500: Memory, Materiality and the Landscape* (Palgrave: 2018), ch. 4; Peter King, 'Decision-makers and decision-making in the English criminal law, 1750–1800', *Historical Journal* 27 (1984), 25–58; Peter King, *Crime, Justice, and Discretion in England 1740–1820* (Oxford University Press: 2000).
52. Hobsbawm and Rudé, *Captain Swing*, appendix II ('Summary of Repression').
53. *Maidstone Journal*, 26 October; TNA, HO 52/8, fos 300–301 Rev. Poore, Murston to Peel, 23 October; *Times*, 30 October; *Maidstone Gazette*, 9 November 1830.
54. TNA, HO 52/8, fos 30–2, Rev. Morrice, Betshanger House, nr Sandwich, to Lord Melbourne, 24 November 1830.
55. TNA, HO 52/8, fos 139–40, John Boys, Margate to Melbourne, 12 December 1830. Magistrate Boys sent a constable to Dover with a warrant for Brown's arrest, but believed that it would be necessary to secure a state warrant to bring him back to Britain for trial.
56. *The Times*, 29 November; KHLC, Q/SBe/122, Depositions of labourer Bartholomew and innkeeper Moors, 10 December 1830.
57. Griffin, *The Rural War*, ch. 11.
58. Keith D. M. Snell, 'Deferential bitterness; the social outlook for rural proletariat in eighteenth- and nineteenth-century England and Wales', in Michael Bush (ed.), *Social Orders and Social Classes in Europe Since 1500: Studies in Social Stratification* (Longman: 1992), 158–84.
59. See: C. Z. Barnett, *'Swing!' A farce, in one act* (J. Duncombe, 1831); R. Taylor, *Swing: or, Who are the Incendiaries? A tragedy [in five acts, in prose and in verse]* (R. Carlisle, 1831); 'Francis Swing' (pseud.), *The History of Swing, the Noted Kent Rick Burner. Written by himself* (R. Carlisle: 1830); G.W. (Gibbon Wakefield: pseud.), *A short Account of the life and death of Swing, the Rick-Burner; written by one well acquainted with him* (London: E. Wilson, 1831), 19th edition, includes the supposed 'confession' of Thomas Goodman, now under sentence of death, in Horsham jail,

for rick-burning; Francis Swing, *The Genuine Life of Mr. Francis Swing* (W. Joy: 1831); Anon. ('Swing'), *A letter from Swing to the people of England* (T.G. Lomax: 1830); E. Wakefield, *Swing Unmasked; or, the causes of rural incendiarism* (E. Wilson: 1831); J. Parker, *Machine-breaking and the changes occasioned by it in the village of Turvey Down. A tale of the times* (Parker and Rivington: November 1831).
60. *Times*, 3 January 1832.
61. Edward Palmer Thompson, *The Making of the English Working Class* (Victor Gollancz: 1963), 12.
62. Ricouer, *Memory, History, Forgetting*, 149.
63. Rothberg, *Multidirectional Memory*, *passim*.
64. Paul Connerton, 'Seven types of forgetting', *Memory Studies* 1 (2008), 67.
65. Mike Hawkins, *Social Darwinism in European and American Thought, 1860–1945: Nature as Model and Nature as Threat* (Cambridge University Press: 1997). On the influence of the concept in intellectual history, see James Campbell and David N. Livingstone, 'Neo-Lamarckism and the development of geography in the United States and Great Britain', *Transactions of the Institute of British Geographers* 8 (1983), 267–94.
66. Ian Dyck, *William Cobbett and Rural Popular Culture* (Cambridge University Press: 1992), 126–7.
67. James Jasper, *The Art of Moral Protest: Culture, Biography, and Creativity in Social Movements* (Chicago University Press: 1997), 20.

Afterword: Landscapes, Memories and Texts

Andy Wood

This volume forms a powerful antidote to the view that human life is determined by apparently impersonal forces such as price movements and demographics.[1] Rather, it represents a decisive statement as to the political agency and cultural creativity of working people over five hundred years of English history. Throughout, the radical imagination is at work. Memory appears as politicised: detailed examples of early modern commoners and nineteenth-century radicals mustering memories of earlier struggles in the legitimation of their own conflicts demonstrate the point.

In contrast to the current historiographical domination exercised by global history, many of the stories told here are determinedly local. This is important: this book does not comprise a set of 'case studies' of a pre-determined theme or question. The claims that can be made as to the value of micro-historical studies of ordinary people and their worlds should be ambitious. In a perceptive discussion, Carl Griffin observes that 'studies of popular memory are a vital way in which big stories, which necessarily ride roughshod over difference – whether different experiences or difference over space and time – can be dismantled'. The local emerges from the studies presented here as *the* field within which everyday life unfolded. In this respect, the collection represents a departure from that social-scientific mode of analysis that saw the locality as a methodological

A. Wood (✉)
Durham University, Durham, UK

© The Author(s) 2018
C. J. Griffin, B. McDonagh (eds.), *Remembering Protest in Britain since 1500*, https://doi.org/10.1007/978-3-319-74243-4_10

focus, a way of narrowing the quantity of research necessary for a defined project. Rather, for the historians and historical geographers represented in this collection, the 'local' is a substantive social presence – it is the thing in itself, not just a slice of data.[2]

Local stories matter because they illuminate the worlds within which everyday life was lived. It was also the site within which popular politics was most closely manifest. Briony McDonagh and Joshua Rodda's essay on the deep context of the 1607 Midland Rising allows us to locate that major rising alongside earlier and subsequent village protests that found their way before central courts. Utilising the difficult records of the Elizabethan Star Chamber, this forensic essay represents not just an important empirical recovery, but also a model of how to conduct microhistorical research. Likewise, Simon Sandall's chapter draws on his distinct knowledge of the Forest of Dean. There is a powerful sense in this piece of the richness and texture of local identities and of how a particular sense of place and an embedded social memory underwrote popular agency. The volume presents itself as a contribution to the 'new protest history'. As such, it engages explicitly with questions of agency, power, subordination and resistance. A large question hovers over the local: did it represent a challenge to popular politics, or the basis of that politics? Keith Snell argued that the localism of nineteenth-century rural workers undermined their politics, impairing a wider sense of class identity.[3] In a somewhat similar way, Antonio Gramsci, whose theorisation of domination and resistance forms any starting point for the issues raised in this volume, also understood the local as a limitation to subaltern politics. As Kate Crehan puts it, 'As far as Gramsci is concerned, subaltern people may well be capable of seeing the little valley they inhabit very clearly, but they remain incapable of seeing beyond their valley walls and understanding how their little world fits into the greater one beyond it'.[4] Yet other writers disagree: Mike Savage is just one sociologist who has argued for the local as the basis for class solidarities.[5]

The everyday world experienced by workers was that of the field, the village, the office or the factory. Here, subalterns might engage in those daily moments of resistance described by James C. Scott – resistance that might keep their dignity intact, and which might incrementally shift a local balance of power, but where any wider, strategic challenge was difficult.[6] The political culture of poorer people in the historical past drew upon this engagement with micro-politics. It was also coloured by locally distinct forms of exploitation, subordination and resistance, and might sometimes be built upon a wider critique of that social order.[7] Somewhere between 1789 and 1832, fundamental discontinuities opened up in the political culture of working-class people. It was not just that nineteenth-century radicalism anticipated a wider restructuring of English society in favour of working people and their families. Another historically distinctive characteristic of working-class radicalism lay in the understanding of how that restructuring might be achieved. This represented a break with the past. Early modern plebeian politics also had some rough sense of an alternative world, but this had been confined to the local: to the reordering of the small world of the village, the common, or the town. This could change: but only rarely. There were moments – the 1549 rebellions are the best example – where for a few weeks popular politics became more ambitious. General demands were not as distant as might be imagined from early modern popular politics. In their Mousehold articles, after all, Kett's rebels famously demanded in 1549 that *all* bondmen may be made free, not merely those of a particular village. But what is seen as the 'making' of the English working class represented a fundamental broadening of the imagined and material sites within which plebeian politics worked: class formation occurred in space as well as in time.

Rose Wallis's essay reminds us that elites had their own social memory. Pointing to the ways in which the Norfolk magistracy's actions during the Swing riots in 1830 were coloured by the experience of the 'bread or blood' riots of 1816 and the disturbances of 1822, she illuminates the bitter social conflicts in early nineteenth-century East Anglia. In the later Victorian and Edwardian periods, this was to be followed by the 'revolt of the field', with attempts at forming agricultural trade unions leading to a long history of strikes and lockouts that could devastate rural working-class household economies. An important question concerns the ways in which the early nineteenth-century protests were remembered in the Victorian and Edwardian periods: stories collected in the 1960s by the folklorist Enid Porter suggest that in Littleport (Cambridgeshire) the vicious repression of 1816 quelled rural resistance for generations.[8] If we are to deal with memories of protest, we need often to deal with the experience of defeat, and with the ways in which subordination might be imposed upon working people by a victorious governing class. This, too, should be part of the 'new protest history'.

It may be that historians of popular politics need new sources. Ruth Mather's transformative essay suggests an exciting way forward in studies of popular memory. Her argument that the home formed a key location in which memory was communicated, nurtured and elaborated is of importance not just for historians of the period spanned by the early industrial revolution.[9] Mather's suggestion that memories of critical events such as Peterloo were maintained in domestic pottery, and hence that radical memorialisation was embedded in the material practices of the proletarian home, is significant enough in its own right, representing a different way of thinking about the making of the English working class. But for historians interested in the communication of custom, folklore and local tradition, it has added import. Witnesses in customary disputes repeatedly made the point that they had learnt about a particular right or entitlement from their aged relatives. And broader instruction in historical narratives may have been formed within the family: Samuel Bamford discusses his early instruction in English history as taking place within his childhood home. Affective ties based upon kinship and household therefore formed part of the social web within which memory was communicated and given meaning. Here is an opportunity: further research on the relationship between family, kin, community and memory would be very valuable, especially in contexts where entire communities were engaged in persistent struggles over issues such as common land, employment rights or working conditions.[10]

Many of the essays in this collection present powerful examples of earlier resistance becoming embedded in local memory. Sandall's study shows convincingly how solidarities in the Forest of Dean were generated in the articulation and defence of custom, and the ways in which these inflected notions of entitlement and local belonging. In the remembered history of perhaps every village, certain individuals stood out: Nicola Whyte presents us with memories of 'stowte' John Bussey who 'cared not for the lord' and who continued to assert his entitlements on Mousehold Heath. Memory, a number of the chapters assert, had a politics. The historiographical convenience that separates the early modern and modern periods can be frustrating in this context. More research needs to be conducted into how the plebeian solidarities of the 1500–1770 period fed into radical, Chartist and socialist politics in the nineteenth centuries.

There are few too social historians researching the period 1500–1900. Why not? The consequences of engaging with this great arch might be revolutionary for our understanding of the political culture of English working people. The sources are there to do it, and with a local or regional focus, and a clear sense of questions, this could make for an amazing project. Medievalists manage to work across this kind of span of time to great effect. Early modern and modern social historians – perhaps especially those of rural communities – ought to speak to each other more. Perhaps this excellent collection, with its wide focus, might mark the beginning of such a conversation. Fundamental to this is the question of how political activity was spatially imagined. An important aspect of the reformulation of social identities in the early industrial revolution lay in the articulation of *national* class loyalties. The new modeling of working-class memory was an integral part of this process of class formation. In this collection, Poole shows clearly how memorialisation fed into radical politics and proletarian solidarities. Yet senses of a national radical history developed alongside the endurance of powerful local memories. The large-scale enclosure of common land in the late eighteenth and nineteenth centuries was a fundamental part of this story. Enclosure, of course, had a long history, and for centuries generated angry protest; but there was something distinctly aggressive about large-scale parliamentary enclosure that imprinted itself on working-class memory as a moment of profound rupture. More work on working class and radical discussions of enclosure would be really valuable: it seems to have been represented and remembered as a watershed moment, a moment of permanent discontinuity and a formative experience in the politics of many rural communities.

Enclosure shattered taskscapes – by which I mean the spatial organisation and experience of labour, and of movement upon the land – and it remodelled social relations. In some places, senses of entitlement might be obliterated, especially where the destruction of common resources was followed by increased in- and out-migration following the generation of a mobile agricultural workforce. This, too, was a form of alienation, and there should be ways of charting its meanings.[11] Part of the history of memory is, as a number of pieces in this volume emphasise, a struggle against forgetting.[12] And as anthropologists and archaeologists have argued, and as a number of pieces in this collection testify, early modern popular memory was embedded in a distinct sense of the land. Elly Robson has recently written very powerfully about the ways in which 'early modern landscapes [were] socially constituted', engendering distinct 'ways of seeing and knowing' and supplying the 'critical means by which spatialized social relations were produced, reproduced, defended and transformed'.[13] In many of the pieces in this volume, there is a similar appreciation of the ways in which landscape was imbricated in local struggles, as in many instances conflicts over (for example) gleaning, fuel rights, pannage or pasture reveal contending understandings of the material world.

As Nicola Whyte's brilliant essay demonstrates, landscapes were palimpsests: the map of Mousehold Heath drawn in 1589, along with its attendant depositions, illuminate not just the environment of that late Tudor taskscape, but also its prior *meanings* – the pit where Lollards and Protestants had been burnt; the Oak of Reformation, under which Kett's rebels had gathered; the site of the discovery of the body of St William of Norwich, which resulted in England's first pogrom; pre-reformation chapels; lime pits exploited by poor people from the suburb of Pockthorpe; sheep-runs used by wealthier farmers. As the depositions set before the Court of Exchequer revealed, and as the map produced in those proceedings made clear, late sixteenth-century Mousehold could be read and experienced in multiple ways: as a memorial to earlier events in the history of the city that adjoined it; as a body of resources; as a landscape of multi-dimensional conflict between lords, sheep farmers and the poor. Whyte's methodological achievement, in reading cartographic and textual evidence alongside one another, is to reconstruct something of the manifold meanings that lay upon the land, and how ordinary people encountered and experienced it.[14]

Which leads us to questions of sources and methods, and to the recoverability of the subaltern voice. Heather Falvey's contribution develops a legalistic re-reading of the witness testimonies (depositions) that social historians (myself included) have utilised. Implicitly, her chapter represents the empirical lintel of this collection. It poses a basic question: how, as historians of protest and memory, are we to access those subjects prior to the advent of mass literacy? In her search for 'authenticity', Falvey shows that depositions were multi-vocal: they contained the words not just of the witness (deponent), but also of the authors of the interrogatory, the commissioners for depositions and the clerk of the court. The same may also, in different forms, be true of depositions taken before church courts, criminal courts and borough courts. But is the search for 'authenticity' in the early modern legal process the best place from which to start? At the centre of this view of court testimony sits some notion of the modern subject. Yet, as regards manorial and parochial custom, the historian is more often confronted with collective opinion – what contemporaries called the 'common voice', 'common repute' or 'common rumour' of a 'neighbourhood' or 'country'. It is for this reason that depositions concerning local memory are so repetitious – only secondarily are we encountering the voice of the individual witness. Perhaps this is especially true of issues such as communal boundaries and use-rights, where deponents repeatedly emphasised how collective opinion was habitually and repetitively inscribed, year on year, in perambulations, labour and instruction by elders. Visions of landscape in depositions, then, form *memory texts* within communities in which memory was more often conceived in collective terms than in our own individualised sense of the concept.

Falvey's striking essay opens up a new areas of potential research. In addressing questions of authorship, she makes us think more carefully about our own ideas concerning the 'voice of the country'. Falvey's chapter implicitly addresses the power relations inherent in the legal narratives on which we depend, and the question of agency within the historical record.[15] These are big questions, and demand an approach that links social, legal and local history.

Perhaps more than anything else, this collection suggests that, at least for the 'new protest history', the cultural turn of the 1990s is over. What we have in this remarkably rich volume is a new social history of protest that is about culture, memory, belief, landscape, economics, politics and social structure all at once. Rather than taking yet another one-dimensional 'turn', this seems to me to be the way forward in historical research: we need a social history that strategically integrates all aspects of human behaviour and mentalities in pursuit of worlds that we have lost.

Notes

1. Jeremy Boulton observes that in the early modern period 'The fortunes of labouring people were ultimately determined by population trends' ('The "meaner sort": labouring people and the poor', in Keith Wrightson (ed.), *A Social History of England, 1500–1750* (Cambridge: 2017), 314). The chapters gathered in the current collection suggest a very different picture.
2. This is true of some important recent work by contemporary social historians: see, for instance, Ben Rogaly and Becky Taylor, *Moving Histories of Class and Community: Identity, Place and Belonging in Contemporary England* (Palgrave Macmillan: 2009); Ben Jones, *The Working Class in Mid Twentieth-century England: Community, Identity and Social Memory* (Manchester University Press: 2012).
3. K. D. M. Snell, 'The culture of local xenophobia', *Social History* 28.1 (2003), 1–30.
4. Kate Crehan, *Gramsci, Culture and Anthropology* (University of California Press: 2002), 104.

5. Michael Savage, 'Space, networks and class formation', in Neville Kirk (ed.), *Social Class and Marxism: Defences and Challenges* (Routledge: 1996), 58–86.
6. James C. Scott, *Domination and the Arts of Resistance: Hidden Transcripts* (Yale University Press: 1991).
7. For a study that emphasises both the formation of subaltern politics within a locality, and the practical difficulties it faced in advancing beyond that locality, see Anthony E. Kaye, 'Neighbourhoods and Nat Turner: the making of a slave rebel and the unmaking of a slave rebellion', *Journal of the Early Republic* 27.4 (2007), 705–20.
8. For popular memories of the 1816 Littleport riots, see Andy Wood, 'Five swans over Littleport: fenland folklore and popular memory, c. 1810–1978', in John H. Arnold, Matthew Hilton and Jan Rüger (eds), *History After Hobsbawm: Writing the Past for the Twenty-first Century* (Oxford University Press: 2018), 225–41.
9. For more on memory and the home, see Carolyn Steedman, *Landscape for a Good Woman: a Story of Two Lives* (Virago Press: 1986); Joëlle Bahloul, *The Architecture of Memory: a Jewish–Muslim Household in Colonial Algeria, 1937–1962* (1992; Eng trans., Cambridge University Press: 1996).
10. Dave Douglass's essay is full of implications: '"Worms of the earth": the miners' own story', in Raphael Samuel (ed.), *People's history and socialist theory* (Routledge: 1981), 61–7.
11. That utter alienation is made clear in Carl J. Griffin, '"Cut down by some cowardly miscreants": plant maiming, or the malicious cutting of flora, as an act of protest in eighteenth- and nineteenth-century rural England', *Rural History* 19.1 (2008), 29–54.
12. I draw here on Milan Kundera in his *Book of Laughter and Forgetting* (Penguin, 1980, 3): 'The struggle of man against power is the struggle of memory against forgetting'.
13. Elly Robson, 'Improvement and epistemologies of landscape in seventeenth-century English forest enclosure', *Historical Journal* 60.3 (2017), 604.
14. Mousehold Heath cries out for a long-term social and environmental history. Whyte's essay in this volume is, amongst other things, a highly significant contribution to the currently limited literature on urban commons. On this subject, see most recently Christian D. Liddy, 'Urban enclosure riots: risings of the commons in English towns, 1480–1525', *Past & Present* 226.1, (2015), 41–77.
15. The best discussion of these issues is John Arnold's inspirational book, *Inquisition and Power: Catharism and the Confessing Subject in Medieval Languedoc* (University of Pennsylvania Press: 2001).

Index[1]

A
Abthorpe (Northamptonshire), 61
Acquitted felons of 1794, 197–200
Adstone (Northamptonshire), 57, 59
Alford, Robert, 120
Archer, John, 160, 164, 166, 178
Ashmore, Wendy, 48n12
Ashton, Thomas, 3
Ashworth, Gregory, 187, 209n1
Assize, 57, 66, 107, 162, 163, 169, 170, 171, 174
Attleborough (Norfolk), 164–165, 172, 175
Aubrey, John, 221
Auslander, Leora, 137
Authorised heritage discourse, 187
Autobiographical memory, 25

B
Badby (Northamptonshire), 57, 58, 71, 76n47
Bamford, Samuel, 136, 143–144, 193, 240
Barker, Robert, 97, 98
Barnes, Donald, 3
Barton Seagrave (Northamptonshire), 66, 78n75
Battle of Barnet, 190, 191, 194
Battle of Bossenden Wood, 219
Bekesbourne (Kent), 228
Bell, Duncan, 10
Benefield (Northamptonshire), 57
Berkshire Special Commission, 226
Bletchingdon (Oxfordshire), 64
Bohstedt, John, 157n56, 221
'Book of Dennis,' 109, 129
Borrow, George, 44
Bossingham (Kent), 227
Boycott of goods, 138, 148–150
Brandon (Suffolk), 162
Brandreth, Jeremiah, 193
Braunston (Northamptonshire), 56, 75n26

---

[1] Note: Page numbers followed by 'n' refer to notes.

© The Author(s) 2018
C. J. Griffin, B. McDonagh (eds.), *Remembering Protest in Britain since 1500*, https://doi.org/10.1007/978-3-319-74243-4

Bridge (Kent), 228
Bristol, 11, 110, 219–220
British Museum, 145, 146
Brockmeier, Jens, 9
Brooks, Chris, 102n20
Brown, Alex, 228
Bryson, W.H., 85, 101n11, 101n13, 102n23, 102n24
Bulmer, Martin, 110
Bunhill Fields, 212n48
Burgh St. Peter (Norfolk), 176
Burston (Norfolk), 188
Burton Latimer (Northamptonshire), 66
Burwash (Sussex), 219

C
Cambridgeshire, 161, 171, 239
Carlile, Richard, 194, 195, 203
Cawston (Norfolk), 172
Chancery, 58, 66, 78n75
Charlesworth, Andrew, 4, 221, 232n9, 233n29
Chartism, 1, 7, 11, 14, 41, 141, 150, 155n23, 188, 196, 197, 199–204, 206–208, 211n28, 212n47, 212n49, 213n64, 213n67, 215, 217, 240
Chase, Malcolm, 147, 155n23, 219
Cherry Orton (Huntingdonshire), 75n26
Cheshire, 139
Chippenham (Wiltshire), 221
Clare, John, 12
Clark, Anna, 4, 154n5
Class-consciousness, 179, 180
Cobbett, William, 164, 174, 195, 196, 198, 201, 203, 231
Coke, Edward, 13
Collective cognition, 119
Collective memory, 11, 25, 26, 128, 217
Colonisation of memory, 8

Commemorations, 2, 5, 6, 7, 10, 11, 16, 25, 29, 44, 138, 140, 142–148, 151, 187–191, 194, 196–201, 204–208, 218
Commoners, 13, 29, 31–32, 34–35, 38–39, 56, 91, 96, 98, 104n45, 117, 237
Commoning, 41, 45, 77n53, 109, 131n17
Common rights, 33, 43, 54–56, 59, 61, 66, 68–72, 74n8, 75n19, 83, 108, 110–113, 116, 131n17
Commons, 11, 29, 33, 36, 42, 46, 54, 56–58, 61–62, 65, 68, 79n83, 90, 98, 112, 115–116, 191, 239–241
  Intercommon, 42
  urban commons, 244n14
Commotion time, 6, 28–34, 45, 55, 73n8, 216, 219
Community, 7, 11–13, 15, 34, 38, 42, 45, 57, 63, 71, 103n31, 108, 110–111, 113,-114, 116–122, 124–125, 127–129, 137, 175, 216–219, 221–225, 227–231, 240
Community feeling, 110
Community history, 8, 221
Community memorials, 7
Community memories, 7, 11, 222–224
Community solidarity, 110
Conflicts, 2, 5–7, 13, 17, 27–30, 33, 42, 84, 112, 119, 188, 191, 194, 195, 206, 217, 219, 237, 241, 242
Connerton, Paul, 218
Constitutionalism, 208
Contestable heroes, 194–197
Conway, Brian, 9
Cornwall, 220, 224
Cotesbach (Leicestershire), 63, 77n53, 77n54

Cottesbrooke (Northamptonshire), 63, 65
Counter-memorials, 8, 11, 15, 21
Counter-memory, 218
Counter-space, 26, 34–39, 46
Courts of conscience, 84
Crace, Jim, 220
Crehan, Kate, 238
Cultural hegemony, 10
Currents of Radicalism, 206
Custom, 5, 13–15, 32–35, 38, 39, 58, 75n19, 82, 88, 106n4, 108, 112–114, 116, 119, 120, 122–129, 240, 242
Customary law, 109
Customary rights, 32, 34, 35, 58, 59, 108, 114, 120, 124
Customs in Common, 15

D
Dalling (Norfolk), 172
Daniels, Stephen, 18n5, 73n7
Darvall, Frank Ongley, 3
Daventry (Northamptonshire), 61
Davis, Natalie Zemon, 84
Dean Reafforestation Act of 1668, 107, 126
Declaration from the Dispossessed, 7
Declaration from the Poor, 7
Deller, Jeremy, 6
Depositions, 81–83
 and corresponding interrogatories, 86–89
 evidence for, 83–86
 evidence related by complainant, 93–94
 evidence related by defendants in affidavits and, 91–93
 evidence related by witnesses in affidavits and, 89–91
 falsification of evidence and, 94–96
Derbyshire, 91, 93
Derrida, Jacques, 232n14

Despard, Colonel, 196
Dimaggio, Paul, 119, 120
Diss (Norfolk), 162–163, 166
Dissonant memory, 201–209
Docking (Norfolk), 172
Dolan, Frances, 83, 86, 99
Domestic space, 11, 16, 114, 135–138, 140, 143–144, 148, 150–152, 191, 240
Dorset, 188
Downham (Norfolk), 162, 169
Duchy of Lancaster, 86, 91, 95
Duddington, 56
Duffield (Derbyshire), 93, 96, 97
Duffield Frith (Derbyshire), 91, 96, 99
Dwelling, concept of, 27, 36, 39, 42, 46, 50n40
Dyck, Ian, 231
Dyndor, Zoe, 12, 224

E
East Tuddenham (Norfolk), 172
Edinburgh Convention, 192
Elham (Kent), 227–228
Ely (Cambridgeshire), 162–163, 169–170, 174, 179
Emmet, Robert, 189, 190, 212n49
Enclosure, 4, 8, 28, 30, 36, 38–40, 42–43, 53–56, 58,–59, 61–72, 74n11, 76n43, 79n86, 83, 90–91, 93, 96, 98, 104n46, 108, 113, 116–117, 126, 220, 241
Enclosure riots, 4, 55, 58, 61–63, 66–68, 89, 91, 117
Epstein, James, 211n24
Essay on Sepulchres, 203

F
Falvey, Heather, 15–17, 227, 242, 243
1549 Rebellions and the Making of Early Modern England, The, 5–6

Farnham, (Surrey), 222
Faversham (Kent), 223
Finedon (Northamptonshire), 56, 59, 75n26
First Reform Bill, 219
Fisher, Chris, 133n66
Food riots, 3, 4, 165, 215, 216, 220–221
Ford (Wiltshire), 221
Forest of Dean, 107–134
Forgetting and memories, 215–231
Formal narratives, 25
Foscote (Northamptonshire), 61
France, 217, 228
Free miners, 111–128
Free Mousehold, 34, 36
Frentress, James, 25
Friedland, Roger, 120

G
Gale Jones, John, 195, 198, 199, 208, 212n48
Gallow (Norfolk), 166
Gloucestershire, 17, 76n50, 107–129
Godoy, Richard, 110, 111
Godwin, William, 203
Goody, Jack, 122, 123
Grafton Underwood (Northamptonshire), 70
Gramsci, Antonio, 10, 238
Great Houghton (Northamptonshire), 64
Griffin, Carl J., 14, 16, 79n83, 160, 237, 244n11
Griffiths, Claire, 5
Guilsborough (Northamptonshire), 56, 65

H
Habitus, 13
Haddisoe (Norfolk), 172, 175

Halbwachs, Maurice, 9, 21n31, 25, 26
Halifax Female Reformers, 141, 151
Hall, Robert G., 14, 217
Hamble (Hampshire), 224
Hammond, Barbara, 3, 6
Hammond, John, 3, 6
Hampden Clubs, 194, 196
Hampden, John, 189, 192, 203, 205–208, 213n63
Hampshire, 223–224
Hardscrabble heritage, 7
Hardy, Thomas, 192, 198, 202, 212n48
Herefordshire, 119
Hertfordshire, 17
Harrison, Rodney, 188
Harvest, 220
Haselbech (Northamptonshire), 62, 63, 76n43
Hay, Douglas, 4, 179
Heritage and protest, *see* Protest heritage politics
Heritage from Below, 6
Heydon (Norfolk), 172
Hillmorton (Warwickshire), 77n54
Hindle, Steve, 1, 5, 54, 62, 68, 100
Historical memory, 25–27, 191, 194, 208
Historical remembrance, 26, 29, 30
History and National Life, 8
History, of protest, 3–6
Hobhouse, Henry, 169, 170, 177
Hobsbawm, Eric, 3, 4, 6, 8, 217, 228
Holdsworth, W.S., 85
Holt (Norfolk), 162, 164
Horsham Political Union, 234n44
Hound (Hampshire), 224
House of Commons, 182n18
Hoyle, Richard, 112
Hudson, William, 224, 225, 230
Hunt, Henry 'Orator,' 135, 138, 142, 146, 149, 151, 194, 195, 201

I

Immortal memory, 195
Incendiarism, 11, 163, 165, 174, 216, 222, 223, 224, 227–229
Individual memory, 10
Indulgence, 166, 193
Industrial heritage, 188
Ingold, Tim, 36, 39, 42
Inquisitions of Depopulation, 55, 65, 67, 71
'Inscription for an Ice House,' 191
Intangible heritage, 208, 213n70
Invention of Tradition, The, 8
Irmingland (Norfolk), 165
Isham (Northamptonshire), 66
Isle of Wight, 223

J

Jacobin heritage, 192
Jerne, Christina, 7
John Frost Square, 188
Johnson, Nuala, 10
Jones, Ernest, 203
Judicial decision-making, 160
Jurica, A. R. J., 124

K

Karr, David, 189
Kean, Hilda, 188
Kuijpers, Erika, 14
Kelmarsh (Northamptonshire), 65
Kenn (Somerset), 224
Kent, 116, 220, 223, 227–229
Kettering (Northamptonshire), 63
Kett, Robert, 27–30, 32, 38, 45
Kett's Rebellion, 28–36, 236, 242
King, Peter, 160, 223, 227
Kings Lynn (Norfolk), 170
Kings Sutton (Northamptonshire), 56

L

Lamarckism, 231
Landscapes, 2, 5, 10, 12–14, 16, 26–30, 32–36, 38–47, 48n12, 53–55, 57, 71–72, 73n7, 82, 99, 107–108, 118, 120, 190–191, 194, 203, 224, 230, 237–244
  signifying, 190–194
Large, Peter, 111
Lefebvre, Henri, 26
Legal depositions, 15, 81–106, 227, 242–243
Legg, Steve, 218
Leicestershire, 53, 55, 62, 63, 74n11, 76n43, 76n50, 77n54, 77n55, 78n75
Leigh, Mike, 6
Les Cadres Sociaux de la Mémoire, 9
Leveller movement, 188
Liberalism, 198–200, 205–207, 212n48, 231
Lilford (Northamptonshire), 59
Linebaugh, Peter, 4
Lingwood (Norfolk), 166
Litchborough (Northamptonshire), 58
Litigation, 119–128
Little Houghton (Northamptonshire), 68, 71
Little Walsingham (Norfolk), 170
Littleport (Cambridgeshire), 162, 169, 239, 244n8
London, 16, 67, 72, 84, 128, 140, 145, 190, 192–193, 195, 197–199, 201, 208, 212n47, 228
London Corresponding Society (LCS), 197–199, 205, 207, 208
Loveless, George, 226
Lowenthal, David, 188

M

McCalman, Ian, 190
McDonagh, Briony, 16, 17, 238
MacMaster, Neil, 42
Magna Carta, 193
Making of the English Working Class, The, 3
Manchester, 42, 135–136, 138–142, 147–149, 153, 188, 201, 203–204,
Manchester Observer, 140, 141, 148, 149
Mandler, Peter, 8
Manning, Roger, 4, 113
Mansfield, Nick, 208
Marshall, Peter, 85
Martin, John, 55, 58, 59, 61, 63, 66
Material memories, 39–45
Mather, Ruth, 11, 16, 17, 239, 240
Mayfield (Sussex), 227
Memorialisation from below, 11
Memories of protest, in here-and-now, 6–8
Memory of the People, The, 2, 12
Memory politics, 8–10
Memoryscapes, 12–14
Memory Studies (journal), 8
Memory texts, 243
 See also specific entries
Middleton (Lancashire), 138, 143, 193
Middleton (Northamptonshire), 70
Midlands Rising of 1607, 53–55
 history of protest, 56–60
 remembering of, 67–70
 year of rising, 61–67
Mine Law Court, 109–111, 119–129
Mnemonics, 12, 13, 22n49, 57, 120, 224, 230
Modernity, 14, 26
Modern memory, 8, 14
More, Thomas, 37, 39
Morgan, Alison, 156n36
Mousehold Heath, 27–28, 45–47, 242, 244n14
 commotion time and, 28–33
 as counter-space, 34–39
 material memories and, 39–45
Muir, Thomas, 191, 192, 200
Muskett, Paul, 160
Myth, significance of, 9, 200, 223, 229
Myths We Live By, The, 8

N

Namier, Lewis, 3
Natural History of Wiltshire, 221
Navickas, Katrina, 17, 42, 136, 140, 221
Neeson, Jeanette, M., 4
Neville, Alexander, 29
New and Impartial History of England, 193
Newcastle, 220
Newnham (Kent), 221
Newnham (Northamptonshire), 57, 71
New Poor Law (1834), 225, 226
Newton (Northamptonshire), 53, 54, 62–64, 66, 70, 72n1, 76n43, 77n52
Nora, Pierre, 8
Norfolk, 25–52, 159–185
Northampton, 63, 69
Northamptonshire, 53–80
North Walsham (Norfolk), 164, 166
Norwich, 27–32, 34, 37, 40–42, 162–165, 167, 170, 174–175, 178, 179, 242
Nuttal, William, 201

O

Oak of Reformation, 242
Occupational flexibility, 114
Occupy camp, 30
Occupy movement, 7
O'Connor, Feargus, 200–202, 208, 212n47
Official memory, 11, 161, 178, 180, 218, 232n9
Oldham (Lancashire), 222
Orlingbury (Northamptonshire), 66
Oundle (Northamptonshire), 53, 58, 69, 70
Oxfordshire, 64, 188

P

Paine, Tom, 140, 189, 190, 193–195, 203, 208, 211n24
Papley (Northamptonshire), 59, 60
Paternalism, 179
Peacock, A. J., 160
People's Park movement, 42, 43
Perambulation (of bounds), 15, 35, 37, 38, 56, 243
Peterloo massacre, 6, 7, 11, 16, 20n18, 135–158, 188–189, 193, 204, 208, 222, 240
Peterloo, memorialisation of, 6, 7, 11, 16, 20n18, 135–138
 boycotting as form of, 148–150
 in commemorative material culture, 142–147
 gendered nature, 150–152
 massacre and six acts, 138–140
 through radical child-rearing, 140–142
Pilton (Northamptonshire), 64
Pittock, Murray, 136, 144
Pockthorpe (Norfolk), 39, 42, 43, 45

Politicisation of memory, 26, 159, 219
Pollmann, Judith, 1, 14
Poole, Steve, 6, 11, 16, 17, 152, 219
Poor Man's Guardian, 201
Popular Disturbances and Public Order in Regency England, 3
Popular memory, 15, 30, 54, 72, 128, 163, 218, 221, 223, 231, 237, 239, 241
Porter, Enid, 239
Primitive Christian Society, 41
Primitive Rebels, 3
Protest heritage politics, 187–213
 acquitted felons of 1794, 197–200
 contestable heroes, 194–197
 landscape, signifying, 190–194
 statues, memorials and dissonant memory, 201–209
Protest narratives, 168–180
 See also specific entries
Purgatory of Suicides, The, 206
Pytchley (Northamptonshire), 62, 66, 76n43

Q

Quaife, G.R., 84
Quarter sessions, 128, 164, 168–171, 179

R

Radical constitutionalism, 189
Radical politics, 6, 7, 16, 68, 110, 111, 126, 135–153, 164, 178, 189–209, 221–222, 225, 234n44, 237, 239–241
Radstone, Susannah, 26
Randall, Adrian, 4, 221
Ranger, Terence, 8

Reed, Mick, 4
Reepham (Norfolk), 172
Reform riots, 11, 220
Republicanism, 195
Ricoeur, Paul, 218
Riot Act (1715), 6, 107, 139, 172
Rioting, *see* Enclosure riots; Food riots; Reform riots; Swing riots
Roberts, Matthew, 197, 213n64
Robertson, Iain, 6, 7, 11, 17, 42, 219
Roberts, Paul, 1
Robson, Elly, 241
Rodda, Joshua, 16, 17, 238
Rogers, Nick, 219, 220
Rothberg, Michael, 225
Rothwell (Northamptonshire), 62
Roughton (Norfolk), 176–177
Rousso, Henry, 217
Royton (Lancashire), 221–222, 230
Rudé, George, 3, 4, 217, 219, 228
Rule, John, 4, 220
Runnymede camp, 7
Rural Constabularies Act of 1839, 225
Rushton (Northamptonshire), 62–64, 76n43

S
Samuel, Raphael, 8, 188
Sandall, Simon, 16
Sans-culotte philosophy, 191
Savage, Mike, 238
Schwarz, Bill, 26
Scotland, 4
Scott, James C., 2, 79n87, 221, 238
Shackel, Paul, 188
Shangdon (Leicestershire), 78n75
Shared memory, 10
Sharp, Buchanan, 4, 116
Shepherd's Life, A, 225
Short, Brian, 22n51

Shutlanger (Northamptonshire), 61, 62, 76n46
Skilled Labourer, The, 3
Skimmington (custom of), 115, 132n28
Slack, John, 4, 147
Smith, Ernest A., 155n17
Smith, Laurajane, 187, 188
Snell, Keith, 179, 229, 238
Social conflict, 5–7, 27, 29, 33, 219, 239
Social dislocation, 216
Social dysfunction, 215
Social memory, 238, 239
  See also Community memories
Somerset, 180, 220, 224
Southey, Robert, 190–194
Spain, 112, 197
Spenceans, 190, 195–200, 202, 204, 207–208, 210, 211n28
Star Chamber records, 55, 56
Stevenson, John, 4
Stoke Bruerne (Northamptonshire), 61, 76n42
Stowe (Northamptonshire), 58
Stretton, Tim, 103n33
Suffolk, 162
Sumartojo, Shanti, 10
Surrey, 7, 223, 227
Sussex, 220, 227
Swaffham (Norfolk), 170
Swing riots, 14–16, 159–180, 225–230, 234n44
Sykes, Julia, 3
Syresham (Northamptonshire), 56

T
Tarlow, Sarah, 12, 51, 224
Taskscapes, 2, 10, 12, 42
Texts, 237–244

See also specific entries
Thelwall, John, 189–194
Thirsk, Joan, 115
Thompson, E. P., 3–6, 9, 13, 15, 215, 221, 223, 229
Thompson, Judith, 191
Thompson, Paul, 9
Threshing machines, 161–162, 164–168, 171–172, 225–228
Throwley (Kent), 229
Tolpuddle (Dorset), 5, 10, 160, 188, 208, 226
Towcester (Northamptonshire), 76n46
Town Labourer, The, 3
TUC, 5
Tunbridge, John, 187

U
Underdown, David, 4, 119

V
Vichy Syndrome, 217
Victoria County History, 8
Village Labourer, The, 3
Villiers, Edward, 115
Vincent, Henry, 204

W
Wales, 4, 188, 205, 224
Wallis, Rose, 14, 16, 239
Walsingham (Norfolk), 170
Walter, John, 4
Waltham Chase (Hampshire), 222
Warren James, 107–110
Warren James 'riot,' 107–110, 129
Warwickshire, 53, 55, 62–63, 67, 76n49, 77n54
Wasing (Berkshire), 226
Welham (Leicestershire), 63
Wells, Roger, 4, 215, 219
Westminster, 84–86, 92, 96, 198
Whelan, Yvonne, 11
Whinburgh (Norfolk), 172
Whittlesey riots and depositions, 81, 82, 87–89, 91
Whyte, Nicola, 5, 10–12, 14, 16, 85, 240, 242
Wickham, Chris, 25
Williams, Gywn, 3
Wiltshire, 201, 224–225
Windsor (Berkshire), 222
Winstanley, Gerrard, 7, 68
Winter, Jay, 26, 30
Witness testimony, 84, 85, 89, 99
Wood, Andy, 1, 5, 10–13, 15, 29, 34, 38, 54, 58, 85, 121, 161, 216
Woodbastwick (Norfolk), 35, 36
Worcestershire, 76n50
Working class, 43, 44, 188, 189, 196, 202, 204, 213n64, 239–241
  home, late-Gregorian, 135–153, 154n6
  movement, 208
  terminology of, 153–154n4
Work of forgetting, 215–236
Wrightson, Keith, 4
Wymondham (Norfolk), 28

X
Xenophobic paranoia, 165, 174, 179

Y
Yorkshire, 41, 203

CPSIA information can be obtained
at www.ICGtesting.com
Printed in the USA
LVHW07*1442120718
583539LV00006B/7/P